AUDEN AND THE MUSE OF HISTORY

AUDEN
AND THE MUSE OF HISTORY

SUSANNAH YOUNG-AH GOTTLIEB

STANFORD UNIVERSITY PRESS
Stanford, California

Stanford University Press
Stanford, California

© 2023 by Susannah Young-ah Gottlieb. All rights reserved.

No part of this book may be reproduced or transmitted in any form or by any means, electronic or mechanical, including photocopying and recording, or in any information storage or retrieval system without the prior written permission of Stanford University Press.

All quotations from Auden's manuscripts and typescripts are printed with the permission of the Estate of W. H. Auden.

Printed in the United States of America on acid-free, archival-quality paper

Library of Congress Cataloging-in-Publication Data
Names: Gottlieb, Susannah Young-ah, author.
Title: Auden and the muse of history / Susannah Young-ah Gottlieb.
Description: Stanford, California : Stanford University Press, 2022. | Includes bibliographical references and index.
Identifiers: LCCN 2022022189 (print) | LCCN 2022022190 (ebook) | ISBN 9781503633155 (cloth) | ISBN 9781503633926 (paperback) | ISBN 9781503633933 (epub)
Subjects: LCSH: Auden, W. H. (Wystan Hugh), 1907-1973--Criticism and interpretation. | English poetry--20th century--History and criticism. | Literature and history. | LCGFT: Literary criticism.
Classification: LCC PR6001.U4 Z696 2022 (print) | LCC PR6001.U4 (ebook) | DDC 811/.52--dc23/eng/20220525
LC record available at https://lccn.loc.gov/2022022189
LC ebook record available at https://lccn.loc.gov/2022022190

Cover design: Rob Ehle
Cover photo: W. H. Auden, poet, St. Mark's Place, New York, March 3, 1960. Photograph by Richard Avedon. Copyright © The Richard Avedon Foundation.

Typeset by Elliott Beard in Adobe Caslon Pro 10.5/15

For Peter
And for my children, Inbo and Zoli

CONTENTS

Acknowledgments ix
Abbreviations xi

Introduction 1

Part I

1. States of Marriage 35
2. Poetry, Prose, and a Forgotten Practice 68
3. "Civilization Must Be Saved" 90

Interlude: The Falling Empire 123

Part II

4. Isotopes of Love 155
5. From Poem to Volume 187
6. Anthropology, Hell, "Good-bye" 211

Coda 239

Notes 245
Index 281

ACKNOWLEDGMENTS

Much of the research for this book was conducted with the materials in the Henry W. and Albert A. Berg Collection of English and American Literature at the New York Public Library, and I thank Carolyn Vega for her help in navigating the archive. Edward Mendelson, Auden's literary executor and most important critic, has responded to queries, both large and small, with tremendous kindness and unflagging generosity over the years. My indebtedness to his earlier scholarship and editorial work is immense.

I am grateful to Whitney Quesenbery, whose gift of her father's Auden library and papers was a surprise delight, and Erin Harris for permission to reproduce Richard Avedon's beautiful portrait of Auden. I thank Erica Wetter for believing in this project and expertly ushering it through the publication process, Caroline McKusick and Gigi Mark for their detailed attention to the manuscript, and Carly Bortman for her superb work preparing the index.

At Northwestern University, the Weinberg College of Arts and Sciences and the Alice Kaplan Institute for the Humanities have provided much needed support for the completion of this volume. The staff in the Department of English and the Comparative Literary Studies Program have likewise been indispensable, especially Kathleen Daniels, Sarah Peters, and Nathan Mead.

I am also very grateful for invitations to speak, listen, and learn as I thought through some of the issues that form the core of these pages. I thank, especially, Homi Bhabha for including me in the multiday conference *Poetics of Anxiety and Security*, co-hosted by the Serpentine Gallery and the Birkbeck School of Law in London; Daniel Heller-Roazen for inviting me to deliver one of the Christian Gauss Seminars in Criticism at Princeton University; Weigui Feng for his gracious welcome to the Department of Literature and Theory at Beijing Normal University; and Fergal Gaynor for eliciting an "Exploded Lecture" for the Avant Contemporary Arts Festival in Cork, Ireland.

At Northwestern, my departmental colleagues, the Poetry and Poetics collective, and my Drinking Gourd crew have provided countless opportunities for collaboration and conversation. I thank especially John Alba Cutler, Katy Breen, Nick Davis, Harris Feinsod, Reginald Gibbons, John Keene, Jules Law, Susan Manning, Susie Phillips, Alessia Ricciardi, Laurie Shannon, Julia Stern, Ivy Wilson, and Tristram Wolff. For the many ways they have enriched and enlivened my own scholarly, creative, and personal landscape over the years, I thank Chris Abani, Tatsu Aoki, Peter Howarth, Ken Krimstein, Maureen McLane, Sharlyn Rhee, Ed Roberson, Nancy Teinowitz, and Steve Young.

I am blessed to have shared decades of sustained and sustaining friendship with Richard O. Block, Bob Gooding-Williams, Sara Gooding-Williams, Sarah Young Imbert, Bruce M. King, Dermot Moran, Man Wei Tam, and Myung Choe Tam. For their abiding humanity, humor, and love, I am ever grateful.

Throughout his life, my father, Ferdinand Gottlieb, insisted in his slightly irregular English that you could dream big and endure much as long as you have "a family what loves you." I am grateful every day for the incalculable gift of my family's love. Thank you to my mother, Bernice Gottlieb, my brothers, Peter and Richard Gottlieb, their wives, Jeri Riggs and Leslie Gottlieb, their children, Degen, Michael, Bobby, and Samantha Gottlieb, and my in-laws, Norma and Steven Fenves. Finally, my deepest thanks belong to my husband, Peter Fenves, my loving partner in everything and best friend for more than twenty-five years, and to my children, Inbo and Zoli Gottlieb Fenves, who refresh the world every day with their impish brilliance.

ABBREVIATIONS

The following sigla are used for Auden's writings throughout the volume.

ACW *A Certain World: A Commonplace Book*. London: Faber & Faber, 1966.

AS *As I Walked Out One Evening: Songs, Ballads, Lullabies, Limericks, and Other Light Verse*. Edited by Edward Mendelson. New York: Vintage International, 1995.

AT *Another Time*. London: Faber & Faber, 1940.

Berg W. H. Auden Collection of Papers in the Henry W. and Albert A. Berg Collection of English and American Literature at the New York Public Library.

CP *Collected Poems*. Edited by Edward Mendelson. New York: Vintage, 1991.

CP45 *Collected Poetry*. New York: Random House, 1945.

CSP *Collected Shorter Poems, 1927–1957*. London: Faber & Faber, 1966.

DH *The Dyer's Hand and Other Essays*. New York: Vintage International, 1989.

DM *The Double Man*. New York: Random House, 1941.

EF *The Enchafèd Flood: or, The Romantic Iconography of the Sea*. Charlottesville: University Press of Virginia, 1950.

xi

FBA (With Louis Kronenberger). *The Faber Book of Aphorisms*. London: Faber & Faber, 1970.

FTB *For the Time Being*. London: Faber & Faber, 1945.

HC *Homage to Clio*. London: Faber & Faber, 1960.

JW (With Christopher Isherwood). *Journey to a War*. 1939. Reprint, London: Faber & Faber, 1970.

Lib *The Complete Works of W. H. Auden: Libretti and Other Dramatic Writings, 1939–73*. Edited by Edward Mendelson. Princeton: Princeton University Press, 1993.

LI (With Louis MacNeice). *Letters from Iceland*. New York: Paragon, 1937.

LS *Lectures on Shakespeare*. Edited by Arthur Kirsch. Princeton University Press, 1994.

MY "*The Map of All My Youth*": Early Works, Friends and Influences (Auden Studies 1). Edited by Katherine Bucknell and Nicholas Jenkins. Oxford: Clarendon Press, 1990.

N *Nones*. New York: Random House, 1951.

NYL *New Year Letter*. London: Faber & Faber, 1941.

O *The Orators*. 1932. Reprint, New York: Random House, 1966.

Plays *The Complete Works of W. H. Auden: Plays and Other Dramatic Writings, 1928–38*. Edited by Edward Mendelson. Princeton: Princeton University Press, 1988.

Prose *The Complete Works of W. H. Auden: Prose*. Edited by Edward Mendelson. 6 vols. Princeton: Princeton University Press, 1997–2015.

S *Spain*. London: Faber & Faber [1937].

SC "*In Solitude, for Company*": W. H. Auden After 1940 (Auden Studies 3). Edited by Katherine Bucknell and Nicholas Jenkins. Oxford: Oxford University Press, 1995.

SH *The Shield of Achilles*. London: Faber & Faber, 1955.

SM *The Sea and the Mirror.* Edited by Arthur Kirsch. Princeton: Princeton University Press, 2003.

SP *Selected Poems.* Edited by Edward Mendelson. New York: Vintage, 1979.

SW *Secondary Worlds.* London: Faber & Faber, 1968.

AUDEN AND THE MUSE OF HISTORY

INTRODUCTION

Against the Big Lie

"Civilization must be saved, even if this means sending for the military, which I suppose it does."—With this proposition, spoken by Herod the Great in *For the Time Being*, W. H. Auden presents an exemplary version of what poetry, in his view, can hope to undo: it can defend language against the Big Lie, which begins in the conviction that "civilization"—in Herod's case, a colonial outpost of the dominant imperial power of the day—is a function of state-sanctioned violence. Concentrating on Auden's work from the late 1930s, when he seeks to understand the poet's responsibility in the face of a triumphant fascism, to the late 1950s, when he begins to discern an irreconcilable "divorce" between poetry and history in light of industrialized murder, this study reveals the intensity with which Auden struggled with the meanings of history in both his poetry and his prose reflections. Denying that poetry is in any simple way causally connected to historical events, while simultaneously rejecting the doctrine of "art for art's sake," Auden's engagement with the problem of history distances him from the temptation to conceive of poetry—his own and others'—as an esoteric or sacral occupation that, outside the public view, magically leads to some sort of salvation or Truth that is not available to a public at large. The struggle against the Big Lie cannot be conducted simply through secular argumentation, supported by the armature of the "liberal *Aufklärung*" (*Prose* 2:39), nor through its opposite, that is, a return to earlier forms of religious life, including the form of religious life to which Auden was himself returning in this very period. Historically engaged poetry is needed when the Lies grow to such proportions that they are at the core of political life. Such was the case, as Auden saw it, in the late 1930s when this study begins. "The muse does not like being forced to choose between Agit-prop and Mallarmé" (*Prose* 3:189), Auden writes with characteristic lucidity, and this account of his complex relation to the muse of history seeks to elucidate the probity, humor, and technical skill with which he responds to the reality of history and to show, in turn, how Auden's work, including a series of poems that has hitherto attracted little critical attention, helps us see dimensions of the struggle against the Big Lie today.

This study comprises two main parts. The first treats principally poems and prose monologues Auden wrote during the Second World War, while the second revolves around poems and prose reflections from the 1950s. The aim of Part I is to describe how Auden develops a literary practice that is genuinely responsible to history, first, by distinguishing historical events from natural processes and social cycles, and then, above all, by recognizing that the forces of fascism that must be defeated, including its rhetoric, are not simply alien elements that have nothing to do with the personal and political lives of those, like Auden, who see themselves as resolutely anti-fascist. Following this first part, an Interlude offers a concentrated analysis of a single poem, "The Fall of Rome" (1947), in which Auden's confrontation with the legacy of modernist poetry (especially that of Baudelaire, Kipling, Yeats, and Eliot) expresses itself in a multi-temporal image of imperial domination that eerily survives through its seeming demise, opening the way to a vista that stretches beyond human history. Part II is correspondingly concerned with a single volume, *Homage to Clio* (1960), in which Auden elaborates the complexity of his commitment to creating a poetic practice that understands itself as so fully responsible to history that it begins to question the discipline of historical studies.

Homage to Clio is filled with some little-studied, generally overlooked, often dismissed, yet nevertheless marvelous poems. One of the aims of the ensuing pages is to alert readers to the crisp brilliance of these poems, which may not immediately register as among Auden's most moving or memorable, but which offer rich rewards to those who are open to the almost intractable perplexities of the problem of poetry's relation to history. Considered afresh from this perspective, this work invites a reconsideration of Auden's later poetry, not only by reading poems carefully in isolation but also by showing how they contribute to Auden's attempt to create a poetry that is "true" to history. Analyzing *Homage to Clio* as a whole demonstrates that Auden, through the very tenacity of his dedication to the "Muse of the unique / Historical fact" (*HC* 17), recognizes an estrangement between poet and historian that affects every element in the final poems of that volume, including, as I argue, an "unwritten poem" that would have directly addressed the culmination of a culture of hate, which is to say, precisely the kind of culture in which little lies grow big. The final pages of this study are concerned with the consequence of this absence, as Auden describes his decision to return to the "guilt culture" of his adopted home in post-Anschluss, postwar Austria. Here readers can see the limits of a poetry whose commitment lies in being true to the—multiple, self-divided—muse of history.

Against Grand Narratives, While Gleaning Insights from a Few of Them

"Poetry makes nothing happen," Auden writes in his 1939 "In Memory of W. B. Yeats." This negative affirmation is as well-known as any line of twentieth-century English verse. Many similarly resonant lines emerge from the pages of Auden's *Collected Poems*. Even as critics have often seen him as a fundamentally apolitical poet—or, more exactly, a poet who first adopted and then, in the late 1930s, abdicated the role of political poet—lines from his poetry appear to be just as often invoked in moments of both personal and political crisis. With respect to personal crises, it is doubtless impossible to verify this claim, although the first chapter of this study analyzes a scene in late twentieth-century popular culture where Auden's words reverberate with profound personal crises that, through their expression, become a small yet far from insignificant element of a major change in law and therefore in public life. With respect to political crises per se, however, sufficient evidence for the claims of Auden's voice can be found by recalling the renewed attention to "September 1, 1939" prompted by the events of September 11, 2001. It was not simply the coincidence of dates, nor simply that Auden situates his poem about the first day of the Second World War in one of Manhattan's "dives." It was, above all, his conviction that his voice freely had to respond to historical events. For Auden, the emotions occasioned in one of the dives on this particular day must find poetic expression; otherwise, the war that "officially" began on September 1, 1939, would already be lost—with the Nazis victorious. From this perspective, there can be little doubt why certain lines from Auden's poetry tend to be evoked during critical moments, whether personal, political, or both at the same time: such moments are what much of his poetry is "about." A cursory review on Twitter of #Auden on the eightieth anniversary of the beginning of the Second World War leaves no doubt that this day, September 1, is remembered in the English-speaking world less for the invasion of Poland than for Auden's poem. Long before Twitter and Facebook feeds existed, Auden worried about the alacrity with which some of the lines of his early poetry lent themselves to every sort of political program—with the concluding stanzas of "Spain, 1937" as the last and most chilling example. Something approaching the opposite characterizes much of his later poetry: even as certain lines continue to direct themselves toward critical moments and historical themes, the poems as a whole exhibit an aversion to making poetry into a vehicle of anything that could be mistaken for propaganda. Of course, no words can be fully protected from use as propaganda, including modern techniques of advertisement. Nevertheless, Auden sought to make it difficult for his poetry to be used for such purposes, going so far as to excise "September 1" from his *Collected Poems* for this reason. For him, the anti-slogan, "Poetry makes nothing happen," remained valid.

The starting point for this study, then, is this: Auden's poems resonate with moments of both personal and political crises because his poetry is always in a certain state of crisis—precisely the crisis that derives from its interrogation of the function of poets who, as Hölderlin wrote, find themselves "in destitute times." In a passage from a 1955 BBC broadcast that became the nucleus of his prose collection *The Dyer's Hand*, Auden borrows the lexicon of the Eleatic sages of ancient Greece that existentialists like Sartre had recently revitalized: "Essentially poetry is an affirmation of Being, and the main negative motive for writing it [is] a dread of non-being. . . . For [the Poet], therefore, anything which has a history, which changes, contains an element of non-being, which resists poetic expression. His very medium, language, is ill-fitted to describe becoming" (*Prose* 3:541). Yet, as Auden notes in the same section of that 1955 radio broadcast, "What Is Poetry About?," the ancient Greek conception of the poet's function is no longer viable. This "no longer," which is emblematic of historical change, contains both a fact and an imperative. Despite his unwavering contention that poetry affirms Being, Auden resolutely refuses to affirm what this implies: that poets should affirm the status quo. Poetry changed as a result, losing its earlier function; but this change does not help the poet find a new function. This, for Auden, is a major perplexity: the premise is right, while the conclusion is wrong. Change is not only possible; it is necessary whenever and wherever conditions are oppressive.[1] All of this is said, of course, in highly abstract prose, which Auden often repeated with slightly different formulations, particularly in his later essays and reviews. The poet is there to affirm Being. So says the prose writer. Yet Being as it currently stands, the status quo, wracked as it is by injustice, must be changed. This the prose writer says, too. Yet again—as both the poetry and prose writer say—poetry makes nothing happen. The prose writer sometimes finds a solution, while the poet tends to intensify the perplexity. This study concentrates on the poet, even as it often refers to the prose writer, because the perplexity is an existential matter for the poet alone.

There would be no discord between prose writer and poet if the poet found a function for poetry from within the general concept of history propounded by the prose writer. Such might be said of Auden's early work, when he tentatively allied himself with Marxism, although, of course, the relation of Auden's poetry to his political allegiances was vexed from the very beginning of his career as a poet. This study begins with poems written after he departed Marxism. Auden did not inaugurate or consummate this departure by writing a critique of Marx or a condemnation of Marxism. The absence of a vociferous "reckoning" with Marx and Marxism can be explained from two perspectives: first, his commitment to Marxist politics was always tenuous at best, and second, he continued to believe that on certain crucial matters, Marx was unquestionably right.[2] More to the point, Auden remained faithful to certain elements of Marx's understanding of history, even as this faithfulness required that he depart from Marxism as it was known to his contemporaries. One of these elements can be found in the famous opening of *The Eighteenth Brumaire of Louis Bonaparte*, where Marx emphasized that historical events do not take place only once and thereafter disappear into the irreality of the past: on the contrary, occurrences become historical because they are entangled with previous ones; historical events are thus characterized by their topicality, happening "now," just as much as in the past, which is itself changed as a result of its mingling with the emergent moment.[3] Auden can be seen to apply the latter element of Marx's work to the former one and to draw a conclusion that stands in conflict with classical forms of Marxism: history, as such, can never be a matter of laws. To represent historical events in law-like terms is to deny their inherent density, and reduce them to the unidimensional plenitude of Being, even when Being is identified with matter and the resulting materialism is given a dialectical spin.

One further aspect of Marxist historiography remained very much a part of Auden's thought: its appreciation of small changes in the forces of production, including, for instance, "Methods of dry farming" (*HC* 7), to quote from the short poem that prefaces *Homage to Clio*. In drawing attention to changes in farming methods, Auden practices something like "microhistory," before that approach became a scholarly ethos.[4] And this practice derives at least in part—but perhaps in full—from his exodus from the grand narrative of Marxism, whereby human beings finally achieve their freedom from the "iron laws" of history when the proletarian revolution eliminates all traces of social classes and thus class conflict. For the Auden under study in this volume, there are no laws of history; history is, rather, that strange thing which is lawless yet not therefore chaotic or simply inchoate. In the late 1930s, searching for this "thing," Auden began to look far afield from Marxism for historians who conformed with his basic conviction that history had to be distinguished from nature, even if human beings are always also natural beings who discover, for instance, more efficient methods of farming in slowly drying climates.

Only rarely does Auden express interest in academic historiography, and so far as his reviews are concerned, he avoided popular histories that emphasized either "great men" and "decisive battles" or—doubtless worse—secret agreements and hidden forces. As for grand historical narratives that attracted a wide-scale readership, Auden was noticeably unmoved. Reminiscing in the 1950s about the decline in Otto Spengler's popularity, Auden noted that "most of my generation read *The Decline of the West*" (*Prose* 4:129); but the evidence suggests that he was among those who did not. As for Spengler's popular post–First World War counterpart, Arnold Toynbee, Auden wrote the following in an undated letter to Elizabeth Mayer: "Am starting to read *A Study of History* (six volumes). So must you if you haven't. It is a major work, I think."[5] Not a single word, however, can be found referring to *A Study of History* in any of his published writings.[6] This indicates at the very least that his hesitation was well grounded: here is a grand narrative, to be sure, but grand narratives as such do not sustain his interest.

With scant attention to academic historiography and little regard for many of the histories that attracted popular attention, Auden turned his attention in the late 1930s and early 1940s to a few grand narratives, each of which was incompatible with the others. What attracted him were not these narratives per se but, rather, their ability to identify certain overlooked or underestimated events that began a tradition whose consequences express themselves in contemporary crises. One of these projects belonged to Eugen Rosenstock-Huessy, whose *Out of Revolution* made a strong impression on Auden as soon as it appeared in the late 1930s. Another project was undertaken by Denis de Rougemont, whose *Love in the Western World* began to inform Auden's conception of post-classical European civilization when it was first published in the early 1940s. And a third was Charles Norris Cochrane's *Christianity and Classical Culture*, which Auden reviewed in 1944, concluding with an explicit appeal to the topicality of the principal event under examination, namely Augustine's reconceptualization of the social order: "Our period is not so unlike the age of Augustine:

the planned society, caesarism of thugs or bureaucracies, paideia, scientia, religious persecution, are all with us. Nor is there even lacking the possibility of a new Constantinism" (*Prose* 2:231). In Rosenstock-Huessy's work, Auden discovers the inception of a revolutionary tradition in the events surrounding the eleventh-century Investiture Controversy, whereas in de Rougemont, he discovers the beginning of romantic love in the new genre of song invented by twelfth-century troubadours. The novelty of these events derives in part from the fact that none of the relevant agents meant to do what they could be seen in retrospect to have accomplished: Pope Gregory VII did not want to begin a revolutionary tradition when he fought for his right to name local bishops without imperial interference, and the troubadours of Provence had no intention of creating a kind of love that was unknown to classical and early-Christian civilizations alike. Thus did a group of poets make something happen: they inaugurated a new epoch of love, our own—but without intending to do so.

The obscurity of such historians as Cochrane, de Rougemont, and Rosenstock-Huessy is doubtless one of the reasons why the ideas of history that Auden began to explore in the late 1930s have generated little critical attention. Most of the other scholars in whose work he could be said to discover "history" are similarly neglected in the early twenty-first century. This is perhaps not altogether accidental, for, even though the scholars whose work attracted Auden's attention had sometimes acquired a broad reputation at the time—this applies to de Rougemont, less so to Cochrane and especially to Rosenstock-Huessy—he nevertheless recognized the strangeness or, perhaps better said, the sheer indigestibility of their work. Like Edward Casaubon in Eliot's *Middlemarch*, they rode their hobbyhorses to death, or at least rode them to the point where even their most sympathetic readers, Auden included, become exhausted. Rosenstock-Huessy, for instance, wrote history backward: *Out of Revolution* begins with the Bolshevik Revolution and concludes with the Investiture Controversy. Cochrane, for his part, proposed a ponderous, tripartite, quasi-dialectical schema whereby "Reconstruction" leads to "Renovation," which, in turn, results in something called "Regeneration." The indigestibility of the work from which Auden began to develop his own ideas of history guaranteed that, far from coalescing into a method of historical research or a grand narrative that would supersede all previous ones, these ideas would remain his own, bound up with the memory of a few cherished authors, whom he preferred to keep for himself, as he openly admits in reference, first, to Rosenstock-Huessy (who is still largely unknown) and, then again, to Hannah Arendt (who definitely is not).[7]

The point of collecting such cherished books, however, is the very opposite of esotericism or "secret histories." There is nothing hidden about the insights that can be teased out of *Love in the Western World*, *Out of Revolution*, or *Christianity and Classical Culture*. Nor does Auden aim to make himself into one of Shelley's "unacknowledged legislators of the world" on the basis of the historical works he holds dear: "'The unacknowledged legislators of the world,'" he writes in *The Dyer's Hand*, "describes the secret police, not the poets" (*Prose* 4:474; cf. *Prose* 2:348). Far from straightforwardly affirming the assortment of historians who, as it were, replaced Marx, Auden disentangles a few of their claims from the explanatory arguments and apologetic purposes out of which they emerged, so that they can be seen for what they are: flashes of insight that help to illuminate where we are now.

Traveling, Silence

History, for Auden, was not simply a matter of reading historiographical investigations that could be clearly distinguished from his own experiences. Like the Dionysus-inspired poets to whom Hölderlin refers in "Bread and Wine" when he describes his friend's answer to the question of what poets are for "in destitute times," Auden found himself "drawn from land to land" from the late 1920s onward. Unlike the poets invoked in Hölderlin's poem, however, his journeys led him away from sacred fervor—and any trace of the thought that poets retain a hidden cultic function. In the late 1920s he entered into the tumultuous world of Weimar Germany, coming into contact with the work of its cultural icons, which resulted in such Brechtian ballads and Weill-like cabaret songs as "Miss Gee," "James Honeyman," and "Victor." Beyond the poems that specifically reflect his experience in the strife-torn streets of Berlin, he regularly included in his poems of the 1930s names of places and persons that were closely linked with the conflicts and events of the period—names such as Hitler, Mussolini, Nanking, and Dachau. After a brief trip to Portugal to visit Christopher Isherwood and a much longer journey to Iceland with Louis MacNeice in 1936, Auden traveled to Spain in 1937, where he worked as an ambulance driver and propaganda broadcaster on the Republican side. In early 1938 he also traveled to China, which was engaged in a fierce war against the invading Japanese Imperial Army, where he saw, photographed, and recounted in verse and prose certain events of the war. Both trips occasioned major poems, "Spain" in the first case, and his sonnet sequence, "Sonnets from China," in the second. Writing to his friend E. R. Dodds about the rationale for his dangerous trip to Spain, he announced the credo that gave direction to his travels for a time: "I am not one of those who believe that poetry need or even should be directly political, but in a critical period such as ours, I do believe that the poet must have direct knowledge of the major political events."[8] Beyond the publication of "Spain" as a pamphlet, the proceeds of which were donated to the Spanish Medical Aid Committee (an international organization supporting the anti-Franco cause), Auden was silent about what he had seen during his time in that country. And by 1940 he began to reevaluate the credo he had so confidently expressed in his letter to Dodds, writing the following in a review of Alvah Bessie's memoir of the Spanish Civil War, *Men in Battle*: "In the Munich crisis I listened to the radio with happy excitement, secretly hoping there would be a war, a hope for which I found excellent political reasons. This September, whenever I listened to the radio I started to cry. My attitude had changed because the personal problem which in 1938 was still unsolved and which in despair I was looking to world events to solve for me, was solved this year" (*Prose* 2:41).

In 1945 Auden returned to Germany, this time as a Bombing Research Analyst in the absurdly named Morale Division of the U. S. Strategic Bombing Survey. His job was to interview German civilians about the effects of Allied bombing on their morale.[9] About this morbid business Auden said little and wrote nothing. Despite an agreement he had made with his friend James Stern to write a book about the scenes of devastation they witnessed together, he kept his silence in both prose and poetry—and, so it seems, in personal conversations as well. It is as though the silence that unexpectedly descended upon him as he reflected on his experience in Spain grew more resolute in response to the catastrophes of the World War: "During these months," Stern wrote, "we were continually together, under circumstances about which I was to write a book but of which Wystan in the years to come could very rarely be persuaded to speak. He did, however, while awaiting my arrival, write to Tania [Stern's wife] in May 1945: 'The work is very interesting but I am near crying sometimes. . . . The people . . . are sad beyond belief.' The main purpose of this letter, I should add, was to ask Tania, whom Wystan had entrusted with power of attorney, to send a cheque for $100 to the sick wife of . . . a refugee who was in Dachau."[10]

The silence that descended on Auden in conjunction with his work with the Morale Division of the Strategic Bombing Survey affected the basic character of his subsequent travels. He continued to undertake journeys, to be sure; yet none of their destinations could be readily described as the sites of "major political events" or, indeed, places where the word *historical* would generally apply, except of course in microhistorical terms. And this is at least in part because Auden had begun to alter his idea of history—not drastically, to be sure, but in subtle manner, as he further developed the lines of thought that led him to discover an event of the utmost importance in, for instance, the Investiture Controversy. Even a focus on an event of this kind, however, became suspect in his view, for the event could still be localized—in this case, localized in Pope Gregory VII's cloister, which begins the "Post-Vergilian" section of "Memorial for the City"—but only because it opens up a crevice in social-political space in which two conflicting domains split apart a cloistered room, one associated with "home," the other with "Rome." As early as 1941, and in response to objections about his move to the United States at a "destitute time" for his British homeland, Auden rejected any suggestion that history belongs to a particular locale. In a letter to his friend Stephen Spender, he described a maturation of perspective that renders deliberate pursuits of so-called historical sites dubious at best, evil at worst; for the desire to see such sites suggests that they harbor a magical power of attraction: "You are too old a hand to believe that History has a local habitation any more" (*MY*, 76–77).

The desire to go to locations where History is happening is based on a paradoxical demand over which Auden gradually gained control: the locations were specific, but History (capital H) is general, and because History was the purpose of the journeys, the specificity of the places was reduced to variables in equations that were supposed to express the historical form of an era. Auden's participation in the Morale Division of the Strategic Bombing Survey must have confirmed his growing doubts about the rationale for his trips to Spain and China—a rationale perhaps never more perfectly and thus more disgracefully expressed than in a remark he made to Christopher Isherwood eight years earlier when they were first contemplating their trip to China: "We'll have a war all of our very own."[11] Auden came to reject the appalling foolishness of such pronouncements. It is one thing to say of Rosenstock-Huessy that he wants to keep his works for himself, but it is something altogether different to say this of a war. Even if the remark to Isherwood is accorded a generous interpretation and understood as nothing more than an expression of a desire to draw the attention of English-speaking audiences to the horrors of Imperial Japan's aggression, it nevertheless operates with the presumption that such attention would confer a reciprocal benefit on them, the travelers whose discovery of a major historical event would be akin to discoveries in the natural sciences, as on a trip to the North Pole, for which credit can be claimed. This goes against the spirit of what draws Auden into the study of history. And he soon turns away from anything of the kind—so much so that no trace of either that tone or the underlying sentiment can be found in the writings that follow upon his demoralizing experience with the Morale Division.

Overview of the Argument

The first chapter begins with Auden elevated to the position of sage, whose words are cited in two cases of popular culture and at similar moments of personal crisis. The advice he gives, as it turns out, is "get married!"—which is a traditional imperative in one case, transformative in another. The first case occurs in Mitch Albom's bestselling book and subsequent film dramatization *Tuesdays with Morrie*, which reaches its climax when

Morrie, near death, quotes a line from "September 1"—"we must love one another or die"—in his effort to convince Albom that the only answer to his midlife crisis lies in forging a marital commitment. The second case is the popular film *Four Weddings and a Funeral*, the unexpected climax of which makes a subtler yet similar assignment of purpose to Auden's poetry, for a recitation of "Funeral Blues" functions as a substitute for the marital vows that the film's gay characters are barred from declaring for each other. This scene represents a public demand for marriage equality. Jim Obergefell, whose case before the Supreme Court established marriage equality in the United States, publicly represented his own experience of marital love through a comparison with "Funeral Blues"—which shows how Auden's poetry helped make something happen without intending to do so. The point of reflecting on these popular appropriations of Auden's poetry is not only to draw attention to its persistent topicality but also to sketch in miniature the conception of history in relation to poetry that Auden developed in the late 1930s and early '40s. After describing Auden's own experience of marriage, divided as it was between legality (with Erika Mann) and reality (with Chester Kallman), the chapter concentrates on two epithalamia he wrote around 1940, where he discloses an affinity between marriage and poetry that derives from the circumstance that each is accomplished with "conscious artifice," as he writes in the second epithalamium under consideration, "In Sickness and in Health." An analysis of this poem reveals how it clarifies the historical character of the event it honors: marriage can be seen to transcend all natural and social cycles without incurring the accompanying illusion that this newly gained transcendence represents a condition in which anyone becomes magically immune from suffering and further change. Marriage, in short, is—and represents the model of—a historical event that accords with the poetic vocation of celebration, because change in this case promises to have been motivated through love.

The second chapter considers a paradigmatic case, for Auden, of a writer who devotes considerable energy to making things happen. The writer is Voltaire, and what he wants to bring about is nothing less than the flourishing of democracy—so Auden surprisingly claims in a 1939 review essay, even as he also emphasizes that Voltaire would never have described his intentions in this way. Auden is attracted to the figure of Voltaire not only because his work represents an eighteenth-century version of *littérature engagée* but, above all, because he accompanied his polemical writings with an attempt, late in his life, to found a semiautonomous community in the Swiss canton of Ferney. The community as it appears at the beginning of Auden's "Voltaire at Ferney" emerges as something akin to marriage writ large: all its members reciprocally support one another, with shared happiness as their common goal. According to Auden's most incisive contribution to political theory of the period, happiness is conducive to democracy, insofar as those who see themselves as happy are more inclined to engage with others, regardless of their assumed and imputed identities. Chapter 2 elucidates "Voltaire at Ferney" by comparing its portrait of the *philosophe* with a contemporaneous portrayal that appears in the final section of what is generally seen as one of the founding documents of Critical Theory, Theodor Adorno and Max Horkheimer's *Dialectic of Enlightenment*. Drawing out the distinctions between these two portraits of a thinker-poet who ceaselessly seeks to "crush the infamy" shows how Auden develops a version of critical theory that can be seen to rival the one proposed by its originators. The Voltaire constructed by Adorno and Horkheimer is a unified and consistent figure, whose thought is so supremely "hard" that it can withstand the deceptive allure of compromise with the status quo. Voltaire, for them, thus becomes an idealized image of critical theory. The image of Voltaire that emerges in Auden's poem is very different, for, unlike Horkheimer and Adorno, Auden does not make Voltaire into an image of his own identity as either poet or thinker. Not only does the Voltaire of "Voltaire at Ferney" differ from the image of Voltaire Auden paints in the prose of his review essay; the Voltaire of the poem also differs from himself, with his life split between Paris-based polemics and Ferney-based practice. Absorbed in the "verses" responsive to the destitution of his times, Voltaire becomes a configuration of poetic as well as cosmic divisiveness.

The third chapter turns to Auden's poetic prose, specifically, three prose monologues he embeds in long poems and verse plays he wrote during the period in question. What unites the three monologues is Auden's reassignment of each of them to figures who are the opposite of the figures for whom each speech was originally conceived. All three monologues thus evince a certain fluidity and instability in matters of political and religious identity. This chapter takes its point of orientation from Auden's eviscerating review of Harold Laski's 1941 manifesto *Where Do We Go from Here?* Horkheimer, for his part, fully approves of Laski's attempt to chart a way forward from the impoverished conditions in which the coalition of antifascist forces currently finds itself. Not so Auden—but not because he is any less opposed to fascism at every point where it appears, including in its rhetoric of "movement." Rather, Auden objects to the form of the question itself, which should ask, instead, "Where are we now?" In order to grasp the current situation in genuinely historical terms, Auden argues, we must recognize that the forces that must be defeated are not some alien elements to which he and like-minded compatriots or comrades are immune. Auden makes this point in a particularly provocative way when he says of Hitler that "he has pushed liberalism to its logical conclusion" (*Prose* 2:106). Illuminating Auden's mode of argumentation with Slavoj Žižek's "defense of lost causes," Chapter 3 proposes that a thought of this kind, whereby political antitheses are implicated in each other, stands at the basis of the change in identity that each of the three prose monologues underwent. The first is a call to a worldwide counterrevolutionary action, which was first conceived as the voice of an Armament Manufacturer but eventually became the voice of a Vicar; the second is a soliloquy that Auden originally began in the voice of the prototypical convert Saint Simeon the Righteous, but which turned into the musings of Herod, who, prompted by his order to massacre the indigenous peoples of his imperial outpost, declares himself a "liberal" (*FTB* 117) compelled to make this decision because otherwise "civilization" would be lost; and the third is an address that Auden began as a song sung by Ariel but completed as Caliban's prose address to the audience.

In the case of the first two monologues, the reversal in the identity of each speaker indicates that the Other is not simply outside but also interior to the self—and indeed a self with which Auden identifies: in one case, an Armament Manufacturer turns into a Vicar, who, as such, stands in for the Church; in the second case, which can be seen as the mirror image of the first, the murmurings of the first Christian convert slip into the voice of the imperial regent who wants to kill the one to whom the convert turns.

In following the traces of Auden's composition, the chapter shows how these two speeches present themselves as defenses of so-called civilization when, in fact, they are violent responses to the fluidity and instability of identity based on the self-serving distinction between "civilization," which represents the inside, and "barbarism," which consists in everything else. The third speech is different, first of all in its language. The language of the Vicar becomes progressively more crazed; the language of Herod is "rational" in the manner of a colonial bureaucrat who was trained in classics at a British public school; but the language of Caliban is so magnificently ornate and magisterial that, as he notes, the audience will gather only a vague idea of what he is saying. In this way, Auden responds in advance to a famous question posed by Gayatri Spivak, "Can the subaltern speak?"[12] The thought that Self and Other are implicated in each other generates the belief that every Other is, after all, comprehensible, and something like "mutual understanding" is always possible. Caliban's address to the audience indicates otherwise. At issue in his address is the "gap" (*FTB* 56) in which it occurs—not only the narrow space separating the actor from the audience but also the vast gulf separating a colonial subject from those who oversee him. Caliban's speech converges on the status of this gap, which cannot be bridged simply by recognizing its existence. Writing near the end of the Second World War and the beginning of postwar conflicts over decolonization, Auden produces his most trenchant response to the question he poses in response to Laski, "Where are we now?"

The first three chapters of this volume are concerned with Auden's poetry and prose from around the beginning of the Second World War to its end, and each of them analyzes that work under a broadly conceived optic: marriage, critical theory, and prose monologue. The second part of this study, also comprising three chapters, concerns the contents of a single volume, *Homage to Clio*, where Auden collected much of his poetry from the 1950s. The Interlude concentrates on a single poem, "The Fall of Rome," which Auden wrote midway between those under discussion in the two parts. The primary purpose of undertaking a detailed commentary on a single poem at the center of the book is to develop *in concreto* Auden's relation to his major modernist predecessors, each of whom expressed anxieties about the collapse of Roman (European, Western) civilization. As the Interlude demonstrates, "The Fall of Rome" responds to Baudelaire, especially his idea of "correspondences," which Auden at once adopts and radically transforms; to Kipling, especially his conception of discipline as all-purpose remedy for social and political collapse; to Yeats, especially his image of an eternal Byzantium that lies beyond Roman-Western history; and to Eliot, who, following Baudelaire, creates a multi-temporal poem, which, unlike Auden's compact poem, is composed of "fragments" intended to reflect the degradation and fragmentation of Indo-European civilization. Without being attachable to an -ism of its own, "The Fall of Rome" strikes at the core of all these versions of modernism: Baudelaire's Satanism, Kipling's racial imperialism, Yeats' occult obscurantism, and Eliot's anti-Semitic Constantinianism. The chapter argues that the poem locates at its center what "Roma" is missing: its reversal, hence "revolution," in *amor*. From its title to its haunting final lines, where Auden encompasses the collapse of the Empire in a vast vision of nature running wild, the poem discerns a division in life itself: as a loveless Rome falls, reindeer roam.

The fourth chapter, beginning the second half of this book, picks up at the point in European history where the Interlude concludes—with the emergence of the so-called Middle Ages after the fall of the Western Roman Empire. Auden does not accept the notion of a stagnating "middle" period separating the dynamism of Mediterranean antiquity from the dynamism of Western European modernity. On the contrary—and in accordance with the distance he takes from certain Enlightenment schemata—Auden is attentive to the traces of fundamental changes in a supposedly static, religiously oriented culture. It is for this reason that around 1940 he became absorbed in Rosenstock-Huessy's and de Rougemont's *magna opera*, each of which seeks to show that twentieth-century European civilization has failed to discover an effective response to the political and social innovations of the eleventh and twelfth centuries. De Rougemont's discovery of the origins of romantic love is of particular importance for Auden, since it touches on a question that is of the utmost personal as well as political urgency: What are the "isotopes" of love? Tracing the manner in which Auden's poetry of that period (the late 1930s and early 1940s) tends to pair the figure of Eros with a variety of "isotopic" companions—including

Agape and "dust" (hence, death) but also, more surprisingly, Aphrodite in the moving conclusion to "In Memory of Sigmund Freud"—the chapter describes the basis for Auden's second reception of Freud's thought, which occurred in the early 1950s, when he was asked to review a spate of books about the origins of psychoanalysis.

What Auden discovers in Freud's early writings is an exemplary historian who, against his will (for he had wanted to be a scientist in accordance with the Helmholtzian model), reluctantly recognizes the irreducible character of the "historical fact." As the chapter argues, Auden is proceeding along a similar path from a different direction—but without undergoing a similar transformation of his "professional" identity and without performing a poetic equivalent to the abandonment of the "seduction theory." Whereas Freud becomes a historian, despite his desire to found a science of the mind, Auden, now in his mid-fifties, is and remains a poet who is called upon to recognize, above all, the historical reality of traumatic events and their lingering effects. The questionable constancy of this stance affects every stanza of the first poem he writes in honor of the muse of history, "Homage to Clio," which begins with an image of the poet holding a book in his hand, as though he had inherited the iconic accoutrement of the classical muse of history. By recognizing that Clio can no longer be seen as an Olympian agent of heroic commemoration, Auden does not close the distance between himself and the muse whom he seeks to honor; on the contrary, Auden experiences a widening of their distance from each other. The dynamics of the muse's family change accordingly: her siblings are no longer the other eight muses; rather, they are two powerful Olympians, Aphrodite and Artemis, who govern the cycles of Eros and Thanatos respectively. As for Clio's erstwhile mother, Mnemosyne, Auden pluralizes her into "our recollections." Chapter 4 concludes by showing that the tension between the poet and the muse of history concentrates itself into a specifically poetic form of recollection: the selection of the poems to include and exclude from a potentially monumentalizing volume called *Collected Poems*.

The fifth chapter takes its point of departure from the second poem in *Homage to Clio*, "Reflections in a Forest." The arboreal silence that prompts this poem not only recalls the scene with which Dante begins the *Com-*

media but also functions as a figuration of social-political silencing under the domination of upward-striving, "straight" conformity. The silence of the muse (history) and the silence of the forest (nature) thus echo each other, and the chapter proceeds to examine the remaining poems in Part 1 of the volume, which introduces two more versions of Clio, with each of the resulting three versions being incompatible with the other two. Along with this dizzying diversity of Clios, Auden presents the figure of a major poet, namely Virgil, who, as Auden argues in contemporary prose reflections, "betrayed the muse." For Auden, betraying the muse of poetry is, however, a positive feature of Virgil's poetic accomplishment, because the function of the muse in classical culture derives from a conception of the cosmos in which nothing can ever change; under these conditions, poetry acquires the sole purpose of helping mortals bear their inevitable suffering. In "Secondary Epic" Auden thus addresses the principal poet of the Roman Empire and implores him to stop writing poetry: "No, Virgil, no." As the chapter argues, this redoubled "no" does not mean, "do not betray the muse" but, rather, "do not betray your betrayal" with stanzas glorifying imperial reign as the end of history. A trace of this "no" then occupies the Interlude through which Auden separates the two parts of *Homage to Clio*. Borrowing his Interlude's title, "Dichtung und Wahrheit," from Goethe's autobiographical reflections, Auden produces fifty Wittgenstein-like "grammatical remarks" in response to a question about whether poetry can be radically historical; specifically whether a particular "I," the poet himself, can create a poem that precisely expresses his love for an irreplaceable, singular "You" whom he expects soon to reencounter. In seeking to work out in prose form the relation between language, love, and history, Auden discovers that the answer to his question is "no." *Homage to Clio* is thus interrupted by what he calls "An Unwritten Poem," the effects of which spread into Part 2 of the volume, where the figure of Clio vanishes, and the second-person singular "You" begins to disappear as well.

Homage to Clio stands out among Auden's volumes of poetry because it is split in two by this unwritten poem. Not only does the volume show a poet at work, again and again configuring the relation between poetry and history in a variety of poetic forms; it also, and just as importantly, revolves around the discovery of a point where the poet must stop, for the poetic work has reached a limit. The sixth chapter of this study traces the effects of this discovery. The first effect—which Auden describes as such—appears at the beginning of Part 2, where Auden produces a poem that is no longer concerned with the "historical fact" but is dedicated, instead, to the progenitor of natural kinds, namely "Dame Kind." A more extensive though less conspicuous effect occurs, moreover, in the final poems in Part 2, where Auden undertakes a distinctly anthropological turn, beginning with "Limbo Culture." Adopting the voice of an anthropologist, he drafts a report on the far-away land of contemporary U.S. and Western European culture, where both "I" and "you" are replaced by types and averages. Limbo is of course the first stratum of Dante's *Inferno*, and in the subsequent poem, "There Will Be No Peace," Auden goes deeper and reports on an even lower stratum of hell. In "Dichtung und Wahrheit" Auden lightly asks whether there can be such a thing as "Romantic Hate," which would somehow replicate romantic love but in reverse. This brief aphoristic inquiry gains a grim complexity in "There Will Be No Peace," which loses any trace of playfulness and directly addresses itself to those who have momentarily survived a culture that consists in "hate for hate's sake."

And the next poem in the collection, "Friday's Child," which is dedicated to the memory of Dietrich Bonhoeffer (who, as the epigraph notes, was murdered by the Nazis in the Flossenbürg concentration camp), gives hate culture a precise historical index. Beyond demonstrating the intricate interconnections among the final poems in the collection—before the outburst of irreverent humor in "Academic Graffiti"—Chapter 6 reflects on their sequential character in order to show how Auden marks the site of a missing poem that would have proceeded still further than "Friday's Child" into the horror of "hate for hate's sake." It is as though, getting to this point in the volume, the poet tells himself, "no, Auden, no"—do not betray the muse by making a pleasing poem about the industrialization of murder in a death camp. This is the *second* "unwritten poem" in *Homage to Clio*, though Auden does not mark it as such, for even that would be a betrayal; instead, he orders his poems so that Part 1 ends with a love poem he cannot write, and Part 2 with a hate poem he will not write. There is some evidence in his literary notebook of this period that Auden began to draft a poem that would have been dedicated to "the darkness" (in Hebrew, *ha-shoah*); but after a few attempts, spread over several pages, the drafts merge into the opening stanza of "There Will Be No Peace." Regardless of the ultimate status of these drafts, the volume ultimately turns away from its hellish descent in its final poem, "Good-bye to the Mezzogiorno," which in purely formal terms—twenty-three quatrains of syllabic verse—returns poet and reader to the volume's starting point, for this is also the form of "Homage to Clio."

This chapter concludes with a reflection on precisely how "Good-bye to the Mezzogiorno" represents a turning back. The poem's first stanza identifies the destination of this return: back to "guilt culture." In this way, the anthropological turn is complete, as Auden adopts and expands one of the chief concepts of contemporaneous anthropological inquiry. Auden associates his movement to the Mezzogiorno with two other Northern invasions of southern Italy: the Gothic invasions that brought an end to the Western Roman Empire and Goethe's Italian journey—hence, the collapse of classical civilization, vandalizing violence, and cultural achievement all at once. In the background is also, of course, the recent occupation of fascist Italy by Nazi Germany. The return to guilt culture is not motivated by anything Auden did wrong; nor, conversely, does writing poetry confer innocence. In tracing the motivations for this return, which is the subject matter of the poem, the chapter identifies two: one related to anthropology, the other to history. The former consists in a realization that Auden, for one, cannot bridge a cultural "gulf" that separates him from those whom he observes; the latter consists in a reckoning with the consequences of a "divorce." Nowhere in *Homage to Clio* does Auden use the word *divorce*; but it is a primary term in the lectures Auden delivered upon accepting the first T. S. Eliot Memorial Lectureship in 1967. The divorce in question is between the historian and the poet, each of whom must reckon with its consequences—but the poet much more directly than the historian. And the ultimate reason for the divorce is that the poet cannot write a poem about industrialized murder, whereas the historian, by contrast, is called upon to write its history. "Good-bye to the Mezzogiorno" is the culmination of Auden's attempt to honor the muse of history by responding to his separation from her. The poem closes with a memory of "meridian names" that, as the term *meridian* suggests—*Mezzogiorno* is, of course, the term's Italian translation—promises a "great circle" of return: not a remarriage, to be sure; but a re-encounter still.

On Concepts of History

From its first to its last pages, *Homage to Clio* bids farewell to grand narratives, so much so that it includes a poem that parodies the grandest narrative of great and not so great philosophers alike, "The History of Truth." The loss of grand narratives became a famous formula a few years after Auden's death, when Jean-François Lyotard defined "the postmodern condition" accordingly: "Simplifying to the extreme, I define postmodern as incredulity toward metanarratives," more precisely those metanarratives that are matters of scientific or scholarly forms under which knowledge is legitimated.[13] In a similarly simplifying vein, it can be said that this study tracks Auden's experience of arriving at his own version of the postmodern condition, which begins with his decision to depart from Marxism and his corresponding refusal to replace straightforwardly Marxian narratives of historical progress with competing ones drawn from some combination of the natural, social, and human sciences. In this regard, Auden's situation is comparable to that of Walter Benjamin, when, in the same period, he wrote the fragments that would be posthumously published under the title "On the Concept of History."

Auden and Benjamin were, each in his own way, idiosyncratic Marxists long before they undertook a reconsideration of Marxism under the shadow of what would become the Second World War. For both of them, the great danger of constructing "the" concept of history lies in its very success; that is, such a construction would fix the concept of history, fitting together the past with the future, making the present into the proverbial steppingstone on the way to an appointed destination. Neither of them was in any sense anti-progressive, yet both saw the belief in historical progress, which is distinct from progress in the acquisition of knowledge, as profoundly mistaken, for, willy-nilly, it diminishes the importance of the present situation in its immediate, hence non-causal, relation to the past. Benjamin expresses this importance through the image of "now-time."[14] In his prose writings, Auden tends to express it in terms of moral responsibility, which is annulled if certain "forces" are said to be at work in the "movement" from past to future. And in the course of their critiques of progressive ideologies, neither of them shied away from drawing on their intimate familiarity with theological motifs, Jewish and Christian, without, in either case, making theology into the core of a more or less crypto-regressive ideology that aims for the restoration of a theocratic order. Chapter 2 of this study conducts a detailed comparison of Auden's views with the ideas of two of Benjamin's then-associates, Horkheimer and Adorno; but except for a brief description in Chapter 3, of Auden writing in 1940 and formulating a thought strikingly similar to a passage in "On the Concept of History," this study refrains from any further comparison between their reflections on the concept of history.

As is the case with the work of Lyotard and of Benjamin, as well as that of Adorno and Horkheimer, Auden's work can be put into productive dialogue with thinkers whom he did not know and who did not know him. Another prominent example is Michel Foucault—not so much as the author of *The Order of Things* and *The Archeology of Knowledge*, which Auden could have read but probably did not, but as the later researcher into the history of sexuality, published in four volumes: *Introduction* (*La Volonté de savoir*), *The Use of Pleasure*, *The Care of the Self*, and *The Confessions of the Flesh*. The period and subject matter that Foucault examined in volumes two through four—roughly speaking, Greco-Roman antiquity and early Christianity—were of intense interest to Auden. His own research on the transformations of the practices and doctrines of so-called paganism into those of early Christianity was facilitated by E. R. Dodds, whose presence in *Homage to Clio* goes far beyond its dedication page. It is unfortunate that neither of them had a chance to read and evaluate what are often dismissed as Foucault's most boring books. It is unlikely that Auden would have found them so. In any case, for both Foucault and Auden, the changes in late antiquity were of immense importance—not only because they concern the very practice of the self but also because they are traversed by continuities that transformed regimes of speech as well. In a seemingly paradigmatic case of "historical change," when one world seems to have been altogether replaced by another, something else was actually happening, which may be correspondingly related to what is happening today.[15] This is not because "history necessarily repeats itself" but because a clear-eyed view of contemporary changes, which Foucault seeks to accomplish in the *History of Sexuality* by a dismantling of the "repression hypothesis," lets us see the shape of earlier ones, and vice versa.

Auden's understanding of history can also be productively compared to another influential work of the mid-1970s, Hayden White's *Metahistory*. Except for the identity of the philosophers under examination in White's study of the "historical imagination in nineteenth-century Europe"—Marx, Nietzsche, and de Tocqueville—Auden's historiographical canon does not overlap with White's. Auden also did not propose a formal "poetics of history," to quote the subtitle of White's introduction. Yet Auden, who knew the categories of poetics like few others, including other professional poets, informally and indeed spontaneously created such a poetics almost every time he examined a historical study or reflected on something that presents itself as a historical occurrence. He never ceases to show that the poet and the historian stand in something like an arranged marriage, such that the historian can do without the poet—but only at the cost of turning historiography into a version of statistical mechanics, with the result that history as such is lost. What principally distinguishes White's self-contained study from Auden's generally occasional reflections is the latter's fluidity: Auden is acutely aware of the poetics that underlies and sustains historiographical reflection; but at the same time, congruent with his own agility as a poet, he does not see this poetics as fixed. He thus produces a poetics of history again and yet again, each attuned to the historical referent, the "emplotment" of the narrative, and above all, the broader "perspective" under which an occurrence acquires the epithet "historical."[16] This is, of course, not a criticism of White's influential study but only a point of contrast. Auden's knowledge of poetics makes every one of his reflections on history a spontaneous chapter of a constitutively inconclusive metahistory.

Something similar can be said about a more recent contribution to metahistorical inquiry, Giorgio Agamben's *The Time That Remains*.[17] Although—or perhaps because—Agamben does not place this work within the larger *Homo Sacer* project, whose aims it helps to explain, this "Commentary on the Letter to the Romans" represents its metahistorical nucleus. Like White, though for different reasons, Agamben arranges certain poetological categories in order to construct or reconstruct a certain concept of history, namely Pauline Messianism, in which our time reveals itself as the beginning of the end of time. Auden studied the writings of St. Paul at least as assiduously as, and probably more persistently than, Agamben. On the basis of our knowledge of Auden's return to Christianity in the late 1930s, we might expect to find a concept of history that would be permeated by the Pauline conviction that we are indeed living at the end of time. If this were the case, a way could be found for Auden the prose writer to merge with Auden the poet: Both, as students of St. Paul, could forge a Christological-Messianic concept of history. But Auden does nothing of the kind. Auden's Christianity is conspicuous, whereas his Messianism is inconspicuous, and the tension between them is a cardinal element of his varying concepts of history.[18] This, too, is a basic starting point for this study: Auden does not replace Marxism with Paulism. Thus the rhetoric of revelation and the imagery of end times are missing from his encounters with historical matters.

Not an end time but an end space can be seen in the "Altogether elsewhere" that begins the final stanza of "The Fall of Rome," the poem discussed in this study's Interlude. Not only is this "elsewhere" disconnected from the imperial regime; it is likewise cut off from the hegemony of humanity in general: "Herds of reindeer move across / Miles and miles of golden moss / Silently and very fast" (*CP* 333). Auden's work has attracted the attention of contemporary eco-criticism, which has put his evident humanism in a contested dialogue with a variety of eco-critical forms of research, including Animal Studies and the New Materialism.[19] As far as I know, though, the haunting end of "The Fall of Rome" has not attracted such notice, even as it raises some of the basic questions that give shape to the environmental humanities, beginning with this: How "altogether" is the "elsewhere" that Auden images as the limit point of what is here "Rome," which, as the first stanza indicates, includes modern technologies? That is, does Auden imagine nature as in a different regime than that of humanity, or is "altogether" a sign of a certain denegation, in which humanity bears—but, at the same time, denies—responsibility for the flight of the reindeer who sense a catastrophe produced by humanity, regardless of whether a particular regime rises or falls? This study does not pursue this and kindred questions; but its reading of "The Fall of Rome" is placed as an Interlude in part to indicate that the poem poses problems that transcend human-centric history.

A concept of human history that resonates with the second part of this study can be found in some of the more recent inquiries of Judith Butler, especially *Precarious Life*, *Frames of War*, and *Parting Ways*. It is not as though these works are themselves dedicated to constructing a concept of history; rather, one appears almost inadvertently. And this, too, is like Auden's experience, when he almost inadvertently comes across the muse of history in the figure of Clio, who may be a war refugee or a displaced person and lives, in any case, a precarious existence—a life framed by the pages of something like *Life* magazine: "I have seen / Your photo, I think, in the papers, nursing / A baby or mourning a corpse" (*HC* 17). For Butler, a concept of history spontaneously originates from the removal of this mass-mediated and ideologically tinted frame, a removal that she presents through the reality as well as the metaphor of translation: "The *co* of *cohabitation* is . . . the nexus where convergent temporalities articulate present time, not a time in which one history of suffering negates another, but when it remains possible that one history of suffering provides the conditions of attunement to another such history and that whatever connections are made proceed through the difficulty of translation."[20] "Homage to Clio" presents this attunement of one history with another in terms of "music," and the difficulty of translation becomes the difficulty involved in "Making of silence decisive sound: it sounds / Easy, but one must find the time" (*HC* 17). The "but" is essential: among those, like Clio, whose existence is precarious, time is not something that one simply "has," but is something one must search out and find again and again. And it is in recognition of such precarity that Auden develops his most capacious concepts of history, gathered into a volume dedicated to its muse.

Another work of contemporary scholarship gives an exacting point of comparison for the perplexity around which this study revolves: Lauren Berlant's *Cruel Optimism*.[21] In a philosophical sense—Leibniz's "best of all possible worlds," famously parodied by Voltaire in *Candide*—optimism is the very danger that Auden solicits when he uses Eleatic vocabulary to describe the poetic vocation as the affirmation of Being. Auden's prose and poetic portraits of Voltaire, each in its own way, are paradoxical affirmations of a figure who refuses to be an "optimist," for doing so only piles cruelty upon misery. This, though, is all a bit abstract. The proximity between Auden and Berlant is more concretely found in the poems under examination in the second section of this study, beginning with "Homage to Clio," where Auden presents shiny objects of desire, figured in the pursuits of Aphrodite and Artemis, as those that thwart the very possibility of the happiness that is supposed to be secured by the possession of those objects. Auden and Berlant let us see a systematically cruel culture that results from these mechanically produced and sustained cycles of desire, marked by an illusory optimism in the colloquial sense, which is itself predicated on a reduced concept of historical progress, applied now only to the "progress" of individual subjects on the path to a "freedom" (from others) secured via the "free" market. For Berlant, this culture takes hold in the Reaganesque 1980s; for Auden, in the Eisenhowerian 1950s. The last poem in the second part of *Homage to Clio* ends, to be sure, with happiness; but it is a happiness the poet discovers in remembrance, when, while bidding adieu to his "midday" world, he momentarily stands outside the regime of induced desire.

The second section of this study is framed by two discourses that became entangled in heated controversy soon after Auden's death and remain so today. One is the study of Freud, especially as it concerns the origins of psychoanalysis in the abandonment of "seduction theory," that is, the theory that neurotic symptoms emerge from actual childhood trauma rather than imagined scenarios.[22] As discussed at the beginning of Chapter 4, according to Auden, Freud departed from his project of becoming a proto-neuroscientist and became a historian when he made the bold decision to replace seduction theory with a new recognition of the depth and density of psychic life. Auden could scarcely be clearer on this matter in his reviews of Ernest Jones' biography of Freud and associated prose writings of the early 1950s. None of the poems in *Homage to Clio*, however, suggests that the source of trauma is anything but real, that is, public and historical—as, for instance, Clio "mourning a corpse," even if this mourning is publicly mediated by the photographic lens. Around Freud, then, Auden the prose writer and Auden the poet part ways in an exemplary manner. Where does Auden "himself" stand with respect to what came to be known as trauma theory? This study does not seek to answer this question; rather, it places Auden's work, both poetry and prose, at the origin of this controversy.

Another, similar controversy is related to the final poems of *Homage to Clio*, where, as described earlier, Auden undertakes an "anthropological turn." It may be said that the turn to anthropology is somewhat half-hearted or simply playful, as Auden includes the name Margaret Mead in "Metalogue to *The Magic Flute*" and assumes the role of a meta-anthropologist in "Limbo Culture." But the questions prompted by these little-studied poems are closely related to those posed by a series of provocative works that ignited the profession of anthropology, including both the book in which Derek Freeman disputes Mead's account of, to use Auden's words, the "status of the sexes" (*HC* 71) in the account of Samoa that made her famous, and the critique of anthropological reason that Marshall Sahlins proposes in *How "Natives" Think*.[23] Playfully anticipating the kind of attack on Mead's account of sexuality in Samoa that finds expression in Freeman's monograph, Auden pairs Mead with Robert Graves, thus suggesting—lightly, yet also boldly—that she, too, is involved in mythmaking. And "Limbo Culture" can be read as a Rorschach version of the latter controversy: does the poet in the form of a meta-anthropologist assume that all cultures can be described in the same terms, which are drawn from the "First-World" culture that in this case becomes the object of anthropological research, or does the very persona of the meta-anthropologist represent a critique of this universalist assumption? It would be a disservice to the poem to answer the question it prompts. It would not be a disservice to describe how a question of this kind expands—or better expressed, explodes—in the late twentieth and early twenty-first centuries. Yet in this case, as throughout this volume, except for the introductory sections of Chapter 1, which track some prominent traces of Auden's presence in Anglo-American popular culture of the late twentieth century, I practice a kind of scholarly askesis.

Throughout this study, I refer, of course, to the scholarship around Auden, which informs and enriches all my readings; but the point of engaging in something like scholarly askesis is precisely the opposite of what it may seem. Auden's work remains ever-topical, surprisingly so, as demonstrated at the opening of Chapter 1, when "Funeral Blues" becomes an argument for the expansion of marriage equality. And in a different form, as described in Chapter 2 as well as in the previous paragraphs, his work can be seen to anticipate and thus illuminate claims and theorems of contemporary critical theory. Yet the premise of this study is that the relevance of Auden's poetry derives not from a kind of "topicality" that explicitly responds to historical events but from the poet's struggle to reconcile the "conscious artifice" of poetry with the less predictable, often brutal historical realities of his time. Poetry cannot directly intervene in history, nor can it responsibly ignore it or simply make it "more bearable." Auden's prose reflections may sometimes engage in a kind of wooly abstractness that has been the source of complaint and parody since the 1940s; so, too, wrongly, in my view, some of his later poetry has been criticized as fatally ruined by discursivity, pointless rhetoricity, or, in contrast, a cozy silliness that has retreated from the bracing engagement with contemporary history that made his early poetry such a tonic to a generation of readers. But as this study seeks to show through a series of readings that culminate in a concentrated analysis of an extraordinary volume of poetry, some of whose best poems have attracted little or no scholarly attention, Auden is acutely, even painfully open to his world, in dialogue with it, as it were. And the way to see how his poetry is entangled with the world today is by carefully uncovering and describing the voices, events, joys, and calamities to which he responds with "conscious artifice," whose precarious position, stranded between lying and truth, is an integral element of its ever-renewable topicality.

Who Is "Our Native Muse"?

This brings us to one further field of critical theory with which this study intersects. For self-evident reasons, scholars of post-colonial studies have made Shakespeare's *Tempest* a pivotal point of reference. For example, Jyotsna Singh has compiled an extensive network of webpages on the topic, titled "Post-colonial Reading of *The Tempest*" and hosted by the official website of the British Library.[24] Without the medium of the internet at his disposal, Auden posted his own contribution to the post-colonial *Tempest* in his *The Sea and the Mirror,* especially in Caliban's concluding speech, where the "fourth wall" of unidirectional play-acting is breached, as he interrogates imperial culture from within its (representational) midst. Just as Auden's portrait of Herod prompts some of the basic questions Edward Said poses in *Orientalism,*[25] so the speech he lends the figure of Caliban directly addresses the question Sahlins proposed with reference to Captain Cook: how do "natives" think? Having Caliban speak—although perhaps not think—in the style of the late Henry James is another Rorschach test for Auden's readers, and perhaps also for himself.[26] And at the beginning of this speech, Caliban invokes a muse, who not only prefigures all of those under discussion in this study but also makes us aware of and uneasy about our place as readers in contexts traversed in various divergent ways by colonial conflicts, which is to say, with few exceptions, all of contemporary humanity.

The outstanding quality of "our native Muse" (*CP* 423), according to Caliban, is her universality, more precisely, her all-embracing non-exclusivity. She welcomes everyone and everything into her realm, which can be seen as both the particular theater in which the performance takes place and the globe at large. It soon becomes apparent, however, that in a certain sense, this muse to whom Caliban appeals insists on a principle of exclusivity, after all, for she radically separates herself from another power, a "rival" whom she refuses to call by her "real name" (*CP* 424), presumably because this name is somehow related to a reality that would immediately implode the space of the theater. "Our native Muse" understands the power of her "rival" as a mirror image of her own magic, for she is called "that envious witch," and she is emphatically exclusionary: "*not* sympathizing, *not* associating, *not* amusing" (*CP* 424). As if he were seeking to extend the drama beyond its formal conclusion, Caliban thus suggests the possibility of a new conflict that would give rise to a spectacular sequel—a conflict, this time, between two muses, one of whom is specifically recognizable as a muse and makes everything amusing through the all-embracing magic of representation, while the other is not and does not.

Caliban, for his part, has a special position in relation to "our native Muse," for, unlike everyone else in the recently completed play, he is native to the island represented on stage, and therefore, when he speaks of nativity in this context, the conflict gains a new degree of concretion: the audience's muse may differ from his. Indeed, by turning to the audience at the end of the play, Caliban "himself" could be identified with this other power but for one restraining condition: his breach of the "fourth wall" may itself be nothing more than a theatrical gesture that sustains the audience in its own "native" state of amusement. Not only is it impossible to present this conflict of the muses as such, it cannot be resolved either through the victory of one over the other or with the establishment of some measure of balance. The two powers are too different from each other. Nevertheless, even as the conflict's outcome remains uncertain, its origin is not. The conflict comes about only because Caliban, while native to the island, invokes "our native Muse" in echoing the unspoken thoughts of his audience. In other words, the experience of historical oppression is its origin, not the general condition of being a finite rational creature endowed with the capacity to represent things in speech.

Does all of this mean that the other muse-like power—the one whom Caliban, expressing the anxieties of his otherwise amused audience, refuses to identify by name—should be called "the muse of history"? This is the question around which this book revolves. If the title of this scholarly study were written in the interrogative mode, it might therefore be called *Auden and the Muse of History?* Soon after Auden's death, Derek Walcott wrote an essay titled "The Muse of History."[27] Walcott does not punctuate his title with a question mark, yet its presence becomes legible as soon as he begins to discuss the figure of Caliban:

> New World poets who see the "classic style" as stasis must see it also as historical degradation, rejecting it as the language of the master. This self-torture arises when the poet also sees history as language, when he limits his memory to the suffering of the victim. Their admirable wish to honor the degraded ancestor limits their language to phonetic pain, the groan of suffering, the curse of revenge. . . . Their view of Caliban is of the enraged pupil. They cannot separate the rage of Caliban from the beauty of his speech when the speeches of Caliban are equal in their elemental power to those of his tutor.[28]

An "elemental power" is trans-historical, and in some sense, Walcott argues strenuously in favor of the elemental over the historical—but only if "historical" is understood in such a way that it comes to restrict the possible range of language. Thus, in the conclusion to his essay, as he addresses his ancestors in their radical absence, he identifies the specific elements of that "idea of history" upon which he has cast doubt: "I say to the ancestor who sold me, and the ancestor who bought me, I have no father, I want no such father, although I can understand you, black ghost, white ghost, when you whisper 'history,' for if I attempt to forgive you both I am falling into your idea of history which justifies and explains and expiates, and it is not mine to forgive."[29]

Auden's situation is doubtless far different from Walcott's, and yet the conclusion of "The Muse of History"—which makes some of their differences particularly apparent—captures precisely those elements of the idea of history that Auden finds equally dubious: history, first of all, as the justification of the status quo; history, furthermore, as the explanation in causal terms of why things are as they are; and history, finally, as the rectification of errors or the expiation of sins in accordance with a process that must always be repeated, as each attempt at rectification or expiation generates the need and demand for another. The question, then, is whether there is an idea of history that has nothing to do with justification, explanation, rectification, or expiation. The answer from the perspective of the poems and prose texts analyzed in this volume is: "yes, there is such an idea, and indeed more than one." These ideas emerge from the conflicts presented in the texts, each of which is akin to the conflict Caliban begins to represent when he speaks of "our native Muse" and the members of his audience begin to suspect that the muse of which he speaks may be different from one whom they represent to themselves.

PART I

ONE

States of Marriage

"Auden Said That?"

The greatest lesson of life comes from Auden—sort of.

In Mitch Albom's *Tuesdays with Morrie: An Old Man, A Young Man, and Life's Greatest Lesson*, a line attributed to Auden forms the decisive link between the old and the young man. First published in 1997, *Tuesdays with Morrie* has been translated into more than forty languages and is the most successful memoir in U.S. publishing history, selling many millions of copies. As its first paragraph explains and last paragraph repeats, Albom's book relates his encounter with a retired Brandeis professor of social psychology, Morrie Schwartz, who is dying of amyotrophic lateral sclerosis (ALS): "The last class of my old professor's life took place once a week in his house, by a window in the study where he could watch a small hibiscus plant shed its pink leaves. The class met on Tuesdays. It began after breakfast. The subject was The Meaning of Life."[1] Several years earlier Mitch had written his senior thesis with Morrie as his academic advisor. Upon learning of Morrie's condition from an episode of *Nightline* entitled "Life's Lessons," Mitch, now a sports reporter, visits his dying teacher and finds his own feelings of "confusion and depression" healed under Morrie's tutelage (Albom 44). From the first "class" of their renewed relationship,

Morrie emphasizes that contemporary culture condemns those under its influence to a "*meaningless life*" (Albom 43) and that the confusion Mitch experiences belongs to the entire era—and so, too, does an urgent need for clarity. Mitch, in turn, sees in Morrie someone who, by virtue of his life-affirming wisdom and his proximity to death, can identify those "important things" that can fill the cultural vacuum about which he knows all too well. During the fifth session of their unofficial Tuesday "office hours," Morrie begins to fulfill his former student's expectations. Clarity comes in a line of poetry the retired professor attributes to Auden:

> Love is so supremely important. As our great poet Auden said, "Love each other or perish."
>
> "Love each other or perish." I wrote it down. Auden said that? (Albom 91)

The line in question could scarcely be clearer, for it represents life in terms of a stark decision: love or death. Despite the simplicity of this decision, however, the scene is curiously complex, as if Mitch, against his own intentions, wants to dampen the effect of Morrie's wisdom. That Mitch writes down the line "Love each other or perish" is itself odd—even more so that he *writes* that he writes down this line. As the beginning of the chapter explains at length, the conversation is being recorded, so that Morrie's wisdom may be preserved. The act of writing in these circumstances is less a sign of confidence in the supreme importance of the quotation in question than an indication of a degree of unresolved confusion: "Auden said that?" The confusion in this case cannot be attributed to contemporary culture; rather, it consists in certain philological problems of citation: is Auden the author of the line, and if so, is it correctly rendered? Perhaps under the direction of another Brandeis professor, Mitch had learned and retained a memory of the famous last line of the penultimate stanza of Auden's "September 1, 1939": "We must love one another or die" (*AT* 105). Perhaps Mitch, or his publisher, having done some research, wants to signal an awareness of Morrie's misquotation but nevertheless remain faithful to the words of his teacher. In any case, who would care about such matters when something of great importance, indeed "life's greatest lesson," has just been articulated?

After the events of September 11, 2001, Auden's celebrated poem about the first day of the Second World War enjoyed renewed circulation in the public sphere, as it was widely quoted, discussed, condemned, and defended in newspapers, magazines, television programs, and internet chat groups. And small wonder, given its setting in New York and the concluding lines of its opening stanza: "The unmentionable odour of death / Offends the September night" (*AT* 103). But the poem was hardly forgotten between the date of its publication and the attack on the World Trade Center. Lines from this poem have frequently functioned as cultural touchstones. E. M. Forster, to take one early example, said of the line from which Morrie derives his mantra, that because Auden had written it, "he can command me to follow him."[2] This same line formed the pivotal text of perhaps the most famous television advertisement in the history of American politics: an anti-Goldwater commercial of 1964 that featured a girl with a flower, a mushroom cloud, and LBJ's voice intoning, "We must love each other or we must die." As if in revenge, by replacing the word "ironic" with "a thousand," the speechwriter Peggy Noonan skillfully incorporated the poem's reference to "ironic points of light" into George H. W. Bush's unironic acceptance speech at the 1988 Republican Convention.[3] In a very different political environment, Madonna repeated "we must love one another or die" as the conclusion to the speech she gave during the 2017 Women's March on Washington. Auden, for his part, was disturbed by the capacity of "September 1, 1939," to generate tendentious slogans: "One cannot let one's name be associated with shits" (*SC* 210). Whereas Morrie empties Auden's poem of its political character, LBJ makes it into sheer political rhetoric. And these two gestures go hand in hand: both directly appeal to a nameless and therefore all the more fearsome threat that the poem itself seeks to name. Auden's uneasiness about the poem's astonishing rhetorical power concentrated itself on the line that appeals as much to Morrie as to Madonna. As Auden writes in explanation of his decision to excise the poem from his *Collected Poems*, nothing can save this line from a certain dishonesty: "That's a damned lie! We must die anyway."[4]

As for Mitch's unexpected question—"Auden said that?"—it does not concern so much the truth of the line as its provenance. Morrie, however, who is apparently unaware that Auden repudiated the line in question, responds by reaffirming both its truth and goodness, regardless of its author: "'Love each other or perish,' Morrie said. 'It's good, no? And it's so true'" (Albom 91). Morrie, for his part, does not offer Mitch any theory of truth, nor does he explain further how the goodness of a poetic line is related to its truth; rather, in responding to his student's question, he begins to sketch an alternative poem by means of a metaphor in which love itself becomes a means of flight: "Without love, we are birds with broken wings." At the same time, however, he continues the conversation by making his own homebound condition into a case in point. Love makes flight possible, yet flight also becomes impossible because of love: "Say I was divorced, or living alone, or had no children. This disease—what I'm going through—would be much harder. I'm not sure I could do it. Sure people would come visit, friends, associates, but it's not the same as having someone who will not leave" (Albom 91–92).

For Morrie, the imperative derived from "September 1, 1939" has nothing to do with "Imperialism's face / And the international wrong," to quote another famous phrase from the poem; indeed, for Morrie, the line in question does not even mean what it says, since, to cite once again his own flight into metaphor, birds with broken wings remain alive. Furthermore, the condition of having one's wings broken does not itself imply that one has failed to love; otherwise, Morrie's lessons would be paradoxical, for his own illness began to manifest itself in his legs and made it impossible for him to do what he enjoys most, namely dance. As a last attempt to clarify the vital lesson contained in the line, Morrie turns it into a piece of advice, which has the great advantage of ridding himself of the ambiguities—or incoherencies—that result from the image of broken wings. He advises his student to get married. Otherwise, so it seems, one is at the mercy of friends who, like Mitch himself, stay only for a few hours on Tuesdays.[5]

In the made-for-television adaptation of *Tuesdays*, produced by Oprah Winfrey, Mitch (Hank Azaria) hears Morrie (Jack Lemmon) pronounce the line from "September 1" accurately, but he still raises an objection—and indeed an objection that reflects Auden's own dissatisfaction with the line: "What does that mean? Don't we die anyway?" asks Mitch. In a hushed voice, Morrie explains: "As long as we can love each other, and remember the feeling of love we had, we can die without ever really going away. All the love you created is still there." That the same could be said of any passion proves Auden's point. Despite its rhetorical power, there is something suspicious about "We must love one another or die." After trying to repair the line by turning the "or" into "and," Auden considered eliminating the entire stanza, and then, finding no credible solution, gave up on the poem: there is no alternative to death. In *Tuesdays with Morrie*, the alternative is marriage. Presented in the book as the central topic Mitch wishes to discuss with Morrie, marriage not only defeats death; in the movie version, it has the enigmatic power to replace it—with love forever. Whereas the book anchors the author's moral development in the transformation of his relationship to his distant and dying brother (to whom the volume is prominently dedicated), the film version makes no reference to him. And whereas in the book the author is married, in the film he is single, and his triumphant moral development therefore consists in learning how to commit himself to the woman he loves, so they can finally achieve matrimonial stability. The film thus makes the basic tendency of the book transparent. A poem that begins as an anguished reflection on the Nazi invasion of Poland becomes the occasion for the dispensation of insipid "life-affirming" advice and thus makes the basic tendency of the book transparent:

> "Personally," he sighed, his eyes still closed, "I think marriage is a very important thing to do, and you're missing a hell of a lot if you don't try it."
> He ended the subject by quoting the poem he believed in like a prayer: "Love each other or perish." (Albom 149)

The film version of *Tuesdays with Morrie* alters the book in another manner as well. Instead of simply repeating the mangled line that runs like a leitmotif throughout the story, Morrie accurately renders it: "We must love one another or die." And the movie further emphasizes Auden's importance by placing his poetry at the center of a "living funeral" Morrie orchestrates for himself in advance of his death. Not only does Morrie repeat the famous line from "September 1, 1939"; he recites, with certain additions and subtractions, much of the stanza from which it is drawn. Although the movie corrects the misquoted line from the book, it nevertheless misquotes the stanza as a whole. As published in Auden's 1940 volume, *Another Time*, it reads:

> All I have is a voice
> To undo the folded lie,
> The romantic lie in the brain
> Of the sensual man-in-the-street
> And the lie of Authority
> Whose buildings grope the sky:
> There is no such thing as the State
> And no one exists alone;
> Hunger allows no choice
> To the citizen or the police;
> We must love one another or die. (*AT*, 105)

All the lines after the colon are disturbingly ambiguous. If the colon is read as a full stop, the lines become expressions of the voice that undoes the lie and thus states the truth; if, however, the colon is read as introductory, the subsequent lines become expressions of the "lie of Authority" that the poetic voice seeks to undo. The ambiguity is particularly acute with respect to the line immediately following the colon: "There is no such thing as the State." Does this mean that the state is a fiction generated by an authority that lies outside any governmental or juridical order? Or, on the contrary, is it a lie to say that the State does not exist—a lie that finds expression in modern skyscrapers, which, like cathedral spires, point toward the heavens and thus dissemble their terrestrial character? Similar questions gather around the closely linked line, "And no one exists alone." This, too, could be one of the lies of authority, which seeks to keep its subjects sharply separated from one another; but it could also be read as the fundamental falsehood of the fascist state. For, of course, this is what "fascism" means: only by melding into a tightly wound bundle (*fasces*) can the existence of the *Volksgemeinschaft*, or "people's community," be secure. None of these questions arises in the teleplay of *Tuesdays with Morrie*, of course, but its alteration of the stanza in the context of its interest in Auden's life-affirming message nevertheless—and regardless of what its directors or producers may have wished—brings out something in the stanza that otherwise lies dormant. "All I have is a voice," the Morrie of the movie says. As his children joyfully affirm their intimacy with their father by immediately recognizing the words of their dying father's favorite poet, Morrie repeats the line and begins his recitation:

> All I have is a voice
> To undo the folded lie,
> The lie of Authority
> Whose buildings grope the sky.
> No one exists alone;
> Hunger allows no choice
> To the citizen or police
> We must love one another or die
> We must love one another or die.

So speaks Jack Lemmon, as the camera closes in upon his no-longer-laughing face. Morrie's sanctification thus takes place under the authority of a poet who disavows the very lines the professor makes into his credo. For Auden, "We must love one another or die" is problematic not only because we must all die regardless of whether we love, but also because the political character of the imperative to love remains elusive. And yet, despite its betrayal of a poem that it wants to celebrate, *Tuesdays with Morrie* does something of note. Within the context of "September 1, 1939," as it originally appeared, there is no reason to understand the line "And no one exists alone" in conjunction with the biblical declaration "it is not good for man to be alone" (Gen. 2:18), but insofar as Morrie has become the sage of marriage in the course of his Tuesday afternoon "classes" with his former student, the line can refer to nothing else.

Auden, as it happens, was also interested in Tuesday-centric love. In "Dichtung und Wahrheit," the Interlude he inserted between the two parts of his 1960 volume *Homage to Clio*, he poses the following question to himself: "'I will love you for ever,' swears the poet. I find this easy to swear too. *I will love You at 4:15 p. m. next Tuesday*: is that still as easy?" (*HC* 50). Prosaic though it may be, the phrase "4:15 p. m. next Tuesday" becomes the comical abbreviation for a hyper-awareness of time, which introduces a rift between Auden and "the poet," whose promise of eternal love ignores both time and history—and is empty for this reason. There is, however, a condition in which the phrases "I will love You at 4:15 p. m. next Tuesday" and "I will love you forever" can be perfectly reconciled with each other: when they are combined in a marriage ceremony, whereby the promise to love a capitalized and thus individuated "You" at a singular moment is at the same time a promise to love far beyond this time. In this case, the promise of "loving you forever" is no longer empty. Nor is it easy. On the contrary, swearing to love an individual You at a particular moment of a particular day can not only be much harder than swearing eternal love; because of legal restrictions on potential participants in the marriage ceremony, it may also be impossible. Morrie's desperate advice to get married—"desperate" because it frees him from the interpretative conundrums arising from his own image of a bird with broken wings—would be a sorrowful mockery if Mitch wanted to swear love to a man on some imaginary Tuesday, with Morrie now acting as a state-sanctioned witness of the promise.

Auden concludes "Dichtung und Wahrheit" by explaining that the poem he wants to write, in which the feeling of "I love you" is self-evidently true, cannot be written because words cannot verify themselves. Only actions can serve this function—including the speech act that constitutes a marriage vow. Here, however, there is a condition: the action in question must be allowed; otherwise, the words cannot be verified. Thus does Morrie's elimination of the previous line of "September 1"—"There is no such thing as the State"—acquire renewed significance. For it is precisely the State in modern Western societies that establishes the legal conditions in which the marriage vow can become veridical. Neither Morrie nor Mitch is worried about the status of the State in relation to the imperative that Auden willy-nilly dispenses, for they implicitly accept a State-sanctioned conception of who can marry whom. But the same is not true of another film that reintroduced the power of Auden's voice to a late twentieth-century audience and thus, to some extent, helped make *Tuesdays with Morrie* into the "runaway sensation" that it ultimately became.

From *Four Weddings and a Funeral* to *Obergefell v. Hodges*

The emotional appeal of the "living funeral" staged in the movie version of *Tuesdays with Morrie* is clearly parasitic on the pathos generated by the funeral in the 1994 surprise blockbuster *Four Weddings and a Funeral*, directed by Mike Newell. Both funerals occur in a broader context of reflection on the nature of marriage, both culminate in the recitation of Auden's poetry, and in both cases, the quoted lines provide the emotional and thematic crux of the film. *Four Weddings* was so popular that it helped ignite a kind of Auden renaissance, which led to, among other things, the publication of a volume of his light verse, *As I Walked Out One Evening*.[6] The movie adaptation of *Tuesdays* capitalizes on this popularity by altering the "living funeral" recounted in the book to include the depoliticized stanza from "September 1, 1939." But the *mise en scène* of the two filmed funerals could hardly be more different. *Tuesdays* signals its earnestness by narrowing and maintaining a focus on Morrie's saddened face as he recites Auden's poetry. *Four Weddings*, by contrast, moves in the opposite direction as Matthew (John Hannah) recites Auden's "Funeral Blues" in tribute to his dead lover, Gareth (Simon Callow). Although the camera moves into close-up during certain moments of Matthew's recitation, when he begins the final stanza of the poem, the scene suddenly shifts. The recitation continues, while the viewer sees the mourners preparing for the funeral procession in a setting that visually emphasizes the power of the State, two icons of which loom over the scene of mourning: a chapel on the left and a towering smokestack on the right.[7] The silent dominance of these images provides a visual confirmation of the political realities that circumscribe Matthew's and Gareth's relationship and, indeed, gives the film its arithmetic title. Instead of showing five weddings, the film can accommodate only four weddings and a funeral. Only at a funeral can the love between Matthew and Gareth receive some form of public recognition. As Matthew explains in his eulogy, "Gareth used to prefer funerals to weddings. He said it was easier to get enthusiastic about a ceremony one had an outside chance of eventually being involved in." After having been described by the minister as "Gareth's closest friend," Mathew makes clear—with reference to Auden—that the nature of their relationship cannot be contained by this term: "As for me, you may ask how I will remember him, what I thought of him. Unfortunately, there I run out of words. Perhaps you will forgive me if I turn from my own feelings to the words of another splendid bugger, W. H. Auden. This is actually what I want to say."

The movie's plot is driven principally by the uncertain relationship between a young, commitment-shy British man named Charles (Hugh Grant) and an elusive American woman named Carrie (Andie MacDowell). Charles meets Carrie and almost agrees to marry her at the end of the first of the film's weddings. But the dramatic tension—and indeed the structure of the film as a whole—revolves around the recitation of "Funeral Blues," which begins with a plea for quiet solemnity:

> Stop all the clocks, cut off the telephone,
> Prevent the dog from barking with a juicy bone,
> Silence the pianos and with muffled drum
> Bring out the coffin, let the mourners come. (*AT* 81)[8]

Three of the four weddings begin with the image of the chronically late Charles stopping an alarm clock. The sole exception is the disastrous wedding of Carrie to Hamish (Corin Redgrave), at which Gareth dies while Carrie's oblivious husband drones on about the threat to masculinity during the Thatcher years. This superimposition of death on marriage immediately gives way to the funeral at which Auden's poem is recited. The gray setting of both the funeral and the subsequent discussion it provokes between Charles and his friend Tom (James Fleet) takes its direction from the poem's concluding stanza, as the dominant image shifts from Matthew to the billowing smokestack:

> The stars are not wanted now: put out every one,
> Pack up the moon and dismantle the sun;
> Pour away the ocean and sweep up the wood;
> For nothing now can ever come to any good. (*AT* 82)

The deflationary hyperbole of this lament, which treats the cosmos as a messy domicile, expresses both the depletion and extravagance of mourning: everything is interchangeable; there is no distinction between sublunar and super-luminary spheres; and there is no action that can rectify the wrong, including the wrong expressed in the final line of the penultimate stanza: "I thought love would last forever: I was wrong." In the absence of celestial bodies, the mundane world is drained of value. In the absence of "true love"—to cite Gareth's own toast to marriage delivered in his last moments—anybody seems as good (or no good) as any other. And it was "true love" that Gareth shared with Matthew: "It's odd . . . we never noticed that two of us were to all intents and purposes married all this time. . . . Surely if that service shows anything, it shows that there is such a thing as a perfect match," says Charles to Tom, who then articulates the celestial insignia under which such a match supposedly occurs, "the thunderbolt." But in the mundane grayness of grief, the question "whom should I marry?" yields the answer: marry anyone. And Charles, mourning the loss of Carrie to Hamish, does just that and thus misreads the poem as marital advice.

But it is another kind of reading of Auden's poem that gives shape to the final—and aborted—wedding of the film. On Charles' wedding day, in contrast to the mornings of the previous weddings depicted in the film, he wakes up in bed with Tom. On the mornings of the first two weddings, Charles wakes up alone. Always sleeping late, he arises on each of these earlier mornings yelling, "Fuck!"—an exclamation that he repeats again and again. This chronic oversleeping provides a rationale—or one could say, a cover—for Tom and Charles sharing a bed the night before Charles' wedding to Henrietta (Anna Chancellor). But the suggestion that the funeral for Gareth has altered the character of Charles' sexuality finds subtle confirmation in the subsequent deviation in his choice of profanity. Upon learning moments before his wedding that Carrie has left her husband, he stumbles into a corner of the church and prays: "Dear Lord, forgive me for what I am about to say in this magnificent place of worship." With his hands on the edge of a table and bent over at the waist, Charles then yells with increasing volume and rapidity, "Bugger! Bugger! Bugger! Bugger! Bugger! Bugger!" This exclamation ties Charles' desperation to Matthew's mourning by way of Auden. As moving as Auden's lines are, Matthew's recitation of "Funeral Blues" at his gay lover's funeral derives much of its emotional force from the pathos of identification. Matthew explicitly identifies himself and Gareth with Auden, whom he describes not, like Morrie, for example, as "our great poet," but as "another splendid bugger." And buggery—which not only is not sanctioned by the state but was illegal in England until 1967—becomes a cryptogram for marriage. But marriage in this case does not mean the creation of a new legal entity under the auspices of an invested power, but the experience of "true love" or "a perfect match"—the symbol of which is the thunderbolt.

At Charles' wedding, the articulation of the paradigmatic performative, "I do," does not therefore establish a legal marriage but effects, instead, the dissolution of his relationship to Henrietta. Responding to an objection that the groom really loves another woman, the minister insistently asks, "Do you love someone else? Do you, Charles?" To which Charles responds, "I do." Henrietta punches him in the face with such force he falls to the ground. As if to seal the identification of Charles with the dead buggers Gareth and Auden, the camera moves above his fallen body, which lies senseless on a memorial stone. For a moment, as the camera drifts upward in the cathedral, it even appears as though Charles, too, may be dead—felled by the retrospective recognition of "true love." And when Charles finally proposes to Carrie in a rainstorm, which reprieves the atmosphere of the funeral, the character of their relationship is indistinguishable from that of the "perfect match" between Gareth and Matthew. Charles does not ask Carrie to marry him, but *not* to marry him: "Do you think, after we've dried off, after we've spent lots more time together, you might agree [pause] *not* to marry me. And do you think [pause] *not* being married to me might maybe be something you could consider doing for the rest of your life?" To which she replies, "I do." Their exchange of vows, which constitutes a paradoxical marriage without marriage, takes place outside a legally sanctioned forum, in the absence of a presiding authority, and without any witnesses other than the audience of the film itself.

The audience is also the only witness to the conversation that disrupts Charles' wedding ceremony and halts his marriage to Henrietta. Charles' brother, David (David Bower), is deaf, and none of the friends, still less the bride or the minister, is able to understand sign language. Only Charles can understand David's signing, and even when he translates David's words, his renditions rarely correspond to what David is saying. The audience, however, can read the subtitles. As the author of the screenplay, Richard Curtis, explained in an interview about the use of subtitles to translate the brothers' "secret language": "that was the way it had to be done, because in a way that was the joke, that you, the public, read what was going on, and if anybody else had vocalized what was going on, it would have destroyed the joke."[9] Throughout the film, Charles' mistranslations provide a source of comedy, as when David says about Hamish, "What is it about penises that they get such great wives?" which Charles translates as "it couldn't have happened to a nicer fellow." Only in the scene of Charles' wedding is the conversation between the brothers almost completely without humor. As the restless wedding party waits for the groom, his brother finds him in the vestibule and asks him what is wrong. Charles tells him about Carrie and asks what he should do. David replies with "three options": the first option is to proceed with the wedding; the second is to call it off. And when Charles asks for "the third option," David says, "I can't think of a third." But before the exchange of vows can take place, David interrupts the ceremony by stomping his foot and telling his brother, "I thought of a third option. . . . Will you translate?" As Charles translates David's remarks more or less accurately, it becomes clear, however, that he has not formulated a third option and, indeed, that this option cannot be properly formulated. This is, in a sense, the joke to which the screenwriter refers: no discursive language can capture an option other than the two David previously identified.

The third option would have to consist in neither marrying nor not-marrying—or both marrying and failing to marry. What David articulates is, instead, his own doubt: "I think the groom really loves someone else." As Charles struggles to bring himself to translate this line, David continues to press him with serious statements meant only for him about love, marriage, and the commitment of a lifetime, which culminate in a moment of leavening humor: "And by the way, your flies are open." At this point in the film, the audience cannot confirm the truth of David's irreverent intervention; the frame does not include Charles' pants. Beyond the possible embarrassment of an open zipper, this joking and seemingly unrelated line completes the sexual exposure that has been gaining momentum ever since Charles woke up in bed with another man. Just as we do not know the state of Charles' lower attire, we cannot know in discursive terms the nature of the third option. But just as there is nothing mysterious about "flies," there is nothing enigmatic or ineffable about this option, even if Charles can only formulate it in the awkward language of "not-marrying." Like the "secret language" between David and Charles, only the audience can recognize the continuity between the love of a "splendid bugger" like Gareth and the longing of Charles for Carrie. The "joke" to which the screenwriter refers—a joke in which Charles plays the role of "straight man"—consists in anchoring a filmic epithalamion in the form of a relationship between two "buggers" who cannot wed.

As with the love between Gareth and Matthew, there is no presiding authority that sanctions the non-marriage of Charles to Carrie—save the thunderbolt that concludes the final scene. Nothing is said in response to this image, which gives the film its "romantic" character: the lovers are meant for one another, and the cosmos greets their union. The thematics of the thunderbolt first arise in the discussion between Charles and Tom immediately after the funeral. Auden's "Funeral Blues" ends with a call to blot out the brightness of celestial objects: "The stars are not wanted now: put out every one / Pack up the moon and dismantle the sun" (*AT* 82). The mourners stand under a heavily overcast sky, and its grayness is made ever thicker by a billowing smokestack, which appears as the extinguished thunderbolt of Gareth's and Matthew's love. In this way, the film appears to take its cue directly from Auden. Even in the discussion between Charles and Tom, the mood of "Funeral Blues" prevails, for the thunderbolt functions as the image of immense improbability. That lightning struck in the case of Gareth and Matthew means, moreover, that it cannot possibly strike again. But the film does not remain faithful to "Funeral Blues." All the major characters are eventually struck by lightning, including the previously skeptical Tom, who mutters "thunderbolt city" when he encounters his future wife on the morning of Charles' wedding.

The film seems to pride itself on making a gay relationship into the model of a "perfect match," but in so doing, it ironically anticipates the most lamentable feature of the movie version of *Tuesdays with Morrie*. The latter eliminates the line "There is no such thing as the State" from Auden's

"September 1, 1939," while the former fails to remember that, for Gareth and Matthew, there is only the "third option" and, therefore, none at all: their relationship will not be recognized by the state, and it is recognized as a "perfect match" only in retrospect—after Gareth's death. The absorption of the role of bugger into the character of Charles doubtless challenges the dominant idea of the "romantic hero," but the film nevertheless betrays both of the splendid buggers it celebrates. It betrays the memory of Gareth by failing to reflect on the serious joke he used to repeat: that he preferred funerals to weddings because it is "easier to get enthusiastic about a ceremony one had an outside chance of eventually being involved in." And the film betrays Auden by magically—and therefore deceptively—reanimating the cosmos. As Auden repeats throughout his lifetime, the function of art is to break all magical spells: "Poetry is not magic. In so far as poetry, or any other of the arts, can be said to have an ulterior purpose, it is, by telling the truth, to disenchant and disintoxicate" (*Prose* 4:473). But Carrie's and Charles' irreducibly contingent decision not-to-marry each other for the rest of their lives appears as a delayed acceptance of cosmic necessity. The clocks are never stopped, as the opening lines of "Funeral Blues" commands; the lovers are only late in recognizing that they were, from time immemorial, destined for each other.

In the end, then, *Four Weddings and a Funeral* may betray Auden by suggesting that Carrie's and Charles' decision not-to-marry is nothing other than the cute and complacent acknowledgment that their relation is, in the end, a matter of cosmic destiny rather than individual decision. Beyond this suggestion, however, the film presents itself as an Auden-inspired argument for marriage equality. Carrie and Charles agree not to marry each other because their wedding would yield consummate the legal inequality that generates the "and" in the film's title. Writing a brief essay in *Variety* under the title "Love, Loss and Steadfast Commitment Lead a Nation Forward," Jim Obergefell emphasizes the significance of the film's rendition of "Funeral Blues" in motivating the suit he brought against the State of Ohio in 2013:

> I first heard the poem "Funeral Blues" by W. H. Auden in the movie *Four Weddings and a Funeral*, during the scene in which Matthew

eulogizes his partner Gareth. I was struck by the depiction of them, because they were a "regular" couple who happened to be gay, much like my partner John and I. Until then, I hadn't related to many gay movie characters, but Matthew and Gareth were different, because they seemed so much like us. That scene, and the words of this poem, stayed with me because the thought of losing John, like Matthew lost Gareth, scared me. I understood the widower's wish for everything to stop, for there to be no noise, for the world to mourn.[10]

Obergefell proceeds to describe the origin and repercussions of the cause to which his name has been henceforth linked: how he and John Arthur were married on a tarmac at the Baltimore-Washington airport as they prepared to fly to Ohio, where they would demand that their Maryland marriage certificate be considered valid; and how, as their case wound its way through the courts, their story and their struggle "resonated with people across the country." At issue in *Obergefell v. Hodges* was the plaintiff's effort to be listed as "spouse" on the death certificate that would be prepared for Arthur, who was suffering from ALS. By a 5 to 4 decision the U.S. Supreme Court sided with Obergefell, thus upholding a universal right to marry the person of one's choosing: "The Constitution promises liberty to all within its reach, a liberty that includes certain specific rights that allow persons, within a lawful realm, to define and express their identity."[11] Obergefell does not explicitly say that the image of Matthew eulogizing Gareth played any role in his and Arthur's decision to pursue their case, but Auden's poem as performed in the film guides Obergefell's memorable narrative of the events that resulted in the landmark decision. In writing "Funeral Blues," Auden of course had no intention of making anything happen; on the contrary, the poem is a plea for an end to all happenings, domestic and cosmic. Yet, his poetry helped make something happen. The "something" can be quickly formulated in the legal designation "marriage equality." But what marriage itself means, for Auden, cannot be so easily determined. Perhaps under Auden's influence, Obergefell arrives at a similar ambiguity when he ends his essay for *Variety* by saying, "If that isn't a marriage, I don't know what is."

"What Are Buggers For?"

Soon after Auden married, he got married again—without ever becoming a bigamist in the conventional sense. His first marriage was to Erika Mann, who needed a British passport to escape the Nazis. Mann, an anti-Nazi activist and performer, had initially approached Auden's childhood friend Christopher Isherwood, who refused, after much agonized deliberation, for two distinct reasons: first, he did not want to upset his mother, who still hoped for grandchildren to maintain the Isherwood name; second, he conceived of marriage as the "Other" and had contempt for gay men who wanted to pass as happily married heterosexuals. Along with his refusal, however, Isherwood offered to contact Auden with Mann's request. Upon hearing from Isherwood, Auden instantly responded with a one-word telegram: "Delighted!" The marriage took place in 1935, on the very day in which Goebbels pronounced Erika Mann an official enemy of the state, and it lasted until Mann's death in 1969.[12] At no time was Auden concerned with passing for straight, nor was he ever tormented over the principle that marriage is an alien institution. In the face of Nazi persecution, Auden simply did not hesitate to exploit a legal formality that otherwise remained unavailable, even hostile to him. On the contrary, he even tried to create a kind of spontaneous institution, in which gay men would marry women threatened under fascist regimes: "After all," he said to E. M. Forster, alluding perhaps to Hölderlin's famous question concerning the function of poets in desperate times, "what are buggers for?"[13] The project was not simply a matter of speculation. Forster and Auden arranged at least one more marriage on the model of Auden's own.[14]

Auden's remarks to both Isherwood and Forster, despite their jocular tone, demonstrate that marriage is not, for him, the "Other" from which he must protect himself, nor is it simply the "same," that is, the same institution it would be for a straight man of his social and economic status, for, even as he participates in the institution, he nevertheless questions his own relationship to it. Marriage is both "other" and "same" at once; or more exactly, a dialogue *about* the otherness of marriage is a part of any marriage whose participants do not delude themselves into thinking that the union they are creating is somehow "natural." Not through theoretical reflection on the "meaning" of marriage—as though the meaning of any human institution could be decided once and for all—but through his own practice, Auden thus works out some of the basic positions that later came under intense discussion within LGBTQ communities as the prospect of marriage equality began to come into focus. In word and action, Auden was for marriage.[15] This advocacy was permeated, however, by a recognition that marriage is anything but a natural "given." It is, rather, for Auden, a model of a positive historical decision, that is, a decision in favor of love.

His second marriage—to Chester Kallman—was unquestionably a matter of love, and Auden remained committed to Kallman until his own death in 1973. As for their initial meeting, far from being consecrated by a thunderbolt, it was experienced on both sides as a disappointment. Upon seeing the disheveled poet at a colloquium, "Modern Trends in English Poetry and Prose," held on West 52nd Street in 1939, Kallman acidly declared, "Miss *Mess*!" Kallman had come to the colloquium with his friend Harold Norse, and the two of them had flirted and giggled shamelessly with Isherwood, who gave Norse his card and telephone number. Two days later, Kallman, having appropriated the card, went to visit Isherwood. Auden answered the door, hoping to find the athletic Norse, then turned away, muttering to Isherwood, "It's the wrong blond!"[16] A few months later, however, the two were married with an exchange of vows. As they embarked on a summer-long, cross-country "honeymoon," Auden—but not Kallman—began to wear a wedding ring. This asymmetry reflects the dynamics of their subsequent relationship, as Kallman pursued a variety of sexual partners, even as they continued their honeymoon. When they returned from their trip, Kallman reunited with Norse at the Dizzy Club: a "dive," in Norse's words, that "was the sex addict's quick fix."[17] Auden went to the club by himself the following night where he commemorated the place and date by writing "September 1, 1939," a poem that situates itself in "one of the dives / On Fifty-Second Street" and combines ironic resolutions to remain faithful—"I *will* be true to the wife"—with anguished outrage at "Imperialism's face / And the international wrong."

At this same time, Auden was also faced with a problem of international rights: the mail on his return included a letter from the U.S. immigration authorities, informing him that he had violated the terms of his visa. Because the quota on British immigrants had not been filled—in contrast to the status of refugees of many other nationalities seeking asylum—Auden was able to cross over to Canada and legally return to the United States, where seven years later, he became an American citizen.[18] By virtue of his British citizenship, he did not need to marry anyone in order to settle in the States; but among his reasons for changing his citizenship, none is perhaps more important than his marriage to Kallman. As Auden wrote to his brother shortly after meeting Kallman: "This time, my dear, I really believe it's a marriage. The snag is I think I shall have to become an American Citizen as I'm not going to risk separation through international crises."[19]

The peculiarity of these concurrent, but not competing, marriages reflects the manner in which the marital state is, for Auden, at once immensely serious and entirely frivolous. This is true of both marriages: Mann needed to wed in order to escape the death camps, but the marriage itself was nothing more than a legal formality; and despite the fact that Auden was deeply committed to Kallman, their relationship often resembled the comic operas on which they collaborated—so much so that Auden once described himself after one particularly tumultuous episode in their marriage as "stripped of self-control and self-respect, like a ham actor in a Strindberg play" (*Prose* 3:579). The combination of seriousness and frivolity is doubtless due, in part, to the doubleness of marriage itself: it can be both a legal institution and an ethical decision, and the two need not overlap. Indeed, the two forms of marriage may be positively opposed to each other—or, as they were for Auden, happily divorced. Something does, however, unite these two forms of marriage: the absurdity of voluntarily making oneself subject to another's will. In the case of the marriage to Mann, the other will is that of the state, which reserves certain rights for, and imposes corresponding duties on, the partners to the legal institution it authorizes; in the case of the marriage to Kallman, the other will is that of the lover, whose independence is irreducible. Auden celebrates this mundane absurdity and enacts on its basis an unlikely defense of marriage. Just as he famously revives traditional poetic forms in the service of an eminently modern idea of art as radical disenchantment, so he creatively refashions the conventional forms of marriage in opposition to international wrong and for the sake of a decision in favor of abiding love.

A Mann and Kallman

In the early years of the Second World War, as Auden, who was still wedded to Erika Mann, exchanged vows with Chester Kallman, he wrote two epithalamia that reflect the relation between his two marriages: one celebrates an imperium without passports, while the other affirms a union without license.[20] The first marriage poem, "Epithalamion," was written for "a Mann"; the second, "In Sickness and in Health," was dedicated, several years after its composition, to the Mandelbaums, a couple Auden met at Swarthmore, who hoped that the dedication would somehow heal their faltering marriage. The marriage apparently collapsed; but the poem is surprisingly free from any thought of failure: "['In Sickness and in Health'] is an almost unique example in its century of a memorable poem about marriage that is not about a marriage's failure."[21] What the two poems—and their dedications—have in common is the *man* of Kallman, who is mentioned by name in neither but whose love is nevertheless transparently inscribed in both.

"Epithalamion" tenuously tries to unite Auden's two marriages—one legal, the other ethical—in the hopes that the act of marriage itself might "redeem the State." "In Sickness and in Health" is without this hope and leaves only a trace of the legal formality of marriage in the words of its title, which are drawn from the Anglican liturgy. Unlike that later marriage poem, "Epithalamion" was composed specifically for the bride and groom to whom it is dedicated on the occasion of their wedding in November 1939. The Mann in whose honor the poem is written is not, however, Auden's wife, but her sister, Elisabeth, who was marrying the anti-fascist activist Giuseppe Antonio Borgese. In the first stanza of the poem, Auden drops their first names, speaking only of "A Borgese and a Mann." By virtue of antonomasia, two proper names turn into abstract nouns that connote two nationalities and pose one of the major questions of modernity: What is the difference between the human being ("Mann") and a bourgeois citizen

("Borgese").²² At a time in which Mussolini and Hitler had united for the purpose of world domination—"While explosives blow to dust"—the marriage between an anti-fascist Italian and an anti-Nazi German could be seen as the image of "another time," to quote the title of the volume of poetry that Auden concludes with "Epithalamion." The German-Italian union could even be seen in retrospect as one of the "ironic points of light" about which Auden writes in the last stanza of "September 1, 1939," a poem that was originally dedicated to Thomas Mann and that, like "Epithalamion," appears under the rubric of "Occasional Poetry" in *Another Time*.²³ And just as the Italian noun *borghese* is the name of an erstwhile revolutionary class that had more recently become the focal point for the debate about the emergence of fascism, so the German noun *Mann* assumes a triple function in the poem: it names the famous family of Auden's wife; it means the male of the species ("der Mann"); and it encompasses anyone who is defined by his or her social function ("das Man"). The multiple meanings of this marriage to "a Mann" generate the image of a unified world that, for now, can only be cultivated poetically:

> Happier savants may decide
> That this quiet wedding of
> A Borgese and a Mann
> Planted human unity; (*AT* 112)

Auden's two marriages are joined in this image of "human unity," which has overcome the opposition between "human being" and "bourgeois" that Marx famously describes in his early writings. The structure of the poem is correspondingly proleptic, for it projects "happier savants," whose felicity consists in their ability to draw the "map of knowledge" without concern for the shape of political or ideological geography. No longer "occupied" by "Battle's stupid gross event," they may "see / . . . all national frontiers melt / In a true imperium." "Epithalamion" thus serves as a cultural counterpart to Auden's spontaneous project of using the institution of marriage to save those, like his wife, who are threatened by fascist imperialism. The seeds of the "true imperium" already take root in the polyglossia of the first stanza, in which words of English, French, Italian, and German origin are seamlessly combined. In this polyglot context, the wedding of a man to "a Mann" also evokes Auden's utterly non-bourgeois marriage to Kallman and anticipates an institution that is as open and unpoliced as the imperium the poem imagines. The anticipatory character of "Epithalamion" is not, however, an expression of sheer wish fulfillment; it is motivated by two practices that, in combination, are supposed to be able to reconcile "Hostile kingdoms": art and marriage. Art brings order to "Fighting fragments" and transforms "the sights of war" into the vision of a symbolic "dove." Responding to the Italian origin of the bridegroom, Auden chooses as his exempla Dante and Leonardo, each of whom sees earthly redemption "bound by love." Similarly, marriage brings order to Eros, which is otherwise prone to perpetual strife. And "Epithalamion" as a whole seeks to unify—one might even say "marry"—these two practices, so that the union of a Borgese with a Mann may be the vital equivalent of the verbal artifact that celebrates their wedding—a concluding prolepsis of another time: "Symbol now of the rebirth / Asked of old humanity."

The practice of art is not, however, equivalent to the practice of marriage. The ability to create art is tautologically restricted only to artists, whereas the ability of individuals to enter into a state of matrimony is restricted by both the rule of law and the contingencies of love. The argument of the poem—and the poem presents itself as a didactic exposition of European history, from the high Middle Ages to the Renaissance, Reformation, Enlightenment, and beyond—is something like the following: when all restrictions are removed on marriage, and marriage itself constitutes an "ethical resolve / Now to suffer and to be," to quote the penultimate stanza, then it will be a singular form of art, which, unlike every other, can be practiced by all. The penultimate stanza thus emphasizes the category of universality, as it transforms the creative capacity previously reserved for Dante and Leonardo—that of vision—into a universal ability:

> All the peoples see the sun,
> All the dwellings stand in light,
> All the conquered worlds revolve,
>   Life must live.

If anyone—regardless of his or her nationality, regardless of his or her legal status, and regardless of his or her gender identification—can marry "A Mann," the ordinary sight of the sun will be equivalent to the artist's vision of the dove. In both cases, peace will shine forth. But the term "All the peoples" does not specify anyone in particular, and it is not true that *everyone* can see the sun. A certain blindness to individuals is signaled by the generic title "Epithalamion," and is likewise contained in the very formula that makes Auden's poetic celebration of the wedding of Elisabeth Mann and Giuseppe Antonio Borgese into an epithalamion pure and simple, namely "A Mann," which transforms the name of a specific individual into the designation of a trans-bourgeois and indeed potentially infinite class: "All the peoples." The same blindness then makes itself emphatically felt in the final line of the penultimate stanza, where "Life"—but not any individual human life—must tautologically live.

The final stanza of "Epithalamion" registers the effect of this attempt to unify the practice of art with that of marriage by representing a wholly unrestricted form of marriage as a universally available form of art. But the bid for unification ironically produces a radical division. The poem articulates an insuperable distinction between a subsolar sphere, which everyone inhabits, and heaven, which belongs solely to naturally gifted artists. And whereas each of the artists is duly named (Mozart, Goethe, Blake, Tolstoi, Hölderlin, and Wagner), those who lack their capacities but are nevertheless entreated to redeem the State, not only remain nameless but are, surprisingly, juvenilized, as well:

> Vowing to redeem the State
> Now let every girl and boy
> To the heaven of the Great
> All their prayers and praises lift:

At the end of "Epithalamion," marriage vows explicitly turn into universal political avowal. This transformation elucidates the enigmatic line of "September 1, 1939" that proclaims the absence of the State: there *should* be no such thing as the State; it should be redeemed of its statehood; border guards should disappear, as the "Happier savants" associated with the "true imperium" replace the ignorant agents of imperialism. The transformation of the proper name Elisabeth Mann into the common noun "Mann" accomplishes its end. And the vow that concludes Auden's celebration of marriage no longer has anything to do with the words two individuals exchange in giving themselves to each other; instead, this vow concerns everyone—or, more exactly, "every boy and girl." Children, however, are excluded both legally and ethically from the possibility of exchanging marital vows: the law declares them minors, and the "ethical resolve" to which the poem itself gives voice consists, above all, in "censoring the nostalgic sigh." The division into which the final stanza of "Epithalamion" issues thus produces two radically separate spheres, which are united solely by virtue of what they both exclude: no member of either sphere is in a position to get married. The "Great" are no longer able to marry (for they are all dead); those who vow to redeem "the State" are not yet able to marry (for their vows are not deemed to be their own).

The tensions of "Epithalamion" culminate in the poem's final appeal to Wagner, whose enormity Auden later captures in the epithet, "the greatest of the monsters" (*Prose* 5:389):

> Wagner who obeyed his gift
> Organised his wish for death
> Into a tremendous cry,
> Looking down upon us, all
>   Wish us joy.

It is difficult to imagine a more shockingly inappropriate figure to invoke for the concluding lines of a poem celebrating the marriage of two renowned anti-fascists. And this incongruity is further emphasized by the fact that this appeal to a notorious anti-Semite thereby concludes the volume *Another Time*, many of whose poems—"Spain, 1937," "Refugee Blues," "In Memory of Ernst Toller," and "September 1, 1939," to name only a few—specifically repudiate the ideology that began to find a murderously effective voice in Wagner's many diatribes.[24] From another perspective, however, the concluding invocation of Wagner is altogether appropriate, for it condenses into three terse lines the basic theory of art through which the poem seeks to represent the practice of marriage as the "Symbol" of human rebirth. Wagner is, in a sense, the paradigmatic artist: by sublimating the death drive—and it should be noted that the poem immediately preceding "Epithalamion" in *Another Time* is "In Memory of Sigmund Freud"—he gains entrance to heaven. His "gift" helps define the sphere to which boys and girls are then entreated to "lift" their voices. The grand sublimation of Thanatos in the work of art thus gives direction to correspondingly lesser sublimations of Eros in the practice of marriage. If the cultivation of art can redeem a Wagner from some particularly vicious tendencies—so the suggestion goes—the act of marriage can accomplish something similar for all of those who are not "great" either in artistic talent or destructive impulse.

The precise formulation by which Auden characterizes the outcome of Wagner's particular form of sublimation—"a tremendous cry"—indicates, however, that he entertains some doubt about its success. A "tremendous cry" can doubtless describe the voluntary expression of a consummate artist, and since Auden proposes that opera, from Gluck's *Orfeo ed Euridice* (1762) to Verdi's *Otello* (1887), be understood as the articulation of "*wilful* feeling" (*Prose* 2:401), there is good reason to read the phrase in this manner. Yet, "tremendous cry" can be read in a completely different manner—as either uncontrolled wailing or histrionic howling.[25] If, moreover, the sublimation of Thanatos is thwarted by the ambiguity of this cry, so, too, is the corresponding sublimation of Eros, which does not express itself in a marital vow but, rather, in a political oath that can scarcely be considered effective, for it is sworn only by children. Eros, in short, is so successfully sublimated by the poet that it disappears from "Epithalamion" altogether.

Sublimation Is Not a Solution

A sublimation of Eros modeled on the sublimation of Thanatos may be nothing other than the work of Thanatos, and the mythic representation of that "sin of the high-minded, sublimation" (*CP45* 32)—to quote from Auden's "In Sickness and in Health"—can be found in Wagner's *Tristan und Isolde*.

"In Sickness and in Health" makes no distinction between a higher realm inhabited by the Great and the lower sphere of ordinary life; but in one place—in conjunction with Wagner once again—it critically retains the rhetoric of greatness: "Tristan, Isolde, the great friends." What is missing in this succinct expression of the form of passionate non-marriage against which "In Sickness and in Health" as a whole directs itself is the "*und*" in the title of Wagner's opera: there is no "Tristan *and* Isolde" but only two separate substances, "Tristan, Isolde," whose status as "friends" consists not in mutual respect but, rather, in the narcissistic self-love signaled by its auditory correlate, namely echo. And echo is itself instantiated in the repetitive opening line of the stanza devoted to the myth of grand passion that culminates in Wagner's opera:

> Nature by nature in unnature ends:
> Echoing each other like two waterfalls,
>   Tristan, Isolde, the great friends,
> Make passion out of passion's obstacles;
> Deliciously postponing their delight,
> Postpone frustration till it lasts all night,
> Then perish lest Brangaene's worldly cry
> Should sober their cerebral ecstasy. (*CP45* 30)

By replacing the "*und*" of Wagner's opera with a comma, Auden graphically illustrates the mutual isolation of these exemplary representatives of grand passion. The "and" in the poem's title indicates the precise place in which the missing conjunction can be found: in the marital vow. "In Sickness and in Health" thus distances itself from the high-mindedness of "Epithalamion." Whereas the earlier poem proposes the artistic sublimation of the death drive as a model for the marital sublimation of the erotic drive, the latter one identifies the sublimation of both drives—one sick, the other healthy—as an irreducible impediment to marriage. And whereas "Epithalamion" concludes with a grand theory of art that culminates in Wagner's "tremendous cry," "In Sickness and in Health" first diminishes this cry as "our howling appetites," and then presents a concise reading of *Tristan und Isolde* that sets a "worldly cry" against the greatness of Tristan, Isolde—and especially of Wagner himself.

Auden's reading of Wagner's opera contains in miniature—and in reverse—the structure of "In Sickness and in Health" as a whole. The distillation and reversal manifest themselves most forcefully in the irruption of another voice in the ninth stanza of the poem. By virtue of italics, the speaking voice in this stanza is distinguished from the lyric "I" that speaks in the other fourteen stanzas and corresponds in this way to the "worldly cry" that Tristan and Isolde refuse to heed. The consequential inclusion of this other voice, which separates its account of sickness from that of health, opposes Brangaene's vital exclusion from the affair of the "great friends" in at least three ways: the speaker, while identifiable, is nevertheless anonymous; the voice, while sober, is nevertheless otherworldly; and the poem not only heeds this voice but survives its intervention by making itself into an exponent of its "absurd command—Rejoice." In conjunction with his critique of sublimation, Auden turns to a paradigmatic reservoir of sublime imagery, the last chapters of the Book of Job, with its depiction of God speaking from the whirlwind and asking his creature—without any expectation of response—whether he is powerful enough to "bind the chains of the Pleiades or loose the cords of Orion" (Job 38:31).[26] Retaining the form of the rhetorical question, Auden nevertheless weakens the rhetoric of the sublime by binding the image of the numinous *"whirlwind"* to the lowly diction of a *bricoleur*, whose artistic achievements are scarcely comparable to those of "the Greats" with which "Epithalamion" ends: *"Rejoice. What talent for the makeshift thought / A living corpus out of odds and ends?"* (*CP45* 31). The act of self-consciously binding one single life to another such life—marriage, in short—consists in responding to this voice not by answering its questions but by rendering "makeshift" arrangements enduring by vowing to do so. The very bind between the stanzas recounting sickness and those concerned with health—and therefore the "and" in "In Sickness and in Health"—thus consists in recognizing the distinction between the obstacles by means of which "great friends" postpone the consummation of their grand passion and the binding vow through which lovers create something analogous to the *"living corpus"* made of *"odds and ends"*: a shared "now."

In terms of their dominant modes of temporality, "In Sickness and in Health" has nothing in common with "Epithalamion" and can even be understood as its wholesale repudiation. Whereas the earlier poem synoptically surveys all of European history and looks forward to a future in which the marriage it celebrates will be seen as a "Symbol" of human unity, the later poem acknowledges that things are always only fragmentary, made entirely of *"odds and ends,"* and it embraces no other time than the "now." "In Sickness and in Health" is composed almost entirely in the present tense: Tristan's and Isolde's celibate passion exists in the present, as does the sexual activity of their opposing type, Don Juan, who "haunts the urinals / existing solely by their miracles." The only exception to the "now"-ness in which the poem situates itself can be found in the voice that irrupts in its italicized ninth stanza. The past this voice recounts, however, does not belong to the historical world, but to the primordial time Auden designates with the Hebrew term *tohu-bohu*.[27] The voice speaks in the aorist, but itself emerges in the present: "Yet through their tohu-bohu comes a voice / Which utters an absurd command—Rejoice" (*CP45* 31). Whereas "Epithalamion" makes a spatial distinction between higher and lower spheres, "In Sickness and in Health" paradoxically distinguishes between two orders of "now." The first "now" appears in the first stanza and describes the historical condition of its composition: "Now, more than ever, we distinctly hear / The dreadful shuffle of a murderous year." The other "now" appears in the first stanza after the intervention of the other voice and describes the shape of the marriage vow:

> Rejoice, dear love, in Love's peremptory word;
> All chance, all love, all logic, you and I,
>   Exist by grace of the Absurd,
> And without conscious artifice we die:
> O, lest we manufacture in our flesh
> The lie of our divinity afresh,
> Describe round our chaotic malice now,
> The arbitrary circle of a vow. (*CP45* 32)[28]

For all the complexity of this stanza, the direction of its movement is unmistakable: the stanza represents a defense of marriage. Only in the creative "now" constituted by a marital vow can the primordial chaos, or "tohu-bohu," be tamed. But—and here the complexity begins—there is no assurance that "we" *can* enunciate the vow that separates the "now" of marital union from the "now" of martial conflict. Indeed, as the previous stanza strongly suggests, only another voice—not our own—has the power to separate and rejoin the elements of chaos into a *"segregated charm"* (*CP45* 31). In blunt terms, creation is a divine act, but the union of two individuals, while likewise creative, is contrariwise imperfect. It is without a secure future from the perspective of which, for example, a marriage could be seen as the rebirth of humanity. And this means that the marital vow must and should remain always precarious: "O, lest we manufacture in our flesh / The lie of our divinity afresh." From this stanza onward, then, the poem struggles with the difficult logic of "lest" that first appears in the line describing the refusal of Tristan and Isolde to hear any voice that would divert them from their "natural" course: "Then perish lest Brangaene's worldly cry / Should sober their cerebral ecstasy" (*CP45* 30). Unless the "now" of the vow is continuously created, which requires a word analogous to the one that tamed the "tohu-bohu," we fall prey to "chaotic malice"; unless the precariousness of the vow is constantly recognized, we are in danger of self-divinization. This precariousness is itself demonstrated in the very word that, as the title of the poem suggests, represents the *conditio sine qua non* of the marital vow, namely *and*.

The "and" that fails to bind "Tristan, Isolde" in the earlier stanza appears in this one in the form of "you and I." But this "and" is a sign of both separation and union; it can be read as a conjunction that follows from the three iterations of "all," so that the phrase "you and I" is equivalent to "all the peoples," or as a conjunction that binds "you" and "I" into a singular union, which, as a pair, is separated from everyone and everything else, including from "you" and "I" as separate individuals. Mutual separation—or *"segregated charm"*—depends, however, on separating both "you" and "I" from the two mutually reinforcing forms of passion that stem from, and result in, their separation. Both these forms are consciously refashioned in the sentence of the poem that joins together "you and I." "All chance, all love, all logic" retrieves the repetitive utterance that encapsulates the relation between Tristan and Isolde: "Nature by nature in unnature ends" (*CP45* 30). And "Exist by grace of the Absurd" rewrites the phrase that captures the nature of Don Juan, whose existence lies in the "miracles" to be found in public toilets. The formula "existence by grace of the absurd" is, of course, drawn from Kierkegaard, and so, too, is the suggestion that Don Juan's endless search for miraculous erotic encounters represents a seductive parody of authentic existence.[29] But what cannot be found in Kierkegaard—who, after all, famously renounced his fiancée at the very time in which he insisted that the knight of faith probably looks like an ordinary tax collector[30]—is the sentence with which Auden supplements the first Kierkegaardian formula and condenses his paradoxical defense of marriage: "And without conscious artifice we die" (*CP45* 32).

Auden's defense of marriage does not consist in celebrating fortuitous couplings, which, like strokes of lightning, bring a brief moment of illumination to an otherwise dark existence. Nor does it consist in reiterating the dreary Pauline recognition that Eros must be somehow managed, and for this reason it is "better to marry than to burn" (1 Cor. 7). Nor, finally, does it consist in delineating according to some syllogistic formula the rationale for the union of two individuals—the advantages marriage brings to them, their families, their nations, or civilization at large. On the contrary: "All chance, all love, all logic, you and I, / Exist by grace of the Absurd" (*CP45* 32). Marriage is defensible precisely to the extent that it, too, is absurd. The remarkable combination of solemnity and frivolousness that characterizes Auden's two marriages is not lost in this great poem in defense of marriage. Because the marital vow forms itself in analogy with the divinely creative word, it is solemn; because the union produced by the vow presumes to supplement an already completed creation, it is frivolous.[31] And in both cases it is absurd.

The double absurdity of marriage is captured in the "And" of the line that itself supplements the all-encompassing declaration that chance, love, and logic exist by grace of the absurd: "And without conscious artifice we die." This line can be read both as a dimension of the "lest" logic by which we are enjoined to live, and as a description of the manner in which we die. Both readings depend on an acknowledgment of a fundamental distinction between divine and human forms of creation, which correspond to the two voices of the poem.[32] From the perspective of the first reading, however, "conscious artifice" means, above all, marriage: the union created by the marital vow is precisely not an addition to creation, still less an expression of nature; rather, this supplementary union is, and must be recognized as, wholly artificial—"lest we manufacture in our flesh / The lie of our divinity afresh." From the perspective of the second reading, "conscious artifice" refers to everything created by human consciousness, which is to say, the entire historical world: none of our creations can protect us from death—not even the works of love. And from the perspective of the two readings in combination, "And without conscious artifice we die" revises to the point of rescinding the most famous line of "September 1, 1939": "We must love one another or die."

The two lines are almost diametrically opposed to each other. The "or" in the line from "September 1, 1939" cannot fail to be read as a form of "lest" logic: unless we love one another, we die. If immortality is taken to be the principle predicate of divinity, this thought represents a particularly seductive version of that danger against which the "lest" of the later poem warns: self-divinization. When Auden, dissatisfied with this line, changed its "or" to "and," he doubtless eliminated this suggestion; but in the same stroke he also did away with any basis for the "must" that gives the line its undeniable force. The connective in "We must love one another and die" expresses a relation between the imperative to love and the prospect of death that is scarcely meaningful, for we must do all kinds of things—and die. The emptiness of this "and" may then rebound onto the relation between those who are enjoined to love one another. Auden recognizes such a possibility in the penultimate stanza of "In Sickness and in Health" where he sees that the "circle of a vow" could "wither to an empty nought." "And without conscious artifice we die," by contrast, is not in danger of becoming a hollow formula; rather, it—this line, which is itself the "conscious artifice" about which it speaks—is absurd by virtue of its "And." To be sure, the line retains a suggestion that something of our own making can protect us from death; but it equally declares the very opposite: we die stripped of the things we have made.

The stanza in which this line appears also contains a concentrated theory of art that revokes the one proposed in the final stanza of "Epithalamion." Art does not belong to "the heaven of the Great," and its function does not consist in the sublimation of the death drive, such that models might be found for lesser forms of erotic sublimation. If any verticality remains in this revised theory of artistic creation, it lies only in the slight suggestion that art is a highly conscious form of artifice—a suggestion reinforced by the highly rhetorized lines of "In Sickness and in Health" itself. What the "circle of the vow" creates is precisely that: a circle, which does nothing more than assert itself in the formlessness of space, just as the "now" of the vow, solely by virtue of its faithfulness, maintains itself in the chaotic "now" of political events. But "In Sickness and in Health" nowhere proposes that "this round O of faithfulness we swear" grows beyond itself or that the marriage celebrated in the poem could be seen in retrospect to form the seed of something greater, which eventually encompasses all of humanity. Far from being a symbol of rebirth, as "Epithalamion" cautiously imagines, marriage in the later poem conscientiously prevents itself from reverting to the symbolic function to which its sign, the O, is otherwise consigned: designating nothingness.

Grasping in positive terms the character of this non-symbolic circle, which paradoxically supplements divine creation without adding any new substances, is equivalent to understanding the relation between the creation of art and the practice of marriage. The term Auden chooses in this context is almost shocking: the "circle of the vow" is said to be "arbitrary." This is, in a sense, the last word on the relation between art and marriage. Both are forms of "conscious artifice," but only the vow is designated as "arbitrary," which means that it escapes all efforts at calculation without, however, falling prey to the randomness of either romantic destiny (Tristan, Isolde) or erotic chaos (Don Juan). *Arbitrary* combines the idea of equality with that of equity: it is up to everyone and anyone to create the circle, without reliance on commanding authorities or superior models. The only trace of authority to which the term bears witness can be found in its evocation of the give-and-take of arbitration, which always operates *ad hoc*, without formal rules, for particular occasions, guided solely by a concern for the elusive quality of equity. Everyone is thus enjoined to marry in his or her manner, to his or her liking; and no agent—whether religious, legal, or even aesthetic—is invested with the power to punctuate the present by pronouncing a marriage valid "now." The validity of marriage lies, instead, in its constitutive absurdity: an O that combines the abstract closure of fate with the sensual openness of orality ("O Fate, *O Felix Osculum*") and forms the wholly arbitrary—corporeal, material—center of both the *vow* and the *now*.

TWO

Poetry, Prose, and a Forgotten Practice

For and Against

Among the various notes and drafts that are to be found in the concluding section of Adorno and Horkheimer's *Dialectic of Enlightenment* is a fragment in the form of a dialogue that bears the surprising title "For Voltaire"—surprising at the very least because the point of the co-authored volume, from its first pages onward, is the relentless critique of a concept intimately associated with the name "Voltaire." The very first page of the *Dialectic of Enlightenment* confirms the authoritative status of Voltaire in the eighteenth-century Enlightenment by quoting his characterization of Francis Bacon as "the father of experimental philosophy."[1] This brief account of the parentage of the modern sciences is the starting point for an investigation into the dialectical reversal whereby the attempt on the part of reason to dominate non-rationality turns into a form of self-domination that cannot stop until it annihilates everything it deems different from itself. Yet, at the end of the volume, Adorno and Horkheimer seemingly identify themselves with the figure of Voltaire. A similar surprise, described as such, can be found among the reviews that Auden wrote for *The Nation* around the time—from the late 1930s to the early 1940s—when Adorno and Horkheimer began the conversations that would lead to the

Dialectic of Enlightenment.² In the spring of 1939, under the title "A Great Democrat," Auden reviewed two recent books on the life and thought of François-Marie Arouet, and it is immediately apparent that he, too, is for Voltaire: "Voltaire was not only one of the greatest Europeans of all time but, though he would be surprised to hear it, one of the greatest fighters for democracy" (*Prose* 2:8). Just as Adorno and Horkheimer write a fragment in favor of the great enlightener in the context of a relentless critique of the Enlightenment, so Auden, from a converse perspective, praises the arch-critic of French Catholicism during the period when the Christianity of Auden's own youth was becoming once again an important element in his life.³

Beyond their unexpected praise of Voltaire in the late 1930s, Auden and the authors of the *Dialectic of Enlightenment* are committed to the general project associated with the term *enlightenment* inasmuch as it seeks to dismantle the stratagems by which unjust powers glorify themselves; at the same time, however, they remain wary of any program that attempts to implement this project, for such programs tend to reproduce the very stratagems in question. All three thus ask themselves why attempts to free thought from oppressive schemata result in new and often more insidious forms of oppression. For Auden, Adorno, and Horkheimer, the triumph of fascism throughout the 1930s makes the inquiry into the dialectic of enlightenment an urgent matter. All three recognize that sane reflection on the contemporary world requires nothing less than a rigorous form of political and cultural analysis—one that grasps the current conflict on the basis of deep historical scrutiny and draws on the resources of the European philosophical tradition (not for the sake of its continuation but in order to determine with a degree of precision where its best insights were occluded). Above all, Auden joins the founders of Critical Theory in the urgency with which they seek to understand and articulate why the desire for freedom, which characterizes the best strains of the philosophical tradition from Plato to Hegel, fosters oppression, which fascism represents with a fury.

The overlap between the concerns addressed in the founding documents of Critical Theory and those in Auden's prose of the same period are remarkable, extending from reflections on the status of new music, as also found in Adorno, to evaluations of psychological categories outside the sphere of individual psychology, as also found in Horkheimer.[4] Auden developed a version of critical theory that not only bears comparison with the one that achieved institutional form through the efforts of Horkheimer and Adorno but may in retrospect be seen as ultimately more incisive and far-reaching—not least because the theoretical insights Auden elaborates in his prose are in more or less constant tension with the direction of his poetic vocation. Nowhere is the relation between Auden and the authors of *Dialectic of Enlightenment* more vividly evident than in their similar yet contrasting portraits of Voltaire. This is no accident, for the figure presented in both their portraits is a philosophically infused critic of the status quo; that is, less a founding father of the eighteenth-century Enlightenment than a predecessor of twentieth-century critical theory. As Adorno and Horkheimer compose their fragments in Los Angeles, aware of the power that modern media both defend and exercise; and as Auden arrives in New York, aware that this move, along with a change of direction in his poetry and his return to the religion of his childhood, will be seen as a betrayal,[5] all three find in the figure of Voltaire a fellow exile, a surprising ally, and a model of theoretically informed criticism of contemporary culture and orders: his struggle against the unity of apologetic discourse and the unjust exercise of power reveals an element of the Enlightenment that survives the disclosure of its oppressive origins and tendencies.

The poem that Auden published in *Poetry: A Magazine of Verse* soon after the appearance of his review derives much of its motivation from the depiction of that element of the Enlightenment to which Voltaire—late in his life, alone among the major figures of the French *éclaircissement*, having lost his erstwhile colleagues—remained wholeheartedly committed. The books Auden reviewed provided the biographical material for the ensuing poem, "Voltaire at Ferney," and the review converges with the poem insofar as they both, like Adorno and Horkheimer's fragment, are unmistakably "for Voltaire." But very quickly—by its second stanza—the poem identifies a marked tension in its titular figure. Auden finds in Voltaire's anti-clerical polemics a model of counter-totalitarian insight: "Voltaire saw that those who say that they cannot live without absolute certainty end by accepting some person or institution that offers it. In his day there was only one such offer, that of the Catholic Church" (*Prose* 2:9). In his own day, Auden suggests, similar offers are made not only by fascist and communist propagandists but also through the offices of commercial advertising, insofar as they offer solutions to problems of personal deficiency that they themselves invent.[6] Nevertheless—and this is where the poem parts ways with the review—"Voltaire at Ferney" presents Voltaire reflecting on the validity of a claim that he publicly proclaims. Voltaire thus enters into a dialogue with himself that issues into fragments of past polemics. The two formulas most closely associated with the historical Voltaire—the cultivation of one's garden contra Leibnizian "optimism" and the promotion of civilization against Rousseauvian primitivism—appear in "Voltaire at Ferney" as elements of a dialogue in which the value of polemics (being-against) is weighed against that of advocacy (being-for):

> He would write
> "Nothing is better than life." But was it? Yes, the fight
> Against the false and the unfair
> Was always worth it. So was gardening. Civilise. (*AT* 29).

The "Yes" of this "Against" is what the authors of the *Dialectic of Enlightenment* are altogether for. And for them, the positive slogans associated with Voltaire—gardening, civilization—stand no chance, as it were, against the power of polemics in the broadest sense; they appear as little more than afterthoughts. In the same vein, the fragmentary character of Voltaire's reflections in the poem mirrors the structure of *Dialectic of Enlightenment*, which was originally titled "Philosophical Fragments." When, therefore, the figure of Voltaire emerges in the poem's final section, the dialogue Auden stages in the mind of the great enlightener—"'Nothing is better than life.' But was it?"—can be seen as a model of the dialogue that Adorno and Horkheimer stage under Voltaire's name for the purpose of justifying a critical theory wholly detached from its practical application, whether in the form of private gardening or public civilization:

For Voltaire

Your reason is one-sided, whispers one-sided reason. You have done an injustice to power. You have pathetically, tearfully, sarcastically, noisily cried out against the shame of tyranny; but you have ignored the good that power has created. Without the security that power alone can establish, such good would never have been able to exist. Life and love played under the wings of power; they have also secured your own happiness by defying hostile nature.—What this apologetics declares is at once true and false. Among all significant actions power alone can commit injustice, for only the execution that follows the judgment is unjust, not the speech of the lawyer that is not carried out. Only insofar as the speech aims to oppress and thus defends power rather than those who are powerless does it participate in the general injustice.—But power, one-sided reason further whispers, is represented by human beings. By exposing the former, you make the latter into targets. And after them, still worse will perhaps come.—This lie speaks the truth. When the fascist murderers are already waiting, one should not rouse the people against a weak regime. But silence about infamy does not follow from the alliance with the less brutal form of power. The chance that the good cause will suffer in denouncing the injustice that protects one from the devil, was always less than the advantage that the devil gains whenever one leaves to him the denunciation of injustice. How far must a society have come when scoundrels speak the truth, and it is left to Goebbels to keep alive the memory of joyously performed lynchings. The bad rather than the good is the object of theory, which presupposes the reproduction of life in this or that determined form. Its element is freedom, its theme oppression. Wherever language becomes apologetic it is already corrupted; according to its very essence, it can be neither neutral nor practical.—Can't you just show the good side and announce love as a principle instead of all this endless bitterness!—There is only one expression for truth: the thought that says "no" to injustice. If steadfast support for the good side is not sublated into the negative whole, it turns into its opposite: violence. With words I can scheme, propagate, and suggest; that is the trait through which words, like all actions, get entangled into reality, and this trait is precisely what the lie alone understands. It insinuates that even the contradiction of the established order succeeds in serving incipient authorities, competing bureaucracies, and the perpetuators of violence. In its nameless anxiety, it is able and willing to see only that which it itself is. Whatever enters into its medium—language as mere instrument—becomes identical with the lie, just as things become indistinguishable from one another in darkness. But, whereas it is true that there is no word that the lie could not ultimately use, it is not by means of the lie but, rather, solely in the hardness of thought against power that the goodness of power also shines forth. The uncompromising hatred of the terror wrought against the last creature constitutes the sole legitimate thankfulness for those who are spared. Appealing to the sun is idolatry. Only the sight of a tree withered by the blaze of the sun allows for an intimation of the majesty of the day that illuminates the world without, at the same time, having to set it aflame. (*DA* 195–96, 180–82)[7]

By virtue of its dialogical form the fragment registers a tension internal to the project of Enlightenment. Neither voice opposes the ends of Enlightenment, but only the respondent recognizes critique as a nonmendacious means. The language of critique is not directed simply against barbarism and darkness; it also sees that vocal support for any form of power is malicious, for it inevitably issues into a justification for violence and is thus already on that side. Adorno and Horkheimer are hardly alone among their contemporaries in recognizing the difference between a version of Enlightenment that acknowledges its constitutive limits and a version that wants nothing more of rational inquiry than a means to increase its own power. Both books on Voltaire that Auden reviewed—one written by a Catholic scholar, the other by a "humanist" intellectual—show, for example, a more or less keen awareness of the double-sided nature of Enlightenment.[8] But in "For Voltaire" Adorno and Horkheimer take this split one step further: *only* the side of Enlightenment that speaks in favor of power *can* speak. This statement is not tautological, because it implies that there is another side of Enlightenment, which speaks only by virtue of its silence—a silence that does not harbor complaints about current conditions but is, rather, the only appropriate expression of a revolutionary protest that demands a total transformation of "the bad" into "the good."

Implicitly following a long theological tradition that denies the quality of goodness can appear as such, the authors of *Dialectic of Enlightenment* paradoxically affirm that the good cannot be a subject matter of discussion, not even their own. The non-phenomenal character of goodness means that it cannot become an "object of theory," inasmuch as theory—far from being an exercise of transhistorical reason, which begins without prejudices and assumptions—"presupposes the reproduction of life in this or that determined form" and is therefore oblivious to the badness that would establish the condition for any goodness of which it would speak. In more colloquial terms, Adorno and Horkheimer celebrate the figure of Voltaire as someone who has no positive plans for social-political perfection. Like Marx, who famously disavowed the "utopian socialists" of his era and undertook a critique of contemporary political economy without an image of what the world would be like after the socialist revolution, the figure of Voltaire constructed by Adorno and Horkheimer has no interest in supporting a reform of, say, the Catholic Church, so that its wealth would be redistributed among the poor and its power democratized among its parishioners; on the contrary, all he wants to do is destroy the infamous powers-that-be, come what may. A stark alternative thus emerges, with each of the two voices in the fragment giving voice to one side: either theory, in the broadest sense, encompassing any articulation of a social-political vision, is subordinated to political action in the form of apologetics, or it is altogether severed from action and expresses itself as pure critique.

Adorno and Horkheimer represent the interdiction on positive expression in terms of the medial nature of language: since language can always be transformed into a means to an end, it cannot secure itself against its extreme instrumentalization in the act of lying, and so human language is unfit for the disclosure of goodness. The words by which they communicate this thought recall Hegel's famous critique of Schelling's philosophy of identity—"the night in which all cows are black"[9]—but they apply to all linguistic theories that conceive of language as a means of positive identification: "Whatever enters into its medium—language as mere instrument—becomes identical with the lie, just as things become indistinguishable from one another in darkness. But, whereas it is true that there is no word that the lie could not ultimately use, it is not by means of the lie but, rather, solely in the hardness of thought against power that the goodness of power also shines forth." In this last sentence Adorno and Horkheimer propose a daring distinction, insofar as it conforms to the rationalist program that the authors otherwise repudiate—the distinction, namely, between language and thought. Adorno and Horkheimer do not take the point of this distinction to lie in somehow safeguarding the integrity of pure thinking, still less the unity of the Cartesian cogito; rather, they make this distinction in order to guard "goodness" from being incorporated into an apologetics that, by directing attention to some putative point of light, obscures the injustice of the world. The hardness of this thought alone brings to light the goodness of the thought-object; no words are adequate to the task. The association of the goodness of power with the hardness of thought is, however, disturbingly self-congratulatory—and not only because of the phallic connotations of hardness in close conjunction with the thought of power. It is a statement made by thinkers that hard thought—hence, their own thought—is unqualified goodness. The thinkers say, in effect, "our power is good." Adorno and Horkheimer may not advertise their thought in so many words, but the implication is clear. It could be formulated in syllogistic form: the hardness of thought against power shows its goodness; our thought is directed against power; the power we exercise is guaranteed to be good. By affirming the power of hard thought to bring the goodness of power to light, hard thinkers make their dialogue into a form of self-affirmation.

Ferney, Happiness

For the first few lines, the Voltaire Auden describes in "Voltaire at Ferney" is as seemingly self-satisfied with his own goodness as the co-authors of the *Dialectic of Enlightenment*. This is particularly true in the original version of the poem, which begins in a state of achieved self-perfection: "Perfectly happy now." Nevertheless—and this becomes more evident in the version Auden published in the 1945 edition of *Collected Poetry*—Voltaire's happiness is a function of a positive practice, located in a particular place: his estate in Ferney. Voltaire's attempt at putting his theory of enlightenment into practice subtends the dreary alternative around which the dialogue of "For Voltaire" revolves: either the silent hardness of thought or the loquacious mendacity of propaganda. In "A Great Democrat" Auden offers an abbreviated account of the theory that accords with the practice undertaken by Voltaire late in his life: "Voltaire was no social revolutionary, but within the economic and social conditions of his time, he attempted on his estate at Ferney to create a community of which the members would feel happy enough to allow the spirit of democracy to flower" (*Prose* 2:10).[10] Auden's phrasing is characteristically exact despite its colloquial fluency. Instead of attempting to establish a utopian community in which everyone would be perfectly happy, Voltaire has the much more modest goal of fostering a condition where everyone is—to use a Winnicott-like phrase—"happy enough" to transcend the limits in perception and disposition that arise from persistent misery: "one of the symptoms of happiness is a lively curiosity that finds others as interesting and worth knowing as oneself" (*Prose* 2:10–11).[11] The discourse of symptoms suggests that happiness is akin to illness in reverse. One can be happy without feeling so. And its outstanding symptom, "lively curiosity," functions as the affective counterpart to the receptive act of listening, which, for Auden, is the condition under which "effective democracy" (*Prose* 2:15) spontaneously emerges, always relative to a range of social, historical, and geopolitical conditions.[12]

The practice of democracy—Auden identifies this practice with "an attitude of mind" (*Prose* 2:8) in order to distinguish it from both codified plans and fleeting urges—is constitutively distant from any putative democratic theory. In this regard, Auden agrees with Adorno and Horkheimer's strictest formulation of critical theory. A dogmatic theory of democracy is inconsistent with the "attitude" that supports and guides democratic practices. The Ferney of "Voltaire at Ferney" is not, therefore, formulated in terms of a theory that would demand a specific set of actions; nor does the poem forget the project of cultivating a condition in which "misery, poverty and social injustice" (*Prose* 2:10–11) can be reduced, so that the symptoms of happiness might arise. The extent to which the authors of the *Dialectic of Enlightenment* forget Ferney becomes apparent in their final sentence: the withered tree with which they conclude their fragment overshadows the verdant landscape in which Voltaire invested his last years.

This forgetting of Ferney is doubtless far less sinister than the danger about which they speak in "For Voltaire"—the danger that the memory of "joyously performed lynchings" will be kept alive only by scoundrels, who enjoy such spectacles—but it is menacing nevertheless, for it obliterates the possibility of a practice for which there is only the minimum of theory: happiness allows one to be open to others, whereas misery isolates those who continually experience it. Auden accordingly presents Voltaire's estate as a place for *a little progress*. Nowhere is there the slightest suggestion of a triumphal march of civilization (for this would require a theory, if not an entire apologetics); rather, the progress consists in sporadic growth that remains outside the range of Voltaire's immediate field of vision. The trees that appear in the opening stanza of "Voltaire at Ferney" may or may not be metaphors for human affairs, but this indeterminacy is not critical; what is important is that no formula for the cultivation of trees is credited with the progress of a few—but certainly not all—of the saplings that Voltaire helped sow:

> Perfectly happy now, he looked at his estate.
> An exile making watches glanced up as he passed,
> And went on working; where a hospital was rising fast
> A joiner touched his cap; an agent came to tell
> Some of the trees he'd planted were progressing well.
> The white alps glittered. It was summer. He was very great.
> (*AT* 29)

All of the opening lines of the poem testify to the greatness of Voltaire, including his estate, which appears at first as the manifestation of his greatness. The first five lines, moreover, are marked by caesuras that at once divide the line and show the seamless articulation of the whole. "Voltaire at Ferney," in this sense, opens as though both it and the estate it describes were works of art like those that watchmakers and joiners create: made of parts that form a unified whole. The caesuras do not register as breaks but, instead, mimic the pauses of someone surveying an abundant variety of practices; they seem nothing more than moments in which a joiner might touch his cap to some passer-by and resume his work. The sense of unity and wholeness carries over into the last line of the stanza, which, looking beyond Ferney, departs from the pattern of a single, mid-line caesura and consists in three independent sentences. By virtue of its inclusion in the stanza, the final line suggests that this sense of unity is a cosmic phenomenon that somehow—the specific relations remain obscure—reflects the greatness of Voltaire.

Greatness, however, is not the same as goodness. The suggestion of unity is nothing more: the absence of any connection between the mountainous setting, the particular season, and Voltaire makes it impossible to say that any of these is related to any other. Indeed, the alteration in the pattern of caesuras produces corresponding counter-suggestions: that the glitter of the Alps is wholly distinct from the seasonal situation, and that neither this particular space nor this particular time has anything to do with the stature of Voltaire, whose greatness can be readily proclaimed but not goodness—if he is, indeed, good. Nor does the democratic character of Ferney appear in any positive sense: Voltaire remains lord of his estate; the workers remain his subjects. The first stanza of "Voltaire at Ferney" could scarcely be clearer on this point: "an exile making watches" is nothing beyond his watchmaking; "a joiner" nothing other than a joiner, "an agent" simply an agent. Only Voltaire is distinguished from his station, for he alone has a name, and he alone is said to be happy. And if he alone is happy, then his estate, far from incubating democracy, appears as almost the direct opposite: a community of workers dedicated to the exaltation of the "great man."

Something along these lines may have troubled Auden. In the 1945 revision of the poem he alters the first phrase from "Perfectly happy" to "Almost happy"—which changes the valence of the "now" that concludes each of these phrases: in the first version, it is a climax, whereas in the second, it is an anticipation. Beyond the alteration of the opening phrase, the 1945 version includes one further emendation. Auden eliminates altogether the penultimate stanza, which had originally proposed a minimal theory of injustice that corresponds to the minimal theory of democracy, as it was expressed in the 1939 review:

> Night fell and made him think of women: Lust
> Was one of the great teachers; Pascal was a fool.

How Emilie had loved astronomy and bed;
Pimpette had loved him too like scandal; he was glad.
He'd done his share of weeping for Jerusalem: As a rule
It was the pleasure-haters who became unjust. (*AT* 30)

In an early chapter of his study, Torrey briefly described Voltaire's "scandalous" courtship of Olympe Dunoyer (Pimpette) as well as his elaborate liaison with the Marquise Gabrielle-Émilie du Châtelet as he contrasted Voltaire's concept of happiness with Pascal's: "[Voltaire] differed from Pascal in believing that the goal could in some measure be reached in this life, that there was no other life in which the term happiness had meaning. It is perfectly true, however, that each man sought and found happiness in his own way—Pascal in the abrogation of pleasure and denial of life and Voltaire in the full acceptance of life's realities and society's responsibilities."[13] By presenting through indirect discourse Voltaire's final judgment on his great adversary, "Pascal was a fool," Auden is briefer still; but it is probably not for the sake of brevity that he excised this and the surrounding lines from the poem for its republication in *Collected Poems*.[14] It has been suggested that the reason for this decision lies in Auden's "settled Christian state of mind," which might have been disturbed by "the illegitimacy of Voltaire's amours."[15] It is far more likely, however, that, in 1945, knowing about the Nazi death camps, Auden did not want to include a line that mocked those who mourned for the destruction of the ancient capital of Judea. The opening line of the poem speaks of "now," thus directly connecting the condition of Voltaire at Ferney with the time in which readers encounter "Voltaire at Ferney."

Neither Torrey nor Noyes, strangely enough, offers a single word about Voltaire's well-known antagonism to Judaism; but they were not the only source of Auden's familiarity with the French *philosophe*.[16] Another source was Ezra Pound, for whom Voltaire was an important point of reference, beginning with his 1916 poem "Impressions of François-Marie Arouet," which, like the deleted stanza of Auden's poem, celebrates Voltaire's life-long virility, centered on his pursuit of Gabrielle-Émilie du Châtelet.[17] Pound was drawn to Voltaire for a variety of reasons, but foremost among them was his aversion to Christian ecclesiastic institutions and their supposedly Jewish provenance. He thus translated the article on Genesis in Voltaire's *Dictionnaire philosophique*, where he could find a notable predecessor to his own attitude toward Judaism.[18] Voltaire, for Pound, was a fellow anti-Semite, where the "anti-" here marks something of the same unrelenting negativity that draws the approval of Adorno and Horkheimer. Insofar as the problematic stanza of the original version of "Voltaire at Ferney" not only alludes to Pound's "Impressions of François-Marie Arouet" but also gives the impression that Voltaire's anti-Jewish writings could be justified under the assumption that sufficient weeping had already been done for the Jews, it makes the entire poem appear as though Auden's version of Voltaire tallies with Pound's.[19] In 1945, revelations about the depths and extent of Nazi death camps made any suggestion that there had been enough weeping for Jerusalem outrageous. The only other alteration Auden made when he republished the poem at the end of the Second World War can be understood from the same perspective.[20] It is similarly outrageous to be "perfectly happy now." And so the opening phrase, in which the "now" finds expression, is similarly changed: "almost happy" is now the happiest an Enlightener can be.

Verse Versus Poetry

In "A Great Democrat" Auden reproduces a passage from a letter Voltaire wrote to Rousseau upon receiving a copy of his "Discourse on the Origin and Foundations of Inequality among Human Beings": "Never has anyone employed so much wit in trying to make us witless; the reading of your book makes us want to creep on all fours. However, since it is now more than sixty years since I lost that habit, I feel unfortunately that it is impossible for me to take it up again, and I leave that natural attitude to those who are more worthy of it than you or I" (*Prose* 2:9). Auden's brief gloss on this derisive passage conforms to the theoretical minimalism that governs his concept of democracy: "Rousseau says that civilization is horrible. Much of it is, but not all. We neither can nor want to become savages or babies again" (*Prose* 2:9). The version of Voltaire that takes shape in "Voltaire at Ferney" begins to depart ever so slightly from the one Auden presents in his review of the studies of Torrey and Noyes. Neither an infant nor a "savage," Voltaire is nevertheless not a mature citizen of the city who straightforwardly defends the value of civilization by presenting his own condition as the accomplishment of an allegedly universal telos:

> Cajoling, scolding, scheming, cleverest of them all,
> He'd led the other children in a holy war
> Against the infamous grown-ups, and, like a child, been
>   sly
> And humble when there was occasion for
> The two-faced answer or the plain protective lie,
> But, patient like a peasant, waited for their fall. (*AT* 29)

In describing adults as "infamous," Auden alludes to the phrase for which Voltaire is perhaps most famous: "*Écrasez l'infâme.*" Under the self-evident premise that Voltaire's struggle against *l'infâme* is the counterpart to the contemporary struggle against fascism, a compelling motive for the image of the enlightener as a scheming child can be found throughout Auden's autobiographical reflections. In an early essay that he had wanted to title "The Liberal Fascist"—Graham Greene objected to this title and changed it—Auden produces the memorable sentence: "The best reason I have for opposing Fascism is that at school I lived in a Fascist state" (*Prose* 1:59). He expands on this remark in the first part of *The Prolific and the Devourer*:

> Every English boy of the middle class spends five years as a member of a primitive tribe ruled by benevolent or malignant demons, and then another five years as a citizen of a totalitarian state. . . . When I read in a history book of King John gnawing the rush-mat in his rage, it did not surprise me in the least: that was just how the masters behaved. So, despite all I have learnt since, my deepest feeling about politicians is that they are dangerous lunatics to be avoided when possible, and carefully humoured: people, above all, to whom one must never tell the truth." (*Prose* 2:415)

The infamy of grown-ups requires a strategy of untruth, which Auden cogently represents in the poem as "The two-faced answer or the plain protective lie."[21] Given the massive disparity in degrees of power and means of violence, only certain modes of combative language—"Cajoling, scolding, scheming"—are available as weapons in a "war" that deserves the predicate "holy" because it is not concerned with relative goods such as land, rewards, or privileges but only with a bare minimum of dignified life.

By the final stanza of the poem, Voltaire is no longer the lord of Ferney, whose greatness is reflected in the landscape of his property, nor, any longer, the leader of an army of "children" engaged in a "holy war" against their elders. In the version published in 1945, moreover, he is not only no longer "perfectly happy" but almost altogether unhappy. Isolated from those on his estate, he is now abandoned by the fellow "children" in his battle against *l'infâme*. In "September 1, 1939" Auden says of himself: "All I have is a voice / To undo the folded lie" (*AT* 105). And his figuration of Voltaire appears to follow suit, for he has become an isolated poet who directs his verse against institutions that exercise unjust power and hide their actions through self-glorifying propaganda. Yet "Voltaire at Ferney" cannot, like Adorno and Horkheimer's fragment, be called "For Voltaire." If the poet who wrote "Voltaire at Ferney" were simply *for* the poet he constructs under the name of Voltaire, he would make his poem into a form of self-satisfaction: the poet would imagine a poet as the only uncompromising and uncompromised fighter against mendacity and injustice. But the end of the poem situates the office of poetry in a different light, and it is in reflection on the conclusions to "For Voltaire" and "Voltaire at Ferney" that the distance between their otherwise strikingly similar versions of Voltaire can be most effectively measured. A precarious stance other than "pro" or "contra" traverses the final stanza of the poem. In keeping with the line of thought developed by Adorno and Horkheimer, this stance remains unnamed; against their line of thought, however, this refusal is not represented in terms of the "hardness of thought," which is supposed to lie beyond the mendacious potential of human language. Rather, the relation between the poet who writes "Voltaire at Ferney" and the Voltaire who writes verses against power appears in the legible disjunctions of Auden's own verses:

> Yet, like a sentinel, he could not sleep. The night was full of wrong,

> Earthquakes and executions. Soon he would be dead,
> And still all over Europe stood the horrible nurses
> Itching to boil their children. Only his verses
> Perhaps could stop them: He must go on working.
>   Overhead
> The uncomplaining stars composed their lucid song.
>   (*AT* 30)

The opening and closing stanzas of Auden's poem present two sharply contrasting versions of Voltaire. At the beginning, in daylight, he is the literal observer of an object, namely the estate that he has himself established and which reflects his position in the world. In the end, without any trace of the original happiness, at night, his observation is strictly figural—"like a sentinel"—and what he sees has nothing to do with his estate; nor does it reflect his position. The final simile is therefore entirely unlike the ones that punctuate the central stanza of the poem. Far from being "patient like a peasant," merely waiting for the "fall" of those in power, Voltaire works alone and with only a single certainty: that he—not those in power—will soon die. And instead of being "like a child," who leads an army of children against adults, he is preoccupied by the dangers to which children are exposed. Whether the word *children* in the final stanza should be understood literally or should, instead, be read as a figure for powerlessness cannot be determined. The "nurses" who threaten children are doubtless unlike the nurses who would work at the "hospital" that Voltaire observes under construction in the opening stanza of the poem; but precisely who they are then supposed to represent is equally uncertain. Perhaps *children* and *nurses* should be understood as both literal and figural: the fairy-tale atmosphere suggests that the image of nurses boiling children is a replacement for other kinds of danger; but this atmosphere likewise presents the dangers to which children are exposed in child-oriented terms. This much, however, is clear: the final and defining object of Voltaire's consciousness is not himself; still less is he preoccupied by his impending death; rather, he is acutely aware of threatened life that is not his own.

The final stanza of "Voltaire at Ferney" also registers another kind of alteration. Not only is the Voltaire who "must go on working" far removed from the Voltaire who leisurely surveys his land, he is also decisively different from the Voltaire whom Auden presents in his review of the books by Noyes and Torrey. The review prominently rejects the widespread conception of Voltaire as a pure polemicist whose motto *"Écrasez l'infâme"* was directed at all religious institutions.[22] While emphasizing the critical side of Voltaire, Auden calls attention to several passages of his writing in which his polemical edge—against Pascal's *deus absconditus* in this case—is employed for altogether affirmative ends: "The man was not lacking in reverence who wrote: 'I was meditating last night, I was absorbed in the contemplation of nature; I admired the immensity, the course, the harmony of those infinite globes. . . . One must be blind not to be dazzled by this spectacle, one must be stupid not to recognize the author of it; one must be mad not to worship him'" (*Prose* 2:9–10; Auden's ellipsis). In this passage of Voltaire's *Dictionnaire philosophique*, which Auden draws directly from Torrey's study,[23] sound is allied with sight, as the harmony of the spheres appears in the form of a stellar spectacle. Nocturnal meditation, according to this passage, becomes an occasion for turning away from a world whose stupidity Voltaire attacks and turning toward the cosmos whose divine author clearly manifests himself.

Some of the same language—but none of the reverence—finds its way into the concluding stanza of "Voltaire at Ferney." The setting is again the night, the subject again the object of Voltaire's consciousness; but the object of his consciousness in the poem is radically different from the one that appears in the review. Voltaire no longer has time for the contemplation of the awe-inspiring heavens; on the contrary, acutely aware of both his own death and the wrongs of the world, natural as well as human, he fails to hear—for whatever reason—that "harmony of those infinite globes" from which he can confidently conclude that only an idiot would deny the cosmos its transcendent author. The poet who appears in Auden's poem, in other words, is unlike the writer about whom he writes in his reviews; the poet Voltaire is, rather, something like the thinker for whom Adorno and Horkheimer argue in their fragment: tirelessly negative, without a trace of reverence for an apparently stable order established by higher powers. Auden thus produces two versions of Voltaire, for any veneration of the cosmic author in the poem could not fail to be read as reverence for the author *of* the poem.

The final stanza is the site of a third alteration as well—an alteration that is legible, however, only in the light of a certain continuity. In the first stanza, a watchmaker continues his work, even as Voltaire, who is clearly "above" the craftsman in every sense of the word, makes an appearance: "An exile making watches glanced up as he passed / And went on working." This scene, which first establishes the framework of Ferney, shows the beneficence of Voltaire as lord: he is a gracious host to exiles, and he does not demand of those below him that they show signs of deference to his exalted position. In the last stanza, some of the same language returns, as does the scene as a whole—with the position of the watchmaker occupied by Voltaire, and the position of Voltaire seemingly, but not conclusively, empty. For it is now Voltaire who continues unaltered in his work; indeed, it is necessary that he do so, and there is no indication that the source of this imperative is anyone other than himself. In other words, he freely binds himself: "He must go on working." The aim of his uninterruptible work is, however, the interruption of historical processes: "Only his verses / Perhaps could stop them." What Adorno and Horkheimer affirm of theory applies, word for word, to Voltaire's verse: "Its element is freedom, its theme oppression." And the decisive term into which Adorno and Horkheimer's reflection on theory issues—namely, *hardness*—also finds an equivalent in Auden's poem: to "go on working." Only when the going isn't easy, so to speak, does it make sense to speak of "going on." But "going on" is a practical matter—and eminently so in the formulation "to go on working." By contrast, the theory of "theory" that finds expression in "For Voltaire" has no room for a positive practice. Because theory "presupposes the reproduction of life in this or that determined form," it can conceive of "going on" only as the perpetuation of the conditions it presupposes. Confronted with this theoretical impasse, the authors of the *Dialectic of Enlightenment* latch onto the idea of hard thinking, which is on the hither side of both language and practice. So hard is the "hardness of thought" that it must be impenetrable; otherwise, its goodness would be violated. Because the practice of "going on," by contrast, is directed at the goal of stopping the practices of those who are currently in power, it must be broadly accessible. Such is the reason for Voltaire's verse: "Only his verses / Perhaps could stop them." And the founding of Ferney is a continuation of this poetic labor. Work goes on regardless of whatever catastrophe awaits the worker and whatever calamities may be happening elsewhere in the world—in particular, as described in the first stanza of the poem, the work of horticulture, carpentry, and watchmaking.

Only the first and last workers in "Voltaire at Ferney," however, are explicitly said to go on working, and it is in the light of their work that the tensions of the poem—and of the particular type of practice it illuminates—become legible.[24] In one regard, the first and last workers are alike: one is a watchmaker; the other, whom the poet likens to a "sentinel," could also be called a watchman. In another regard, they could scarcely be more different. Whereas the first "glances up" when the lord who offers him refuge momentarily appears, the last never looks upward. Such is the upshot of Auden's alteration of the image of Voltaire from review to poem. If Voltaire, like the exile making watches, looked above him, momentarily attentive to the lord of the cosmos, this gesture would complete the comparison between the craftsman who takes up residence at Ferney and its owner, who is on the verge of departing from his earthly estate. As a result, it would bind the first image of the poem to the last: the heavenly and earthly spheres would be as harmoniously related to each other as are Ferney's various strata. The structural unity of the cosmos would, in turn, mirror the imagistic unity of the poem. Just as the estate would be seen as governed by a beneficent lord whom his subjects thoughtfully notice without having to perform any specific sign of deference, so, too, would the cosmos of which this estate would be an exemplary instance. The exiled watchmaker would reflect the exalted Watchmaker, who, according to the famous Enlightenment simile, created the cosmos in such a perfect manner that it goes on working without any need for outside intervention.[25] Finally, just as the first and last line of every stanza rhyme, so would the first and last stanzas of the poem harmonize. But such is not the case. The two workers who are seen to go on working remain unlike each other in one decisive regard: the last one does not "glance up." The following analogy—which is attractive precisely because it would make the poem appear as a microcosmos—does not hold: earthly watchmaker is to lordly watchman as lordly watchman is to heavenly Watchmaker. The first and last images diverge, and the poem, far from representing a microcosmos, presents a micro-cataclysm: the rupture of any relation between terrestrial and celestial spheres.

By representing the cosmos as an undifferentiated sensorium—the law of gravity applies to all things in both the sub- and supra-luminary spheres—proponents of the eighteenth-century Enlightenment welcomed a re-division of the world into a moral universe and a natural one. Whereas the moral universe is the subject of critique and discipline, the natural one is a field of observation and control. For the Voltaire who appears in Auden's poem, a total separation between the moral universe and its natural counterpart is the condition under which he can—and must—assume responsibility for his world. Without effective allies, and without any expectation of help from nature or God, Voltaire alone makes use of the tools at his disposal to prevent the massacre of innocent life: "And only himself to count upon" (*AT* 29). The condition in which it makes sense to speak of responsibility, in other words, is the condition in which talk of a single cosmos—even a cosmos separated into harmonious spheres—no longer makes sense. Such is, for Auden, the dialectic of Enlightenment: greater responsibility for the world requires its irrevocable fragmentation. Auden was not, of course, the first to recognize that the separation between celestial and terrestrial spheres was an integral feature of the Enlightenment. The only other verses of his that refer to Voltaire place the lord of Ferney in opposition to a poet who was particularly affected—and offended—by this separation, namely:

> Self-educated WILLIAM BLAKE,
> Who threw his spectre in the lake,
> Broke off relations in a curse
> With the Newtonian Universe,
> But even as a child would pet
> The tigers Voltaire never met. (*CP45* 270)

Even if Blake were able to encounter the "fearful symmetry"[26] that escapes proponents of Enlightenment, the violent manner by which he separates himself from the universe he curses guarantees that he reproduces the very separation that occasions his curse. Not so Auden, whose "Voltaire at Ferney" neither curses nor praises the divisiveness of Enlightenment. Instead of reproducing the separation between moral and natural universe, Auden introduces a corresponding split into the very institution of poetry: on one side is verse, like Voltaire's, that attends to the wrongs of the earth; on the other side is stellar song.

The final line of "Voltaire at Ferney" describes what happens in the celestial sphere, as Voltaire produces his version of *littérature engagée*: "Overhead / The uncomplaining stars composed their lucid song." Nothing in the poem can be counted as preparation for these words. In the concluding line of the first stanza, the Alps are said to glitter, but the line goes no higher. Unlike the Alps, the stellar song is over Voltaire's head in all senses of the phrase: above him, outside his consciousness, and perhaps even beyond his comprehension. This song does not, therefore, belong to Voltaire's Ferney, and the lines in which it appears are, in this sense, cut loose from the poem. And here a final comparison between "For Voltaire" and "Voltaire at Ferney" is illuminating. Both fragment and poem conclude by directing attention to stellar objects, and the specific ones to which they refer correspond to the subject matter into which they issue. For Adorno and Horkheimer, a dialogue on the role of reason ends with an image of the sun, which can both clarify the world and set it ablaze; for Auden, a poem on the role of poetry concludes with an image of stars as composers of their own song. In the fair copy of "Voltaire at Ferney," Auden had originally concluded the poem in this way: "The uncomplaining stars performed their lucid song." For the published version, however, he crossed out "performed" and replaced it with "composed." The alteration is decisive. The notion of the stars performing their song reproduces the age-old doctrine of the harmony of the spheres. In the original version, then, the final line of the poem would reaffirm some version of Voltaire's Deism, according to which God lets the infinitely varied elements of the world perform the complicated composition he created. With the image of the stars composing their "lucid song," by contrast, the poet separates himself from

Voltaire's Deism without thereby stating a doctrine of his own. Rather, the stars become comparable to poets—and yet different from producers of verses, like Voltaire, who understand their task as "complaining" about terrestrial conditions.[27]

In "For Voltaire" the final image summarizes the argument of both the fragment in particular and the *Dialectic of Enlightenment* as a whole: the power of reason can be safely sensed—which is not to say honored—only by attending to those barely standing creatures that are almost destroyed by the very light that grants them life. In the final version of "Voltaire at Ferney," by contrast, the concluding image is not only *not* a recapitulation of the poem as a whole; it sets a part of the poem apart from itself. The stars' "lucid song" has nothing to do with Voltaire's "verses" except, perhaps, insofar as they negate each other: the song is as uncomplaining as the stars that compose it, whereas the verses, as sheer complaint, are uncompromisingly critical. And there is no lucid answer to the following questions: should "Voltaire at Ferney" be understood as verse or as song—or not quite either, or in some sense both? The institution of literature splits apart, and the only manner in which the sundered spheres relate to each other is by way of mutual exclusion: if Voltaire paid attention to the stellar song, the continuity of his verse production would be interrupted, and if the stars could attend to Voltaire's verses, they might well have reason to complain.

THREE

"Civilization Must Be Saved"

Two Versions of the "Real Question"

In March 1941 Max Horkheimer wrote a letter to Harold Laski thanking him for sending a copy of *Where Do We Go from Here?* Horkheimer became acquainted with Laski in the early 1930s, when the offices of the Frankfurt School of Social Research temporarily moved to London, in part through Laski's efforts on its behalf. Written immediately after the Nazis' victory over France, Laski's treatise is subtitled *An Essay in Interpretation* because it seeks to provide an interpretation of modern history that shows how the Nazis were able to succeed in dominating the continent of Europe without, as of the time of Laski's writing, provoking any significant internal or external resistance. The swift capitulation of the French to Hitler's army, for Laski, is a historical sign of a certain rottenness at the core of capitalist liberal democracy. The case of the United Kingdom will be different, Laski assures his readers, for its citizens are well aware of what happens when the Nazis seize control of a country: "Great Britain has come to see that it is for its citizens a question now of victory or annihilation; there is no middle term between the two."[1] Conceived as an amplification of these stark alternatives, Laski's interpretation of modern history is divided into three chapters, with the greatest weight falling on the final chapter, the title of which was reformulated for the treatise as a whole: "What Are We to Do Next?" The next steps in Laski's program involve the essential transformation of liberal democracies from capitalist- to socialist-based economies.

Horkheimer received a copy of *Where Do We Go from Here?* shortly after it appeared and sent Laski a letter of appreciation a few months later with an apology for the delay. Beyond the general turmoil of the times, he explains, "we had a very heavy personal loss to suffer: our staff member, Walter Benjamin, committed suicide after an unsuccessful attempt to cross the Franco-Spanish border."[2] After briefly praising Benjamin for the independence of his intelligence, Horkheimer bemoans how little he himself can do "for the time being," as he strings together a series of theological-political images that express the absence of a critical vocabulary for contemporary events:

> But all this does not imply that we have become passive and gaze into the flames, hands in our laps. . . . You can very well imagine that, in a practical way, we are able to do very little for the time being, except to attempt to pull from the hell of the German orbit as many of our endangered friends as we can. We make every effort. But the impotence of the individual, and the individual institution, in [the] face of the juggernaut, comes more clearly to our consciousness every day.[3]

In the absence of a practical course of action, Horkheimer seeks consolation in its theoretical counterpart: "So we try to continue our theoretical work *tant bien que mal*, and to bring our problem as close to reality as possible." Confronted with the horror in Europe, Horkheimer's apprehensions soon devolve into self-pitying reflections on the supposed danger to which he and his colleagues at the Institute for Social Research will expose themselves as soon as they begin to pursue "the real questions": "Everything that stays aloof appears more superfluous today than ever before, whereas one burns one's fingers as soon as one approaches the real questions."[4] Horkheimer concludes his letter by emphasizing the degree to which he and his colleagues agree not only with Laski's program for social-political transition, but also with the terms in which its way forward is presented: "We sincerely hope that the historical way out, which you point, will be used not only in England but elsewhere."[5]

Auden, too, responds to *Where Do We Go from Here?*—not in a personal letter but in the form of a book review that appeared in the short-lived journal edited by Klaus Mann, *Decision: A Journal of Free Culture*. Auden's response represents an incisive summary of his recent reflections on history, made urgent by the "decision" that his brother-in-law announces as the title of the journal. In schematic terms, the decision in favor of "free culture"—and thus for a certain liberal democracy—cannot be predicated on the conviction that we are unqualified exponents of such culture and therefore know what it should be like. For Auden, these doubts must be expressed, but they cannot simply be masked in the form of banal theological-political images like those through which Horkheimer indicates the absence of a technical vocabulary adequate to the current crisis. Auden's response is starkly different from Horkheimer's, even though, as the opening paragraphs of the review indicate, not only does he agree with much of what Laski writes but—and this is something about which Horkheimer, also living far from Europe, is silent—he also acknowledges the difference between the physical safety he enjoys in New York and the vulnerability of Laski's situation in London during the Blitz: "I wish I could feel more enthusiastic about this book than I do, not only because I agree with nearly everything that is said, but also because in view of what the author and his fellow countrymen are now enduring in the defense of civilization, a certain impudence attaches to any criticism by someone who is not sharing in their suffering" (*Prose* 2:104). Prompted by Laski's interrogative title and the gravity of the historical situation, Auden, like Horkheimer, directs his attention toward a "real question."

Here, however, the similarity between the two responses to *Where Do We Go from Here?* ends. For Horkheimer, Laski's prescription for "the next step" is the primary source of their overall agreement; as the spokesperson for the Institute for Social Research, he is attuned to the possibility of getting one's fingers burned as soon as one goes beyond the aloofness of philosophical reflection and drafts a program for political transformation. For Horkheimer, burned fingers mean nothing other than the loss of financial support. To speak too much of the transition from capitalism to socialism, in other words, is to expose the Institute for Social Research to negative repercussions among its funding agencies.[6] For Auden, by contrast, the "real question" lies elsewhere: "Where-do-we-go-from-here is an unreal question: the only real question, and this itself becomes unreal unless it is asked all the time, is where-are-we-now" (*Prose* 2:107). Auden's review of Laski's work takes its title from this revised question, and it is a vertiginous rhetorical performance. Even as he agrees with the general aims of the book, Auden clearly dislikes it and wants to prevent readers from being blinded to its crucial errors out of complacent identification with its liberal social-democratic goals.[7] Both Laski and Auden recognize the all-too evident failure of capitalist democracy to resist Hitler's rise, and both view debates about the virtues of socialism versus capitalism as secondary matters. Like Laski, moreover, Auden has no sympathy for the kind of contemporaneous proto-fascist political programs that find expression in, for example, Eliot's *After Strange Gods*, to say nothing of explicit appeals to fascism as the necessary replacement for the broken and ailing systems of the Western democracies. But even in the case of Laski's proposed solution to the problem of British social conflict, which involves the demolition of class privileges, Auden's whole-hearted agreement is tempered by a suspicion that the solution, too, evades the "real question," for it will encounter little resistance and requires no decision: "I cannot help wondering if Professor Laski is not at times flogging a dying horse. Whoever wins this war, the Lord Lloyds are lost" (*Prose* 2:105).

Auden sees something that Laski does not: the goal of liberal social democracy becomes an impediment as soon as it is viewed as a "given" and not as a historically bound horizon. Beyond this horizon are others that may be obscured by the necessary struggle against fascism, but the necessity of the struggle does not mean that this occlusion is itself necessary. Without any brash gestures of ultra-left-wing radicality, Auden's review is nevertheless a radical statement that seeks to shake the readers of *Decision* out of their somnambulistic identification with a political creed that sees compromise—concretized in the idea of a liberal democracy that mixes capitalism with socialism—as the ultimate political virtue. Something of Auden's quietly tough-minded reflections can be found in the more vociferous writings of Slavoj Žižek, especially *In Defense of Lost Causes*, the final pages of which emphasize a point that also permeates "Where Are We Now?": "What is unthinkable within [the] horizon of linear historical evolution is the notion of a choice/act which retroactively opens up its own possibility."[8] And in the introduction to *In Defense of Lost Causes* Žižek draws on the image in which this "choice/act" has been framed. Speaking of "Third Wave" social democrats like Tony Blair (who could be seen as a recent heir of Laski's legacy), Žižek seems to follow Auden's path even more fully; he connects the transcendence of the contemporary horizon of political possibilities established by rigid adherence to "common sense" with the Kierkegaardian image that informs all of Auden's work of this period: "The problem, of course, is that, in a time of crises and ruptures, skeptical empirical wisdom itself, constrained to the horizon of the dominant form of common sense, cannot provide the answers, so one *must* risk a Leap of Faith."[9]

For Auden, however, the problem is not the lack of answers but, rather, the pervasiveness of "unreal questions," which make "real questions" appear as problems that require technical-mathematical "solutions." Auden is little inclined toward the kind of obstreperous provocations that characterize much of Žižek's work, not least his defense of certain "lost causes" like Stalinism. Nevertheless, one of the statements Auden makes in the review of Laski's work is every bit as provocative, and arguably more "real," for it is a direct assault on the social-democratic pieties that cast Hitlerism as other-worldly rather than intimately related to its own premises: "The historical importance of Hitler is that he has pushed liberalism to its logical conclusion. He has accepted the psychology of Freud and the Behaviorists. . . . He has accepted the Marxian view of political conduct. . . . He has accepted Locke's view of government as the ringmaster of competing interests, and shown that, on that assumption, the subordination of every interest to the political is perfectly logical. He has, in fact, unmasked the unmaskers" (*Prose* 2:106). Liberalism, according to Auden, cannot conceive of an absolute claim in which individuals at once recognize their own absoluteness and correspondingly recognize other individuals as similarly absolute. On the contrary, all forms of liberalism, especially contemporary social democracy, replace absolute claims with appeals to a putative reality gained by adopting a "historical perspective," in which "here" and "there"—marking the starting and ending points of our journey—are related to each other in the form of a natural continuum: without any gaps and certainly without the need for any leaps on the part of those intent on progress.[10]

Despite his very real doubts about the reality of the questions posed under the rubric of liberal social democracy, Auden does not, however, follow his many modernist contemporaries who fell into the arms of antiliberal doctrines or parties, nor does he ever have the slightest doubt that the struggle against Nazi Germany can rightly be described as the defense of civilization, which is by its very nature *liberal* in the proper senses of the term. Auden's critique of Laski is generated, above all, by his contention that many of his allies in the struggle against fascism do not realize what is required for the defense of civilization, beginning with the recognition that the defense is never definitive and cannot be conducted by reference to its putative "achievements." And this is for a simple reason: regardless of its etymological connection to the city and its protective walls, the category of civilization is not, for Auden, a matter of achievement but is, rather, a way of being—free, open, generous—that makes it possible for human beings to interact with one another in such a way that something like the putative urbanity of "city life" is possible. Civilization is thus a central category of Auden's reflections. It cannot be geographically qualified, as in the term *Western civilization*, and it is positively repugnant to understand civilization as a "burden" that a race—the "White Man" in Kipling's formulation—must bear. Because civilization is unqualified, it is akin to the unconditioned that liberalism in its classical formulations renounces. Understood in this way, however, it is an immanent unconditioned that cannot stand outside history as either origin or goal. Even as Auden recognizes and applauds technological advances that allow greater control over natural forces, he rejects any talk of historical progress from barbarism to civilization. Benjamin famously wrote: "*Even the dead* will not be safe from the enemy if he is victorious."[11] Auden ends his review of Laski's study with a remark that could be understood as that statement's complement: "unless it is realized that the true necessity of which to become conscious is internal and absolute, then, when Hitler is defeated and the external compulsion of war removed, the dead and themselves will once again be betrayed by the surviving" (*Prose* 2:108). To use a phrase that again links Horkheimer's letter to Laski with Auden's thought of the period, civilization is a question always and only "for the time being."[12]

Auden's review of Laski's book is only one of many attempts on his part to pose the "real question" in light of the threat of fascism, not only in terms of its military powers but also, and especially, in terms of its "internal" appeal. The latter is expressed with the utmost urgency when Auden makes the disturbing pronouncement that Hitler takes liberalism to its logical conclusion. With this thought, a comforting moral and political dichotomy collapses, as one pole of an acute opposition is recognized as directly related to the other. A collapse of this kind can be discerned throughout Auden's writings of the period. To conceive of the struggle of civilization against "ignorance and barbarism" as an event that can be successfully completed once and for all, or to see the struggle in terms of a righteous self at a distance from a malevolent other—this is the stubborn delusion around which Auden created three major prose monologues in the 1930s and 1940s. The first takes the form of a sermon he assigns over time to a dizzying array of starkly contrasting characters in different plays and publications of the period; the second is a soliloquy that forms the penultimate section of his "Christmas Oratorio," *For the Time Being*, under the chilling title "The Massacre of the Innocents"; and the third is the concluding address in *The Sea and the Mirror*, a "commentary" on *The Tempest* that was originally published alongside *For the Time Being* in a single volume. As the three monologues make clear, each in its own way, "ignorance" should not be understood in relation to a body of acquired knowledge that constitutes either a secular *paideia* or theological indoctrination; and as for the term *barbarism*, these monologues also make clear that it cannot be simply attributed to modes of unruly or otherwise violent life that are supposedly foreign to whatever is associated with the term *civilization*.

What is immediately striking about all three monologues—and the primary motivation for seeking to understand them in relation to one another—is that in each case, the speaker undergoes a radical change of identity from original conception to final publication, as Auden struggles to find the proper poetic voices to express both a certain dichotomy and its collapse. To be more specific: the first of the monologues consists in a crazed jeremiad for which Auden invents a diabolical figure who sees enmity in the form of the international proletariat. Auden initially assigns this looney speech to an unambiguous champion of counter-revolution, who, as an Armament Manufacturer, has a material interest in fomenting state-sponsored violence; but he then reassigns the speech across several publications, and it ends up in the mouth of a Vicar, whose very title is intimately associated with traditional English religiosity.[13] The second prose monologue is a speech that Auden began to write as the voice of Saint Simeon the Righteous, who received the baby Jesus in his arms at the Temple, but which Auden ultimately published as the soliloquy of Herod the Great, who responds to news of the Christ child with an order to slaughter all the infants in the province he controls.[14] This startling transformation integrates further opposing identities, for, far from being the prototypical madman of the Christian tradition, Auden's Herod speaks the rational discourse of a British colonial administrator and pitifully declares himself a "liberal" at the very moment he authorizes the massacre of the innocents.

The first two monologues are united by the conviction of their speakers that they are agents of civilization—"the civilized globe" (*CP45* 246) in the first case, a "tiny patch of light" (*FTB* 113), in the second—in continual conflict with its irreconcilable enemies. As for the identity of the barbarians, they, too, are different: in the first instance, the enemy of civilization is an international organization of the underclass; in the second, it is the baby Jesus and all those who are susceptible to belief in his divinity. But the basis for the appeals to violent counter-action on the part of the Vicar and Herod remains the same: without the annihilation of the opposing camp, each of them argues, the political-social order with which they identify themselves—ecclesiastical Christian in the first case, Roman imperial in the second—will reveal its vulnerability and thereby succumb to destruction. By having the author of the massacre call himself a "liberal," Auden completes, as it were, the argument he develops in "Where Are We Now?" Under no condition will he present the figure of evil simply as the Other whose identity is altogether different from his own. The Vicar, after all, is a representative of the very religion to which Auden has returned, and something similar is true in the case of Herod: his soliloquy develops out of a meditation in which Auden sought to capture the discovery of his own vocation as a poet and the experience of his return to the church, yet it becomes an apologia for genocide.

The mobility with which Auden repurposes the speech of the Armament Manufacturer and the meditation of Simeon suggests a fluid identity—or nimble power of re-identification—across ideological and religious extremes. Rejecting the pretense that evil is a foreign other, Auden recognizes the concomitant presumption that the other's perspective is wholly accessible and not so different after all. Something else happens in the third and last prose monologue under consideration here: it is spoken by Caliban, who, thanks to the renown of his inventor, is the prototypical colonial subject in English literature. Here, too, Auden began to write Caliban's speech in the voice of his opposite, that is, Ariel. In changing the identity of the speaker, however, Auden was not revealing that the voice of the Other is intimately related to that of the same, which in this case would be something like the voice of "art," understood as a magical power capacious enough to capture every human experience. On the contrary, the change in identity is a direct challenge to the fantasy that Auden's form of art, his poetry and prose, can speak for otherwise voiceless colonial subjects. But what does Caliban say? The figures of the Vicar and Herod say, in effect, that violence is the only "real" answer. Caliban does not affirm the opposite; his speech is not a plea for universal human understanding. On the contrary, in probing the pacifying fantasy of "understanding the other," it becomes something like an extremity of its own—a pole without a corresponding counter-pole, a speech into which Ariel simply vanishes. An echo of this vanishing, spoken by Ariel, completes the "commentary."

The Counter-Revolutionary

Whether presented as a "Sermon by an Armament Manufacturer," a recording emitting from a Gramophone, the effusions of a Vicar, or, finally, as "Depravity: A Sermon"—the genre of the first monologue in which Auden invents a figure who presents himself as a ferocious defender of civilization against a demonic enemy remains constant: it is a sermon, the aim of which is the uplift and strengthening of the faithful. What it reveals instead—to its auditors, if not to the speaker—is the violence required by the sermonizer in upholding his own convictions. It is no accident, therefore, that the monologue floats from one speaker to another: the lack of faith revealed over the course of the sermon corresponds to the fluid identity of the speaker, who is only ever the opposite of what he wants to destroy. And his destructive impulses are directed at many enemies. The only stable element of his identity is a combustible combination of advanced technology and counter-revolutionary fervor. The sermon begins with a review of conservative clichés that are rooted in biblical imagery, but it soon devolves into a crazed manifesto in favor of all-out anti-proletarian warfare. In a series of reflections Auden wrote in the 1930s, he seeks to distinguish art from propaganda in terms of their underlying intentional structures: propaganda seeks to propagate a cause, whereas art—to quote the poem Auden wrote in 1939 on the occasion of Yeats' death—"makes nothing happen" (*AT* 98).

Auden expands on this thought in the concluding passage of his famous essay on Yeats' legacy, written at the same time, with specific attention to the reality and unreality of our questions: "art is a product of history, not a cause. Unlike some other products, technical inventions for example, it does not re-enter history as an effective agent, so that the question whether art should or should not be propaganda is unreal" (*Prose* 2:7). Insofar as the genre of sermon aims to propagate a cause, it is closer to propaganda than to poetry; but insofar as the effect of the sermon rebounds onto the sermonizer, its propagating intention is, as it were, turned around—or, to use Auden's own term in its original Latin sense, "depraved." And this is exactly what happens in "Depravity: A Sermon." The cause for which the sermonizer seeks to mobilize his auditors affects only him. Beginning with sublime imagery drawn from scripture and *Paradise Lost*, the sermonizer poses a question that is every bit as "unreal" as the one Auden identifies in his reflections on Yeats' death: "What was the weather on Eternity's worst day? And where was that Son of God during the fatal second?" (*CP45* 243). By the end of the sermon, the mood and tone of the speech are altogether different. It would be understatement to say that Auden traces the descent of pathos into bathos. As is evident from the progress of the sermon, especially when combined with the stage directions in *The Dog Beneath the Skin*, the aim of strengthening conviction demonstrates only the infantile weakness of the speaker: "O windmills, O cocks, O clouds and ponds. Mother is waving from the tiny door! The quilt is turned down in my beautiful blue and gold room! Father, I thank Thee in advance! Everything has been grand! I am coming home! (*At the end of the sermon, the* VICAR *collapses like a wet rag into his chair and feebly mops his face with a handkerchief*)" (*Plays* 579).

The course of the sermon can thus be described as a vertiginous descent from the sublimity of angelic combat to the clichés of a pastoral life that is even more unbelievable than the traditional imagery of sheep and shepherds. Why—a reader is prone to ask—would the open door be "tiny," and who, after all, would inhabit a "blue and gold room"? Of course, such questions are as unreal as the sermonizer's questions concerning the proto-historical battle. As the stage directions for *The Dog Beneath the Skin* indicate, the Vicar is not even supposed to articulate the final passage; rather, it is to be "*wailed*," as "*saliva runs from his mouth*" (*Plays* 575), thus suggesting that the dog beneath *his*—fawning, counter-revolutionary—skin has been unwittingly revealed. Regardless of which figure or machine intones the sermon, however, its collapse into cliché displays the consequences of being unwilling to ask oneself and one's auditors, "Where are we now?" The sermonizer sees "now" as the site of a struggle that began in proto-history and can end only in an apocalyptic finale, and when, in the end, he returns to his own situation, he somehow sees himself repeating his own proto-history, with mother and father waiting for his glorious homecoming. Thus, a dizzying rhetorical performance devolves from quasi-Miltonic musings about the weather on "Eternity's worst day" to the self-negating silliness of "Everything has been grand!" And the entire sermon works as a warning: here is what happens to political speech when the speaker avoids the question of "where-we-are-now."

The primary dogma of the sermon is a matter of pure logic, so to speak: if, as every believer agrees, Satan is the first revolutionary, then all subsequent revolutionaries—from Adam and Eve to Lenin and Trotsky—are similarly Satanic. The resulting political theory emerges in two steps. The first is expressed in a relatively measured tone, as the sermonizer proposes a traditional form of authoritarianism grounded in the notion of the divine right of kings that is at the same time a justification for the permanent state of military rule: "[God] set over us a kindly strictness, appointed his Authorities, severe but just, a kind of martial law" (*CP45* 245). The sermonizer, however, is unsatisfied with this stale political theory, for it concerns only a past action, not a present condition. As of now—Auden will soon write a dramatic text entitled *For the Time Being*—divine right lies with "the people." The sermon thus traces an arc of conservative political conviction that begins with traditional authoritarianism and ends with fascistic populism. Once "the people" recognize themselves as a divinely motivated natural force, the annihilation of the last, broadest, and most insidious form of revolution will be inevitable. Nature itself will do the requisite job of destruction in the strange form of clever vegetation and aggressive flocks of sheep: "[the enemies] shall be trapped by the stalks of flowers. Sheep shall chase them away" (*CP45* 247).

By the end of his speech, the sermonizer seeks to propagate a populist doctrine that divinizes the action and passion of "the people": "All actions and diversions of the people, their greyhound races, their football competitions, their clumsy acts of love, what are they but the pitiful, maimed expression of that entire passion, the positive tropism of the soul to God?" (*CP45* 247). The implication of this expression of populism as the modern replacement for the divine right of kings is obvious enough: whoever falls outside the range of "the people" always turns toward Satan, which means they can be annihilated because they are mere representatives of negativity. The sermonizer's rhetoric, his own tropes in favor of a divine-people tropism, leads nowhere else. According to the stage directions for *The Dog Beneath the Skin*, by the end of the sermon the Vicar "*has worked himself into a hysterical frenzy*" (*Plays* 575). The Vicar's loss of self-control is a direct consequence of his ever-more fervent advocacy of his cause. The sermon begins with a description of the decision that the angels had to make for or against God; but it comes to an end by insisting that members of "the people" are not required to make a decision at all, for—like heliotropes—they naturally turn toward God. In the absence of decision there emerges a sign of its absence in the very comportment of the sermonizer: he mimics action in the form of frenzy and expresses repressed desire in a fit of hysteria. The content of the desire appears in the final passage of the sermon, where a Golden Age suddenly appears—not the Golden Age of humanity but only of the sermonizer, who sees himself entering a "blue and gold room." This parodic image of the bourgeois interior of a childhood home is what the sermonizer seeks to defend as civilization itself. To the extent that the image of this garish room is either an artful illusion or a pure delusion—and the latter becomes so apparent that Auden ultimately decided that the sermon could stand alone, without stage directions—the sermonizer encounters reality only in the form of his wretched and risible collapse.

The Colonial Administrator

Herod does not so much collapse as recede into whimpering self-pity. Like the sermonizer, however, he understands himself as acting—and suffering—for the sake of a rather small space of civilization, which he calls a "tiny patch of light" (*FTB* 113).[15] With this "patch" in mind, he can justify, or "patch up," any act of violence, even a massacre of innocents. The name of the enemy changes from the sermon to the soliloquy: in the first case, it is the international proletariat, in the second, those who believe in the divinity of a human being who is not himself an emperor. Nevertheless, the basis for the violent reactions of sermonizer and soliloquist remains the same: without the annihilation of the enemy, the civilized space whose borders they claim to protect will become vulnerable and ultimately disappear. Just as the conservative custodian of culture, horrified by images of worldwide active atheism, turns into a fascist proponent of counter-revolutionary civil war, so does Herod, as the champion of a liberal program of enlightenment—emphasizing nothing so much as the emancipation of humanity from magical thinking—become the advocate of mass murder. Here is how the sermonizer imagines what would happen if the revolution succeeds: "I should like just to try and imagine for one moment what the world would be like if this lunacy with its grim fanatic theories were to spread over the civilized globe. I tell you there would exist a tyranny compared with which a termite colony would seem dangerously lax" (*CP45* 246). And here is how Herod imagines the world that would emerge from a revolutionary doctrine: "One needn't be a psychologist to realise that if this rumour is not stamped out now, in a few years it is capable of diseasing the whole Empire" (*FTB* 115). In both cases, the fantasy of a devastated civilization is the basis for devastating violence.

Setting himself against a long theological and literary tradition in which Herod appears as the incarnation of madness, Auden makes the king into the spokesperson for rationality, who, from his own perspective, wants to serve as the able administrator of a stable province of the classical imperium: "And what, after all, is the whole Empire," he asks himself at the center of his monologue, "with its few thousand square miles on which it is possible to lead the Rational Life, but a tiny patch of light compared with those immense areas of barbaric night that surround it on all sides" (*FTB* 113).[16] Herod sees himself as sublimely unaffected by all forms of irrationalism—aware of others' errors not because he is himself in possession of unconditional truth but because he is a disillusioned agent of disenchanted reason. This belief in the power of his mind to rise above the magical thinking of the native population is grounded in a distinction between matter and spirit—a distinction that the "rumour" of Christ's birth disturbs. Here again, Auden's review of Laski's treatise is illuminating, for Laski, as an exponent of the liberal enlightenment, is as committed to the fallacious distinction between matter and spirit as Herod: "'Nothing less,' [Laski] says, 'than a revolution in the spirit of man is necessary if we are to enter the kingdom of peace as our rightful inheritance; and a revolution in the spirit of man, as all history goes to show, must follow, and cannot precede a revolution in the relationships of that material world by the exploitation of which he must live.' This Jam-yesterday-and-Jam tomorrow dualism of spirit and matter, whether one gives precedence to Matter like the Marxists, or to Spirit like the Oxford Grouper, is as dangerous as it is false" (*Prose* 2:107). Without further analyzing the fallacious character of spirit-matter dualism—impractical and out of place in a book review—Auden identifies only its immediate danger: "it deprives man, if accepted in its idealist form, of the will to act, and, if accepted in the materialist form, of the power to make his actions conform to his intentions" (*Prose* 2:107–8).

Both of these dangers are precisely captured in the figure of Herod, whose soliloquy oscillates wildly between calm reflection and petulant complaint. Devoid of any desire for action, his thoughts ultimately issue into a decision that runs directly contrary to its intention, for in seeking to annihilate the threat to the Empire posed by the "rumour" that God has been born, he sets in motion the destruction of the Empire he represents. Laski's error, according to Auden, lies in imagining that the conquest of nature that expresses itself in the notion of material improvement of civilization will naturally lead to a revolution in human spirit. Auden disputes this by noting that the idealism, legality, and technological improvements in European lands from the mid-nineteenth to the mid-twentieth century have done no such thing. He then creates in the figure of Herod-as-rationalist the image of an intellectual aware of this failure who also recognizes that the revolution Laski predicts has not only not come to pass but never will. This, in short, is Herod's predicament, which directly reflects Auden's rejection of Laski's argument, even as he agrees with its social-political commitments: the revolution of spirit that should naturally follow from the process of material improvement has failed, with the result that ever-more-egregious forms of irrational belief emerge anew.

Herod could scarcely be clearer about the relation between his form of disenchanted reason and his disappointment with the results of the rational order of the Empire. At the beginning of his soliloquy, he announces the good news of material progress, expressed through the rationality of city planning, the reasonableness of food prices, and the straightness of roads: "Barges are unloading soil fertilizer at the river wharves. Soft drinks and sandwiches may be had in the inns at reasonable prices. Allotment gardening has become popular. The highway to the coast goes straight up over the mountains and the truck-drivers no longer carry guns. Things are beginning to take shape. . . . Yes, in twenty years I've managed to do a little" (*FTB* 113). And yet, as Herod quickly realizes, none of this matters; that is, the increase in barge traffic has not changed anyone's magical-spiritualist inclinations—and there is no possibility that this situation will change: "Legislation is helpless against the wild prayer of longing that rises, day in, day out, from all those households under my protection: 'O God, put away justice and truth for we cannot understand them and do not want them. Eternity would bore us dreadfully. . . . Look after Baby, amuse Grandfather, escort Madam to the Opera, help Willy with his home-work, introduce Muriel to the handsome naval officer. Be interesting and weak like us'" (*FTB* 114; cf. *Prose* 2:233). All of Herod's monologue stands under the sign of helplessness. Public law is helpless in relation to private longing, and without the possibility of legal authorization for his own actions, Herod sees himself as helpless. From his perspective, where his citadel becomes the ever-shrinking point of "civilized" life—reduced to something akin to the sermonizer's remembered or imagined "blue and gold room"—he has no choice but to eradicate those whose belief runs directly contrary to his own basic assumption.

And yet, even as Auden creates a portrait of Herod that emerges from his critique of those, like Laski, who have failed to recognize that the "liberal *Aufklärung* is wrong" (*Prose* 2:39), his image of the tyrant is equally a self-portrait, and his criticism is equally a self-reproach. This is especially clear when the published version of the soliloquy is compared with the original draft, which, strangely enough, is not written in the voice of the tyrant Herod but, rather, in its very opposite: the voice of Simeon, the prototypical convert in the Christian tradition. In the published version of *For the Time Being* Herod's monologue is preceded by "The Meditation of Simeon," an abstract and rather lifeless section, which, in some respects, reproduces a series of reflections that Auden published elsewhere in his articles and essays of the period. For this reason, "The Meditation of Simeon" has sometimes been understood as a representation of Auden's own philosophical and theological views.[17] The image of Simeon in the draft manuscript, however, presents a more compelling reason to associate Simeon with Auden, for, in the draft, the future convert describes the moment when he realized what his vocation would be, and this passage closely reproduces lines in "Letter to Lord Byron" where Auden describes the moment when he himself realized he should become a poet.[18] This draft version of Simeon's self-reflections begins with almost exactly the same words as the beginning of Herod's monologue. Auden doubtless sees himself in the figure of Simeon; but in the light of the earlier draft version, it becomes clear that Simeon is a starkly divided figure, at once on the point of conversion and on the verge of yielding to Herodian impulses.

The clear delineation between Simeon and Herod in the published version of *For the Time Being* does not altogether blunt this self-division, for, even as the figure of Herod issues the murderous decree, his voice is far livelier, far more engaging, and far more fully realized than the convert's. Whereas Herod is a fully individual character, contending with his unhappy situation in the social-historical world, Simeon remains less a prototype of conversion than a theological-political type, whose conversion is affected by his recognition of the paradoxical character of the Truth. The gleeful energy with which Auden thus animates Herod's monologue, by contrast, conveys something of Auden's own amused like-mindedness. Auden's critical portrayal of Herod is thus also a self-critical portrayal of his own mode of reflection, in which dialectics is entangled with the most recent newspaper reports. This is particularly apparent in the giddy rendering of Herod's fervent—and drolly convincing—rejection of "that incoherent wilderness of rage and terror, where Mongolian idiots are regarded as sacred and mothers who give birth to twins are instantly put to death, where malaria is treated by yelling, where warriors of superb courage obey the commands of hysterical female impersonators, where the best cuts of meat are reserved for the dead, where, if a white blackbird has been seen, no more work may be done that day, where it is firmly believed that the world was created by a giant with three heads or that the motions of the stars are controlled from the liver of a rogue elephant" (*FTB* 114). If, as Auden asserts in his review of Laski's treatise, the question of where we are now can be answered only by each individual and for the time being; and if, as he likewise writes, "the true necessity of which to become conscious is internal and absolute" (*Prose* 2:108), then the resolute condemnation of evil in others—expressed in a generally self-complacent tone—points toward a failure of consciousness that is all the more insidious insofar as it is scarcely recognizable as a failure.

Auden dramatizes such a failure in the opening of the original draft of Simeon's meditation, which he then takes over, with only slight revision, as the opening paragraph of Herod's soliloquy, "The Massacre of the Innocents." The failure is difficult to recognize insofar as it does not express itself through psychosomatic symptoms or dramatizing gestures. In draft after draft of a poem in which Simeon recounts his conversion, the emphasis falls on the conditions of total self-awareness. The initial condition is purely physical: it is a cold, clear winter day, and only in the winter, Simeon says, does he ever feel perfectly healthy. Thus do physical and psychic conditions reflect each other: "Today was one of those days, cold brilliant, utterly still / When the bark of a shepherd's dog carries for miles, / The great wild mountains come up quite close to the house / And the mind feels intensely awake."[19] For the published version of *For the Time Being*, Auden lightly retouches these lines, as he changes the identity of the speaker from convert to tyrant: "To-day has been one of those perfect winter days," Herod says, "cold brilliant, and utterly still, when the bark of the shepherd's dog carries for miles, and the great wild mountains come up quite close to the city walls, and the mind feels intensely awake" (*FTB* 113).[20]

Besides the change from verse to prose and the alteration of the tense of the first use of the verb *to be*, the two versions differ in only one place: the limit of Simeon's world is defined by the edge of his house, that of Herod's world, by the walls of the city. The difference can be described in vocational terms. As a poet, Simeon is primarily a private person, whose powers are determined by the extent of his household; as a representative of the Empire, Herod is a public potentate, whose domain is defined as the walls of the city and thus, by extension, the borders of "civilized" life. The logic of Herod's argument forces him continually to redraw the borderline between civilization and barbarism, until, in the end, the only civilized site is his own citadel. The hyperconsciousness of his opening reflections conceals from him that all his reflections on the defense of so-called civilized life are merely self-reflections on what is required for his own self-defense. And his corresponding praise of the goods of civilization is a case of entertaining but earnest bragging about his own goodness.

Herod's hyperconsciousness thus hides the degree to which his attempt to save civilization is an attempt to save himself. The very grammar in which he casts his decision reveals how he has lost his identity, for he, the active agent *par excellence*, switches to passive voice: "Civilization must be saved, even if this means sending for the military, as I suppose it does. How dreary. Why is it that in the end civilization always has to call in these professional tidiers to whom it is all one whether it be Pythagoras or a homicidal lunatic that they are instructed to exterminate? O dear, Why couldn't this wretched infant be born somewhere else? Why can't people be sensible? I don't want to be horrid" (*FTB* 117).[21] When Herod calls the supposed agents of this protection "professional tidiers," figuring murderers as janitors, he sanitizes language to the point where it is indifferent to such distinctions as killing and cleansing. Not only does he order the military to kill indiscriminately, but he eliminates his own agency in the process. "Professional tidiers" is Herod's last euphemism—a grimly comic farewell, as it were, to the elaborate images of his preceding reflections. As his monologue ends, Herod's sentences shorten; the word *I* emphatically asserts itself; he imagines an interlocutor, who breaks into his citadel-centered hyperconsciousness; and above all, he presents himself as the incarnation of a political doctrine that would be the sign and seal of his goodness.

That doctrine is now identified with liberalism, which hides its own misery in a feeble expression of a desire for universal happiness: "I've worked like a slave. Ask anyone you like. I read all official dispatches without skipping. I've taken elocution lessons. I've hardly ever taken bribes. How dare He allow me to decide? I've tried to be good. I brush my teeth every night. I haven't had sex for a month. I object. I'm a liberal. I want everyone to be happy. I wish I had never been born" (*FTB* 117). The shortest of these concluding sentences of Herod's monologue—"I object"—is the most revealing, for, even as Herod casts himself as the subject of his sentences, the reader can see something else happen: "I" directly abuts "object," as though the subject wanted to say "I is object" in preparation for its rejection of its own existence in total: "I wish I had never been born." This is no empty comment; on the contrary, it precisely captures the underlying desire of Herod's defense of genocide as a step in the advancement of civilization: the civilized life of which he speaks can never be born, for in every birth there is vulnerability and the corresponding need for responsibility and care. In the end, Herod says what he wants: to be birthless. In this way, he would become as eternal as the imperial city he represents. This is the supreme form of *civilization* under a certain interpretation of the word: to be civilized is to make oneself into a *civis aeterna*. The ultimate expression of Herod's desire lies in the murdering of new life.

Herod's concluding proclamation of his own liberalism is as startling in its context as the assertion Auden makes in his review of Laski's book:

"The historical importance of Hitler is that he has pushed liberalism to its logical conclusion" (*Prose* 2:106). The point in both cases is not the replacement of liberalism with an opposing political doctrine. Where Hitler goes wrong, for Auden, is altogether clear, and it accords with Laski's analysis, even if they understand the relevant term in different ways: Hitler is an outlaw.[22] This is not exactly true of Herod. Rather, he becomes an outlaw when he discovers that the revolution in material power over nature does not bring about the kind of revolution in popular belief that would make everyone agree with his beliefs: he does not desire social or political subordination per se, nor does he want to proclaim himself a god; on the contrary, he expresses a desire for universal happiness and seeks to validate this expression by showing how little he has used his own position to make himself happy. The apparent clarity of Herod's proclamation—"I want everyone to be happy"—is obscured, however, by the anonymity of "everyone." If Herod unwittingly reveals his own proximity to "object" at the conclusion of his monologue, so, throughout his reflection, does he see the subjects of his rule as less than fully capable of proposing and pursuing their own goals. The anonymity of "everyone" is a function of their place in the Empire: they are—to use a famous phrase—in the Empire but not of it. In other words, they remain "natives," despite having been born during a time when "Things are beginning to take shape" (*FTB* 113).

Even with increasing signs of public order—swans, for instance, are no longer killed in the parks—members of the subject population either remain in their savage condition or adopt the veneer of culture, which, so Herod imagines, only intensifies their native restlessness. But the discrepancy between the public order of the Empire and the irrationality and inchoate desires of its subject population becomes a matter of immediate and urgent concern in the "rumour" Herod hears on the morning of his meditation. The birth of the Christ child is the defining perplexity of Herod's monologue because the Nativity is a paradigmatic version of native belief, which neither derives from, nor conforms to, the imperial center. Without sentimentalizing the Christmas story, with its pastoral image of the manger, Auden reminds his audience that the Nativity emerges from precisely those dark patches—and people—that, from Herod's perspective, are stubbornly inimical to civilized life as it is defined by the citadel. Auden thus anticipates the argument developed almost forty years later by Edward Said, according to which the administration of a colonial province—unnamed in Herod's monologue—is conditioned by a discourse of enlightenment scholarship that organizes knowledge on the basis of a series of abstractions in such a manner that "the Orient" emerges as a debased derivative of "the Occident."[23] Not only does Auden propose an implicit critique of the orientalist discourses that dominated much of the modernist reimagining of the house of Herod, in which the culture of the Levant in the first century of the Common Era is represented as both outlandishly different from Western European civilization and as a precursor of its new, decadent culture; Auden also reveals how the colonial administrator, aligning himself with the "liberal Enlightenment," sees himself as the exponent of the abstract principles of civilization, which devolve into their opposites as soon as they encounter, in every sense of the terms, native belief.

The Colonial Subject

In the volume Auden published in 1944 under the title *For the Time Being* he includes the voice of a colonial subject: it is not the voice of Mary and Joseph, who are blissfully unconcerned with their position within the Empire, and it is not the "citizens of the empire," who, combined into the fugal chorus and promoted by the Narrator, praise Caesar for having "conquered Seven Kingdoms." Rather, the voice of the colonial subject emerges in the figure of Caliban, whose prose monologue helps conclude *The Sea and Mirror: A Commentary on Shakespeare's "Tempest."* This Commentary, published in a single volume with *For the Time Being* in a work that takes its title from the "Christmas Oratorio," depicts a Caliban who provides a necessary and illuminating counterpoint to the Roman tyrant. Despite their opposed positions in the imperial-colonial hierarchy, Herod and Caliban are alike insofar as each is defined by his educational debts. At the beginning of his monologue, Herod honors those to whom he owes his position, including "Mr. Stewart, nicknamed The Carp, who instructed me in the elements of geometry through which I came to perceive the errors of the tragic poets" (*FTB* 112); while Caliban, of course, is indebted to Prospero for his language. But Herod and Caliban understand the nature and terms of their debts very differently: Herod lightly passes them off in his long, absurd list of acknowledgments, whereas Caliban is deeply ambivalent about the language he learns to manipulate with supreme self-confidence. And the fact that Caliban's use of language is even more impressive than Herod's—Auden famously modeled it after the virtuoso prose style of late Henry James[24]—shows that the tyrant's conception of what "is capable of diseasing the whole Empire" (*FTB* 115) is mistaken.

Herod never imagines that the members of the subject population can forego their hysteria, represented by various manias and superstitions, culminating in the "rumour" he hears on the morning of his monologue. The presence of Caliban in *For the Time Being* shows not only the fallibility of Herod's self-consciousness but also the positive falseness of his citadel-centered perspective on civilization. It is Caliban, not the supposedly sober Herod, much less the maniacal sermonizer, who addresses the question of where we—speaker and auditors alike—all find ourselves. The play is over; the world of which it is a mirror has come to an end, and now we not only must act but must do so in relation to this ending. The question "Where are we now?" finds its most incisive exponent in Caliban precisely because he is barred from indulging in the self-defensive illusion that he represents and protects civilization: if there is to be "civilized" life, it is to be decided now.

In reconceptualizing Caliban as a Jamesian-like speaker—but even Henry James did not speak as he wrote—Auden responds in advance to Gayatri Spivak's famous question, "Can the Subaltern Speak?"[25] Auden's subaltern is without the slightest doubt the construction of an elite imagination, so much so that his extravagantly elevated speech quickly becomes incomprehensible to even the most "educated" members of the audience. This means, in effect, that the subaltern does not speak—or, rather, by speaking an exaggerated version of putatively "civilized" language, he forcefully stages what would otherwise flow unremarkably through the channels of elite cultural institutions; namely, the cultured pretense of affording the subaltern a voice of his own. Rather than presuming to present "native" speech to which he has no access, Auden throws into high relief the very mode through which cultural institutions that presume to represent difference actually absorb and erase it into the dominant discourses of imperial culture. That Caliban's highly wrought speech is confusing cannot be doubted, yet it is likewise clear that he is himself not confused. Rather, he speaks to the audience only because *they* have formed a "confused picture" of the events on stage and cannot find the "all-wise, all-explaining master" (*FTB* 31) to whom they could address their questions. Thus, as is fitting for a "commentary" on a masterpiece, the colonized subject emerges in the place of the colonial master. Something of the relation between master and servant can be found in the relation between the masterwork and its commentary; but it would be a mistake to presume that all master-servant relations can be subsumed under one universal dialectical schema. Yes, the relation of master to servant is an element of Auden's relation to Shakespeare in the composition of *The Sea and the Mirror*; yet his Caliban is categorically different than Shakespeare's. The first difference, to be sure, lies in their respective use of language; but the second, related to the first, lies in Caliban's speech in Auden's commentary being itself a commentary on how the mastery of the servant in the coercive context of colonialism fails to be "generally" understood.

In contrast to the famous Hegelian account of the master-servant relation in which the servant overcomes the master by mastering the negativity through work, *The Sea and the Mirror* not only suggests that the servant does not replace the master but, on the contrary, presents the absence of the master in altogether sober terms—thus without the ravings of the sermonizer or the whimpering of the colonial administrator. Caliban does not enter the stage as the visage of the new master, who has displaced the old rulers; rather, he steps onstage only to overstep its boundaries, thus breaking the "fourth wall" and destroying aesthetic illusion. As for the master, for some unstated reason, he declines to address the "bewildered cry" (*FTB* 31) of the audience, which occupies the position of maniacal-melancholic longing for his presence. The "cry" of the audience associates its members with Herod, as do a number of formulations through which Caliban ventriloquizes their bewilderment, including his description of the events on stage as "the perfectly tidiable case of disorder" (*FTB* 36). And this is the overarching point of Caliban's speech to his audience, traversed as it is by a gap that constitutes the stage itself: you over there, sitting comfortably in your seats, cognizant of your cultural knowledge and confident of your civilized outlook, will not understand what I am saying, not despite but, rather, because of your coercive culture and your equally coercive form of civilization. He does not say this in so many words because if he did so, he would be understood and thus would reinforce the illusion of gapless understanding, without coercion, across boundaries—at once theatrical and imperial. The gap is never more ominously present than in the event of an artistic performance, when the members of the audience, apparently tranquil but in fact anxiously awaiting the presence of the master who will tell them why they are there, choose to forget that they are themselves addressed by those whom they observe across the "proscenium arch" (*FTB* 58). The gap between the "other world" on stage and the world of the audience is doubled and intensified when Caliban speaks, for it is always also the gap between the imperial realm, wherever it may extend, and the colonial subject, who is on the other side.

As the inversion of Herod, Caliban addresses a Herodian-prone audience. Whereas Herod, following Simeon in both the draft and published versions, talks only to himself, oblivious to any gap, Caliban consciously addresses himself to others. A supreme image of the gap appears in the very title, *The Sea and the Mirror*. Herod and Caliban are separated not so much by two verse plays within the same volume as by the breadth of a sea. Herod sees himself as helpless because the subject population will never learn to be civilized; Caliban hopelessly tries to teach the audience that their supposed civilization is infinitely unstable—"hopelessly" because he knows that the audience is barred from learning the lesson by virtue of the very culture that conditions them to remain seated in confused bewilderment during a theatrical performance. What Caliban does, even as he recognizes the nullity of his act, is show that the recognition of a breach—including the temporal rift separating "where we go from here" from "where we are now" and the spatial one between actor and audience—does not constitute its overcoming. Here, for Caliban, is the source of the desire expressed in spiritualist creeds, which are based on the "old fallacy" (*Prose* 2:107) of separating spirit from matter: a gap between the spiritual and material worlds will be recognized, and thus overcome. In Caliban's succinct words, it is a "delusion" to believe that "an awareness of the gap is itself a bridge" (*FTB* 56). The paragraph in which Caliban thus attempts, without hope of success, to disabuse the audience of their faith in the power of recognition begins with his sole reference to his own scene of instruction: "Having learnt his language, I begin to feel something of the serio-comic embarrassment of the dedicated dramatist, who, in representing to you your condition of estrangement from the truth, is doomed to fail the more he succeeds" (*FTB* 55). The difference between truth and estrangement from truth is so unbridgeable that even a term like *gap* ultimately fails to grasp its dimensions, for it suggests that the two termini of the difference are symmetrical: there is truth on one side, estrangement on the other; or conversely, here is the imperial realm, there the far-away site of colonial rule. Estrangement in the case of the sermonizer is populist fascism, and in the case of Herod, justification for genocide. According to Caliban, however, there is really only a single side—that of truth—which means that error is always in error about its own position, deluded into seeking answers to questions about such things as the next step on the way toward the accomplishment of a goal or the way to achieve "cross-cultural understanding."

There is another way in which the movement from error to truth can be conceived—through the experience of a shock beyond what is generally recognized as a "shocking experience." Thus does Caliban suggest that the "madness" of those who seek to overcome the gap between truth and error by creating an artifice such as a bridge "can only be cured by some shock quite outside his control, an unpredictable misting over of his glass or an absurd misprint in the text" (*FTB* 56). Auden was, of course, familiar with a mode of contemporary dramatic theory and practice in which the shock experience about which Caliban speaks is integrated into the de-theatricalizing movement of parekbasis that he executes when he directly addresses the audience. Having worked with Brecht on *The Duchess of Malfi* and having translated *The Rise and Fall of the City of Mahagonny*, *The Caucasian Chalk Circle*, and *The Seven Deadly Sins*, Auden learned, as it were, the principles of Brechtian "learning plays" (*Lehrstücke*).[26] When Caliban tells the audience about their "estrangement from the truth," he is at once invoking and altering the direction of the famous "estrangement principle" (*Verfremdungsprinzip*) through which Brecht sought to destroy the classical theater in its current, bourgeois form. Arguably the most precise formulation of the Brechtian program, however, does not stem from Brecht's own writings about his theatrical practice but from his discussions with Walter Benjamin, who formulated the idea of the "shock effect" in "What Is Epic Theater?"[27] Caliban precisely describes the moment of shock: it is not the sudden breaking of the mirror, which would disclose the truth "behind" it, nor is it the conflagration of the text, which would coincide with the resurrection of the author. The shock does not come with the complete loss of the ability to see or understand but, rather, with the disconcerting experience of being unable to recognize anything "behind" the mirror or understand anything "beyond" the text. What one sees or understands is stubbornly there, unwilling to cede its place to either something like "reality" in the first case or "another mind" in the second.

At the end of his address, while emphasizing that he has made no progress, Caliban indicates that something akin to an advance may inadvertently have been made. To make sense of this advance is remarkably difficult. The final passages of Caliban's address to the audience are among the densest passages of prose Auden ever wrote. This is not because Caliban is trying to be obscure, much less because the colonial subject has begun to rave like the sermonizer or succumbs to doleful self-pity like the imperial administrator; on the contrary. The sermonizer traces the path from traditional authoritarianism to populist fascism; in reverse, Herod begins as a confident exponent of disenchanted liberal bureaucracy and ends as the diffident agent of genocidal violence. Caliban follows no similar path; rather, he remains where he begins: a voice directed at the audience whom he seeks to instruct—though without hope of success—in the unbridgeable character of the gap, here called a "gulf," that separates truth from error, which is also the gap that separates Caliban as colonized from his supposedly civilized auditors. Nevertheless, despite remaining where he begins, he is able to articulate in an entirely negative way something altogether positive, thus a name or pseudonym for truth, which is here called "Wholly Other Life" (*FTB* 58). This phrase resonates with two radically different interpretations. Insofar as "wholly" resonates with "holy," the word corresponds to a theological position like the one associated with Karl Barth's commentary on the Epistle to the Romans, whereby God is acknowledged as "wholly other" and is thus incomprehensible in the highest possible degree.[28] Conversely, though, when "wholly" is not confused with "holy," the phrase designates a form of life or mode of living that is altogether unlike those familiar to the members of the audience, trained as they are to see their civilization as all-embracing. It is at this point, where the intensity of the double "gap" is at its greatest, that Caliban dares to make a positive assertion, in which this other life enters into relation with the life that ascribes the quality of being civilized to its art. The inadvertent "misting" of the mirror becomes the figuration of a greater "blur," and the accidental "misprint" in a text becomes the figuration of a wider "muffling."

> Not that we have improved: everything, the massacres, the whippings, the lies, the twaddle, and all their carbon copies are still present; more obviously than ever; nothing has been reconstructed; our shame, our fear, our incorrigible staginess, all wish and no resolve, are still, and more intensely than ever, all we have; only now it is not in spite of them but with them that we are blessed by that Wholly Other Life from which we are separated by an essential emphatic gulf of which our contrived fissures of mirror and proscenium arch—we understand them at last—are feebly figurative signs, so that all our meanings are reversed and it is precisely in its negative image of Judgement that we can positively envisage Mercy; it is just here, among the ruins and the bones, that we may rejoice in the perfected Word, which is not ours. Its greatest coherences stand out through our secular blur in all their overwhelming righteous obligation; its voice speaks through our muffling banks of artificial flowers and unflinchingly delivers its authentic molar pardon; its spaces greet us with their grand old prospect of wonder and width; the working charm is the full bloom of the unbothered state; the sounded note is the restored relation. (*FTB* 58)

In closing his address, Caliban thus returns to its starting point: the "perplexity" and "downright resentment" (*FTB* 31) experienced by the audience in response to the half-hearted pardon with which Prospero ends *The Tempest*. At the end of the *Dyer's Hand* Auden presents this experience in his own voice:[29]

> *The Tempest*, Shakespeare's last play, is a disquieting work. Like the other three comedies of his late period, *Pericles*, *Cymbeline* and *The Winter's Tale*, it is concerned with a wrong done, repentance, penance, and reconciliation; but, whereas the others all end in a blaze of forgiveness and love—"Pardon's the word to all"—in *The Tempest* both the repentance of the guilty and the pardon of the injured seem more formal than real. . . . [Prospero's] attitude to all of them is expressed in his final words to Caliban: "as you look / To have my pardon trim it handsomely." (*Prose* 3:460)

In keeping with the subtitle of *The Sea and the Mirror*, the final passage of Caliban's speech can be understood as a commentary on the lines Auden singles out in *The Dyer's Hand*. Disposing with Prospero's half-hearted gestures, Caliban revises the blanket pardon with which *Cymbeline* ends, "Pardon's the word to all," so that the word "pardon" is released from the sphere of possession and can be correspondingly qualified as "perfected." Something produced by a human being is called "perfect" if the result of the production exactly reflects the originating intention. A "perfected" word therefore would be one that exactly captures what its speaker intends to say. But this cannot be done—not even by the greatest masters of language, whose words always still call out for a commentary that discloses at once what the words once meant and what they may mean now. An understanding is thus achieved of what not only makes "perfect" understanding between individual human beings impossible but also makes it impossible for the members of the audience whom Caliban addresses to understand where they are—and thus whether they are members of an audience or indeed part of any collective body whatsoever. In the same stroke, Caliban reverses and alters the title of the text in which he himself participates: "the sea and the mirror" becomes "mirror and proscenium arch," both of which are broken, and in neither case is there any assurance that the fragments add up to a whole, whether it be understood as immersive and self-dissolving or solid and self-reflective. It is doubtless for this reason that Auden changed the German translation of "figurative sign" from "*Symbole*," which suggests a lost yet recoverable wholeness, to "*Sinnbilder*," which does not.[30] A word, in short, can be "perfected," Caliban claims, only as long as it is no longer "ours." This is eminently true in the case of the declaration "Pardon," in which, as he pointedly remarks, "all our meanings are reversed."

Caliban has had the estranged and estranging experience of learning language, with the result that he does not accept that any word perfectly captures what its speaker intends to say. With every word, there is also a subtext: the word you encounter is a sign of my power, including the words "I pardon you," which says that "I, the master, am in a sovereign position to effect a reversal of judgment." The "perfected Word" does not have this insidious sub-intention, and it emphatically associates flowers not with nature but, rather, with both art and history under the capacious category of "artifice": "its voice speaks through our muffling banks of artificial flowers and unflinchingly delivers its authentic molar pardon." The voice of which Caliban speaks, which of course is not his voice, is altogether different from the whisper imagined by the fascist and the rumor feared by the colonial administrator, both of whom proposed military means for the annihilation of their respective messages. Regardless of its medium—figured as "muffled banks of artificial flowers"—it is insuppressible, and its "molar" quality points in two complementary directions. On one hand, "molar" is equivalent to adjectives such as "wholesale" or "blanket," and on the other, it suggests a grinding operation, as in the workings of a mill (in Latin, *molar*).[31] The two senses of "molar" thus include the assertion of the whole in abstraction from the parts, and the disintegration of the whole into the smallest parts. In the event of the "authentic molar pardon," everyone is pardoned, regardless of what he or she has done; at the same time, however, the mechanical, grinding, mill-like character of the pardon minutely separates out everyone, disentangling them from the whole, so that pardon may be "the word to all," but cannot be captured by the master-word "pardon"—or any word that we might utter.

By setting out the terms in which the "authentic molar pardon" can be heard, Caliban responds to what Auden calls the "perplexity" experienced by the audience in response to Prospero's pardon at the end of *The Tempest*: the voice issuing an authentic pardon can only be that of "the Word, which is not ours." With this negative clause, Caliban's task as a commentator is done: he has answered the questions that the members of the audience are forced to ask themselves when they hear Prospero's barely credible pardon.

But he does not stop there, with his duty fully acquitted. He continues for two more clauses, as if there were something still missing, even after he has described the terms of the pardon that would be at once complete and perfectly individuated. It is in these final passages that Caliban prepares an exacting version of the question "Where are we now?"—that is to say, a version that is least likely to be transformed into the "unreal question" concerning the steps required for the securing of our goals and accomplishments. There is nothing obviously "political" in these passages, but this, too, is comprehensible from the perspective of the question "Where are we now?": To the extent that politics is represented though political programs, the question cannot be answered by describing the status of this program, and it therefore appears unpolitical. As with the sermon and Herod's monologue, the final passage of Caliban's address is a place where Auden experienced an uncertainty concerning the figure to whom it should be attributed. The following, again, are the final lines of the published version: "its spaces"—the reference is to the "perfected Word"—"greet us with their grand old prospect of wonder and width; the working charm is the full bloom of the unbothered state; the sounded note is the restored relation." However else it may be understood, this capacious scene of greeting is the exact opposite of the "tiny door" into which the sermonizer frantically imagines himself entering, as he addresses the narrow familial bonds of Father and Mother. Here, however, is the version of this greeting in an earlier draft of *The Sea and the Mirror*, as spoken by Ariel:

> The local voice, the visible creation
> Greets us again with its grand old calm.
> Its wonder and width, the working charm
> The sounded note is the restored relation.
> Kiss me Caliban, curse no more,
> The tears that made trouble between us are gone,
> Elsewhere over water in wistful eyes.[32]

The difference between the draft and the final version can scarcely be overstated. Not only does Auden change verse into prose and exchange one speaker for another; even more strikingly, he also alters the identity of the voice to which the speaker refers. In the draft the voice is "local," whereas in the final version it is "not ours." In the original draft Ariel is providing a commentary for Caliban who is presumably prepared to learn about his own location from a disciple of the colonial master: these voices, so Ariel informs him, say that their relation is now restored. As to the question "Where are we now?" the answer runs, in short: all of us have survived the harm, are over the suffering, and are now ready to reconcile, if only you would acquiesce to the voices that you are apparently incapable of understanding without the master's voice to guide you. By the time Auden has worked his way to the final version of *The Sea and the Mirror*, the sense of this passage is altogether different: "the sounded note" is set free from the context of the play, and the "working charm"—which originally did no work in the sentence, as if it were a floating phrase delivered by the consummate charm-worker—becomes the subject of a sentence that replaces the blatant eroticism of "the kiss" with the apparent apathy of "the unbothered state." As with "molar pardon," "unbothered state" is ambiguous, since "state" can refer either to a social-political unit or the condition of an individual. In the former case, the phrase describes a smoothly operating political system; in the latter case, the phrase designates either someone who is free of perplexity or—and this is where the contrast with the eroticism in the draft version leads—someone who experiences agape.

If "the unbothered state" is understood as an efficiently run political order, the "restored relation" has a straightforward interpretation: it is the restoration of the status quo ante produced by a "charm" which "works" by making the subjects of the state forget their perplexities, lulled by the beauty of the "sounded note." If, however, "the unbothered state" is understood as agape, then the interpretation of the passage is considerably more difficult: agape effortlessly expresses itself—"full bloom" is the image—not through words but in the ever so slightly eroticized affect of "charm." And the "restored relation" no longer designates the restoration of an earlier status but almost the very opposite: the restoration of relation is absolutely not a constant of the kind that is attributed to political orders or social conditions; rather, it is there only in the sounding of a note, which can be heard as such only if it is surrounded by silence. Far from being the emblem of continuity, the "restored relation" is structured as constant interruption; it is the name of a "now" that includes the past but does not allow itself to be represented in terms of steps backward or steps forward. Auden's alteration of the passage from verse to prose is comprehensible from this perspective as well. When Ariel sings of the "sounded relation," it is implied that the relation is happening in his voice. When Caliban speaks of this relation, there is no such implication: it is for the audience to decide whether they understood what is meant by this phrase—and thus, in the end, whether they can understand the "unbothered state" as something other than the well-functioning political-social order. The end of Caliban's address to the audience does not indicate that he stands in possession of some knowledge or plan that he would like to impart to the audience; nor is his voice an exemplum of the "sounded note" of which he speaks. He is as distant from the "restored relation" as his audience; but in presenting some tentative terms for this distance, he demands of his audience that they ask themselves where they are now.

INTERLUDE

The Falling Empire

The Front of History

In 1937 the BBC commissioned Auden to write a radio play about Hadrian's wall. For the BBC the commission was simply a part of its educational mission; for Auden, however, the play represented an auspicious occasion that allowed him to develop and summarize his recent reflections on the question of history, organized around the existence of a wall that would supposedly separate the space of civilization from the world of barbarism. Instead of presenting a straightforward narrative, which was probably what the BBC expected, Auden's radio play intersperses the comments of contemporary tourists along with the voice of a narrator and the complaints of certain exemplary figures—from Roman soldiers through Scottish rebels to contemporary archeologists—who are associated with the wall's original construction, its intermittent defense and maintenance, its eventual deterioration, and its fragmentary restoration. As Auden claims in the synopsis for the play, the wall represents "the front of history," and although the front has since moved, "the same issues, of order versus liberty; the State versus the individual . . . still remain."[1] Auden did not republish the play in its original version, but, instead, salvaged only a single song, "Roman Wall Blues," which could scarcely be described as expressing allegiance to any idealized political-theological order, whether Roman imperial or Christian. Whereas the original context of the song made it into an exposition of the distinction between a world under the protection of the Roman imperium and the unprotected space in which barbarians held power, the new context recognizes no such distinction. Thus does Auden, in accordance with the procedure of self-revision that characterized his poetic and poetological reflections throughout his life, preserve a poem from a discarded work while radically transforming its meaning.

Just as Hadrian's Wall itself no longer even pretends to function as a protective shield separating the civilized world from "savage" invaders, so the sense of the song of lament that Auden plucked from his script and published in *Another Time* is no longer governed by the intention underlying *Hadrian's Wall*: "I'm a Wall soldier; I don't know why" (*AT* 85). The primary distinction made by the Roman soldier—beyond the distinction between his own eros-filled life and the absence of erotic pleasure in the life of his Christian acquaintance—has nothing to do with the spatial difference between inside and outside or even the political difference between friend and enemy. Instead, it crystallizes around the temporal difference between the period of enforced service, which is confined to the border of so-called civilization, and the period of freedom, which is unconstrained by any visible limit—and this, despite the limitations to his vision: "When I'm a veteran with only one eye / I shall do nothing but look at the sky" (*AT* 85). Auden thus transforms the difference between the "inside" of civilization and the "outside" of savagery, into the left and right sides of the Wall soldier's non-symmetrical face. And it is by no means evident which side of the wall represents blindness and which side vision. The last lines of the song identify, however, the ultimate object of the Wall soldier's desire: the sky, not as a place of heavenly rest but as a space without boundaries, which is to say, a space without the Wall that defines his function and thus his own identity as well as his song's.

In this regard, the direction of "Roman Wall Blues" runs counter to the explicit intention of the educational project that governs the production of *Hadrian's Wall*. Whereas the radio-play as a whole seeks to represent the "front of history"—where "front" is a term drawn from the martial terminology of the First World War—the Wall soldier wants the concrete form of this "front" to disappear. And Auden, for his part, began to doubt that the "front of history" overlaps with political-national borders, with one side as the guardian of civilization, the other side a font of barbarism. If one were to conceive of history as connected with wall-like places, one would also have to admit that there are places without history, perhaps because they are too "primitive" for anything to be visibly enclosed, or perhaps because civilization has reached a point where no barriers are needed. When Auden left England for America in January 1939, he was widely accused of abandoning his homeland in its time of distress—and thus leaving the place where history was happening for a place that was mercifully free of history-making crises. In response to such accusations, Auden wrote to Stephen Spender in March of 1941, "As a writer and pedagogue the problem is different [than it is for a soldier or air-warden], for the intellectual warfare goes on always and everywhere, and no one has a right to say that this place or that time is where all intellectuals ought to be. . . . You are too old a hand to believe that History has a local habitation any more" (*MY* 76–77).[2] With this judgment, there is little left of the ideological program that underlies *Hadrian's Wall*. Learning about history means giving up childhood fantasies about *genius loci* or "local habitation."

Auden's doubts about the validity of identifying civilization with the construction of protective walls—or any other designation of the "front of history"—became so strong that, by the time he wrote *For the Time Being*, such efforts find expression only in the voice of Herod, who, isolated in his stately citadel, looks for a justification for a genocidal decision: "what, after all, is the whole Empire, with its few thousand square miles on which it is possible to lead the Rational Life, but a tiny patch of light compared with those immense areas of barbaric night that surround it on all sides" (*FTB* 113). Herod's decision to order the mass murder of children as the price of civilization is significantly located not only at the birthplace of Jesus, but also, and equally importantly, at an outer region of imperial Rome at the inception of its empire. Rome, for Auden, is the name for a question that can be formulated in terms of a palindrome that has been associated with the city from classical times onward: where does the domain circumscribed by *Roma*—understood as the city itself, as urban civilization in general, and as the imperial rule that seeks to justify its violent actions in the name of civilization—come to an end and the reign of love (*amor*) begin?

The question posed by the palindrome *Roma amor* is a general one, perhaps applicable to every historical moment dominated by imperial powers; but for Auden, it was particularly urgent during the period from the early 1930s to the late 1940s, with the rise and fall of the Nazi regime—and the beginning of the end of the British Empire. During this period Auden was continually drawn toward reflection on the relation between contemporary geopolitical conditions and the Roman Empire, often elaborating his depictions of Rome with references, sometimes subtle, sometimes overt, to contemporary events.[3] As he writes in the conclusion of his review of Charles Norris Cochrane's *Christianity and Classical Culture* in 1944, "Our period is not so unlike the age of Augustine. The planned society, caesarisms of thugs or bureaucrats, paideia, scientia, religious persecution, are all with us" (*Prose* 2:231). Despite the seemingly jumbled character of this list of historical correspondences, it is a remarkably exact formulation, combining broadly positive tendencies, such as the spread of humanistic education and the advance of technical knowledge, with political travesties and moral atrocities, all prefaced by the ambivalent phrase, "the planned society," which, regardless of whether it is considered positive or negative, stands in contrast to the ungovernable eruption of both erotic and neighborly love.[4]

Although Auden clearly comes to reject the notion of civilization as a stronghold that could be secured by the erection of walls—whether ideological or physical—he nevertheless preserves something from *Hadrian's Wall* beyond "Roman Wall Blues": its complex, non-linear representation of different historical times overlapping one another. The wall, in other words, is not so much a place as a "topos" that can become topical—and the poet can contribute to the demonstration of its topicality. Instead of being "the front of history," the wall is a contingent materialization of different times becoming entangled with one another—sometimes explicitly entangled, which archeological projects try to redress, sometimes implicitly so, as when modern sightseers intermingle with Roman soldiers, with each group carrying out its own distinctive, yet oddly similar role. *For the Time Being* incorporates and develops this lesson of *Hadrian's Wall* into its representation of what it means to exist in more than a single time at once—and thus in history, properly understood. The figure of the Narrator, above all, makes no distinction between the Roman world and its modern counterpart: "These are stirring times for the editors of newspapers: / History is in the making; Mankind is on the march. / The longest aqueduct in the world is already / Under construction. . . . / Our great Empire shall be secure for a thousand years" (*FTB* 90). There is no question that, for Auden, the Narrator is deluded, and the center of his delusion is the belief that the "making" of history is like the construction of an intra-imperial aqueduct or empire-defining wall.

The strikingly anachronistic reference to newspapers indicates that history cannot be represented in rectilinear terms, in which each step of the "march" is comparable to an element of a construction project. The delusion of historical progress that stamps the character of the Narrator—who must, after all, "narrate" events rather than experience them in their irreducible uniqueness—is thus counteracted by notions of historical simultaneity that Auden discovered in a number of radical writers and thinkers of the nineteenth century, including Baudelaire's "correspondences," Nietzsche's "eternal return," and Kierkegaard's "contemporaneity of all believers." The latter is particularly important for Auden. *For the Time Being* represents an advance over the implicit theory of history that governs *Hadrian's Wall* not only because its emphasis on time eliminates the dubious notion of "the front of history" but also, and doubtless more importantly, because it fully subscribes to the thesis that all believers are contemporaneous with one another and that, therefore, from the perspective of faith, nothing separates us from the event around which *For the Time Being* revolves. So thoroughly does the Kierkegaardian concept of equi-contemporaneity permeate the oratorio that the Narrator, too, adopts and transforms it for his own purposes: all those who believe in, or become enamored with, the Caesarism espoused by the Narrator are contemporaneous with one another, so that the "march of history" never stops, even as it fails to achieve any goal beyond the reassertion of similar forms of Caesarian rule under the banner of civilization.

By denying that anything of significance occurred in the two thousand years since the Incarnation and Crucifixion, Kierkegaard not only challenged the bourgeois-Christian establishment of his era and, as Auden dryly notes, accomplished the difficult trick of "making Christianity sound bohemian" (*Prose* 3; 579); he also challenged theologically inclined historians of Christianity to justify their investment in history. For Kierkegaard, so-called primitive Christianity is the only Christianity; everything else is "Christendom," which is its polar opposite. A strict doctrine of the contemporaneity of believers means that faith and certain conceptions of history are mutually exclusive: where there is faith, there is only the Event; where there are events that are amenable to progressive or regressive narratives, there can be no faith. Auden was drawn to Cochrane's *Christianity and Classical Culture* because it gave him insight into ways to affirm Kierkegaard's critique of Christendom without in the same stroke abandoning the concept of history altogether and replacing it with a counter-concept of total contemporaneity in the Moment.[5] The insight consists, above all, in Cochrane's exposition of the irreparable inadequacy of the understanding of love that pervaded ancient Hellenistic and Roman civilizations.

Cochrane's study is concerned with the same events as the first four volumes of Gibbon's *History of the Decline and Fall of the Roman Empire*, and Cochrane can be understood to agree with his eminent predecessor up to a point. Whereas Gibbon attributes the collapse of the Western side of the Roman Empire in large part to the disastrous effects of Christianity, whose anti-worldliness undermined the foundations of the classical world, Cochrane identifies something like a "fatal flaw" in classical civilization from which it could not escape and which, once recognized, precipitated its collapse. As Auden explains in his review, classical culture failed to establish "any intelligible connection between the natural affective bonds and the love of justice" (*Prose* 2:228). For this reason, the collapse of the Empire could never be reversed, not even by the attempt on the part of "the last Caesars to give the dying empire a new lease of life by substituting Christianity for philosophy as a state religion" (*Prose* 2:227). In contrast to Greco-Roman culture, so Cochrane argues—and Auden concurs—the Augustinian version of Christianity has no greater aim than the disclosure of a hitherto unrecognized dimension of love in which the higher sphere of justice becomes bound up with the chaotic impulses of everyday life: Augustine's doctrine of love can thus "make sense of man's private and social experience, [whereas] . . . classical philosophy cannot" (*Prose* 2:228).

In the conclusion to his review, Auden indicates what first attracted him to Cochrane's study beyond the clarity of its exposition of Augustine's thought. In reading the "and" of *Christianity and Classical Culture* as a Kierkegaardian "or," he found his own model of equi-contemporaneity, which differs from both Kierkegaard's anti-historical radicalism and the Narrator's faith in the progress of civilization. Auden ends the review with the aforementioned list of historical correspondences, from "the planned society" to "religious persecution," to which he also adds a possibility that was realized in the Roman Empire and that, for Auden, haunts the contemporary world: "Nor is there even lacking the possibility of a new Constantinism" (*Prose* 2:231). In the event of a "new Constantinism," a religion of love would become a state-enforced ideology or, conversely, a state-enforced ideology would replace the religion of love. The voice of the Narrator gives a succinct description of both ancient and modern forms of Constantinism: "our true existence / Is decided by no one and has no importance to love" (*FTB* 65). Auden, in short, found Cochrane's basic conception of the reason for Roman decline convincing—and it has nothing to do with the advance or retreat of protective walls. Because classical civilization was unaware of any credible connection between the eternality of the supra-lunar sphere and the transitory character of the sublunar sphere; because it correspondingly conceived of spaces in terms of interior (civilization) and exterior (barbarism), it was destined to disintegrate in accordance with the divisions that traversed both its cities and its cosmos.

Correspondences: Baudelaire, Tennyson, Eliot

Auden's reflections on Roman history in relation to the contemporary world, animated by Cochrane's diagnosis of an incorrigible error at the heart of classical culture, culminate in a magnificent poem he published in 1947 under the title "The Fall of Rome." Whereas the speech of the Narrator in *For the Time Being* intermingles the first and twentieth centuries, based on the conviction that the Empire must be making progress (because progress consists in the intensification and expansion of imperial rule), "The Fall of Rome" moves in precisely the opposite direction, which is to say, it begins with stasis. The opening stanza represents a condition of total immobility. The image of the train, by itself, suggests that technology has progressed beyond the level reached by Roman engineering, but in "The Fall of Rome," the trains, as motors of so-called civilization, have stopped:

> The piers are pummelled by the waves;
> In a lonely field the rain
> Lashes an abandoned train;
> Outlaws fill the mountain caves. (*N* 32)

What is striking about this stanza is the absence of any rendering of social conflict. It is as though Auden has decided to begin his poem about the decline of the Empire by suggesting that it was something akin to a natural process, more exactly, a moment in the process when personified nature becomes abusive rather than nurturing. Violent waves and beating rain interact with human beings in the form of punishments, "pummeling" and "lashing" the structures of civilized life that facilitate maritime and terrestrial movement beyond the bounds of natural human capacity. Fields that might once have been contested by the armies of Empire, or populated by the figures and structures of an imperial polity, are "lonely," for the only humans in the stanza have retreated from civilization. From the perspective of nature and its laws, all human beings can be considered "outlaws," for in seeking to transport themselves—across the sea and land—they would flee the natural boundaries that constrain their mobility. The artifacts of their efforts to escape natural regulation are therefore subject to its punishments. And the outlaws who appear in the first stanza can escape this "natural" violence only by feeding themselves to the natural world—filling "the mountain caves"—and thus entering into its metabolism.

Just as *For the Time Being* transforms Kierkegaard's notion of the contemporaneity of all believers, so "The Fall of Rome" revises Baudelaire's notion of correspondences, in which the urban world is suddenly suffused by the glimmer of an archaic past that lies beyond any act of recollection and transcends every horizon of history. Both notions—contemporaneity and correspondence—cancel, in effect, the content of historical reality: if everyone can be present at the Moment, then nothing happens from one second to the next; accordingly, if every meaningful moment stands in correspondence with an element of prehistory, meaning is entirely dependent on these elements and has nothing to do with the actual course of events. "The Fall of Rome" adopts the notion of correspondence but insists on precisely what Baudelaire seeks to deny: all corresponding elements are fully historical. Thus the significance of the train, which ordinarily links points in space ("terminals") just as the Baudelairean correspondences are supposed to link a temporal terminus with an archaic and transhistorical one. The train in Auden's poem does not move from terminal to terminal—linking one place with another—but it does link one historical terminus with another. It is as though the train transports the reader from antiquity to modernity precisely because it, the train, has been abandoned. As they deny the validity of singular historical acts, Kierkegaard, who "makes Christianity sound bohemian," and the bohemian poet Baudelaire also evacuate the ethical sphere of its significance. For Kierkegaard, the ethical is superseded by the religious sphere, and in Baudelaire, ethics is identified with the bourgeois spirit the poet associates with the "Belgians." Kierkegaard doubtless repudiates the aesthetic sphere, but he does so in aesthetically pleasing works, and Baudelaire doubtless promotes nothing so much as "art-for-art's sake," but this credo welcomes a form of religiosity that—to quote perhaps the most famous phrase of nineteenth-century European poetry—glories in "the flowers of evil." Throughout the 1940s Auden wrote extensively about Baudelaire as a "romantic rebel" (*Prose* 2:85), often placing him in the company of his fellow maverick Kierkegaard, but always also emphasizing a certain counter-Kierkegaardian "error" in Baudelaire's thought: unlike the Danish thinker, the French poet "mak[es] a religion of the aesthetic" (*Prose* 2:211) and thus leaves no room for the ethical; hence no room for a decision, on the one hand, and responsibility for what one has decided, on the other.

Auden's most substantial writings on Baudelaire from this period are two prefatory texts he wrote in the 1940s: his introduction to Christopher Isherwood's translation of Baudelaire's *Journaux intimes*, and—more surprisingly—his introduction to *A Selection from the Poems of Alfred, Lord*

Tennyson. In the latter, Auden does not associate Baudelaire with great "rebels" like Kierkegaard or Nietzsche but, rather, with the "provincial Englishman" whose poetry occupies the ensuing volume: "In his basic anxiety about his existence Tennyson is the brother of another and greater nineteenth-century poet, Baudelaire" (*Prose* 2:209). Auden's pairing of Tennyson and Baudelaire is no momentary whim, fashioned out of capriciousness or delivered as a provocative aperçu. In "New Year Letter," written in 1940, Auden lightly juxtaposes Baudelaire and Tennyson (*NYL* 24), and so, too, in *The Enchafèd Flood* from 1950 (*EF* 37).[6] In his introduction to Tennyson's poetry, written in the mid-1940s, Auden quotes as evidence for their affinity a number of stanzas from the two poets, including the following ones from "In Memoriam" and "L'Irrémédiable":

> And crowds that stream from yawning doors,
>   And shoals of puckered faces drive;
>   Dark bulks that tumble half-alive,
> And lazy lengths on boundless shores

> Un damné descendant sans lampe,
> Au bord d'un gouffre dont l'odeur
> Trahit l'humide profondeur
> D'éternels escaliers sans rampe (*Prose* 2:209–10)

The stanza Auden quotes from "In Memoriam" and the one he draws from "L'Irrémédiable" are thematically similar, insofar as both describe a movement of falling in which any attempt to counteract descent only contributes to further decline. Auden expands on this comparison of the two poets' shared sensibility with a discussion of the formal similarities between the two poems—an observation that becomes especially significant as Auden takes over the verse form of "In Memoriam" for "The Fall of Rome." Beyond claiming that the "spirit" of Baudelaire and Tennyson are kindred, Auden emphasizes the correspondence of their "verse technique" (*Prose* 2:210), even though the prosody of French and English poetry differ significantly, since the former is syllabic, whereas the latter has been predominantly accentual-syllabic ever since the regularization of the English line by Chaucer in the fourteenth century. The two stanzas nevertheless demonstrate a formal kinship across languages, with the *rimes embrassées* of Baudelaire's seven- and eight-syllable, four-line strophes revealing a surprising likeness to the iambic tetrameter quatrains, rhyming abba, that Tennyson made his own in "In Memoriam." The thematic and formal correspondences between the two poems reflect, as Auden emphasizes, the kinship between the two poets. And their "brotherhood" is formed around their kindred desire for "magical certainty" (*Prose* 2:212) which has as little to do with modern science as it does with genuine faith—and is the very opposite of taking responsibility for the uncertain predicaments of the historical world.

At the end of his introduction to the collection of Tennyson's poetry, Auden summarizes his assessment of the poet with a biting quotation from Henry James that emphasizes not only the poet's detachment from history but also his irresponsible inability to match his gifts with his expenditures: Tennyson's enchantment with magical certainty, so Auden concludes, resulted in "an infinite torpor, a 'glory without history, the poetic character more worn than paid for, or at least more saved than spent'" (*Prose* 2:212).[7] Auden does not simply repudiate or declare an insuperable distance between himself and the great "brothers" Tennyson and Baudelaire—as though he could surmount once and for all both the imputation of irresponsibility and the temptations of magical certainty. Rather, by adopting the verse form that his predecessors have in common for his own poem "The Fall of Rome," Auden recalls as a present possibility the "infinite torpor" that, for both earlier poets, finds its solution in magical certainty. For Auden, however, Baudelaire's achievement is not entirely defined by the poems collected in *Les Fleurs du mal* but is also—and perhaps more importantly—found in the path leading from the indolence of *Les paradis artificiels* to the final pages of *Journaux intimes*, where, as Auden emphasizes, the poet first and finally begins to assume responsibility for his actions, talents, and debts.

It was in response to a debt of his own that Auden replaced Eliot's introduction to the Isherwood translation of the *Journaux intimes*. In 1930, Auden, out of money, asked T. S. Eliot whether the *Criterion* would be interested in a review of Isherwood's original translation of the *Journaux in-*

times, for which Eliot himself had provided the introduction. Presumably because it would be seen as a conflict of interest, Eliot declined the offer and suggested that Auden, instead, write a longer essay on Baudelaire, which he did not do. Some seventeen years later, however, Auden took up the suggestion, writing an introduction to the Isherwood translation that has replaced Eliot's in subsequent publications. The new introduction does not explicitly respond to the earlier introduction; but the opening images of "The Fall of Rome" can be seen to have their origin in Eliot's citation of a line from a "successor" to Baudelaire: "In a beautiful paragraph of the volume in question, *Mon coeur mis à nu*," Eliot writes, "[Baudelaire] imagines the vessels lying in harbour as saying: *Quand partons-nous vers le bonheur?*, and his minor successor Laforgue exclaims: *Comme ils sont beaux, les trains manqués*. The poetry of flight . . . is, in its origin in this paragraph of Baudelaire, a dim recognition of the direction of beatitude."[8] Auden completed "The Fall of Rome" in January 1947, which is probably also the month in which he wrote the new introduction to the translation of *Journaux intimes*.[9] In perusing Eliot's introduction he would have come across Laforgue's ascription of beauty to "les trains manqués." In contrast to Eliot, who praises "the poetry of flight," even if it is only dimly cognizant of its trans-historical destination, Auden's 1947 poem creates an image of imperial decline in which there is no place outside of history to which one can flee: piers do not connect sailors with outgoing vessels; a train carries no passengers.

The image of an "abandoned train" establishes a correspondence between the last stages of the Roman Empire and the post–Second World War world. But the correspondence is almost the exact opposite of those that inform *Les Fleurs du mal* and its symbolist heirs. An image from the contemporary world is glimpsed in that of the past—and equally importantly, the past that corresponds to the present is not a pre-historical realm, retrievable only in the flash of quasi-mystical insight, but a thoroughly worldly past, the object of historical research as much as poetic appropriation. It is even possible that the opening of "The Fall of Rome" directly responds to Baudelaire's "Correspondances," which famously begins with a description of the relation of nature to humanity that crystallized into a Symbolist motto:

> La Nature est un temple où de vivants piliers
> Laissent parfois sortir de confuses paroles;
> L'homme y passe à travers des forêts de symboles
> Qui l'observent avec des regards familiers.
> [Nature is a temple, where the living
> Columns sometimes breathe confusing speech;
> Man walks within these groves of symbols, each
> Of which regards him as a kindred thing.][10]

The "piliers" of "Correspondances" may have suggested to Auden a graphically similar term: "piers," which extend into the water, just as "piliers" protrude from the ground. Far from being the gateway for the transmission of words—however confused—from the sphere of nature to that of humanity, the piers in Auden's poem are the inert objects of nature's "pummeling." Regardless of whether Auden had "Correspondances" in mind as he was composing the opening stanza of "The Fall of Rome," he radically revises Baudelaire's compositional principle: the correspondences glimpsed in Auden's poem are intra-historical, beginning with the "piers" and continuing to the "abandoned train" that, in contrast to Baudelaire's image of humanity in transition—"L'homme y passe"—suggest nothing so much as human paralysis in response to nature's relentless aggression.

In his introduction to *Intimate Journals* Auden takes the opportunity to reflect on the status and significance of Baudelaire's work in general. In this regard, he follows Eliot, whose introduction is even more invested in a general appraisal of the French poet than Auden's. Eliot, of course, had himself absorbed and even appropriated Baudelaire's poetry, most famously perhaps in the opening section of "The Waste Land," which ends with the concluding line of the dedicatory poem to *Les Fleurs du mal*, "Au lecteur": "You! Hypocrite lecteur!—mon semblable,—mon frère!"[11] When Auden identifies Tennyson as Baudelaire's "brother," he is subtly alluding both to the appearance of this line in *Les Fleurs du mal* and to its reappearance in Eliot's poem. Much may have changed for Eliot between 1922, when he composed "The Waste Land," and 1930, when he wrote the introduction to *Intimate Journals*; but it is very likely that his general assessment of Baudelaire in the latter helps his readers understand why he quotes his poetry in the former. Baudelaire's greatness, according to Eliot, does not derive from the modernity of his poetry but, rather, from his early-Christian conception of evil as a positive force, which no amount of civilizing progress can ameliorate.

Baudelaire thus understood, according to Eliot, that it was better to do evil than to do nothing, because at least those who do evil actually exist, whereas those who do nothing, while believing themselves to be servants of humanity, are no longer even human. Thus Eliot concludes his introduction by observing: "In all his humiliating traffic with other beings, he walked secure in his high vocation, that he was capable of a damnation denied to the politicians and newspaper editors of Paris."[12] Following Baudelaire, even if he turns in the opposite direction, Eliot elevates evil-doing into a threshold experience that, by courting damnation, opens up the possibility of salvation. Read from the perspective of the early postwar years, in which evil-doers of an unprecedented dimension were on trial in Nuremberg—and it is inconceivable that Auden would not have reread Eliot's introduction when he replaced it with his own—the comments with which Eliot concludes his introduction could scarcely be understood as anything but moral stupidity. While giving the impression of being superior to "modern" conceptions of evil, they contribute to the ideological conditions in which intellectuals could glorify horrific crimes for their own sake.

Oddly enough, Eliot's introduction to the *Intimate Journals* says almost nothing about the journals themselves. For Eliot, Baudelaire, as the author of *Les fleurs du mal*, is the exponent of an aesthetic-religious viewpoint in which evil-doing is superior to indifferent self-satisfaction, for genuine crimes against humanity negatively acknowledge the reality of salvation. Auden, by contrast, does take on the journals themselves and even identifies a moment when Baudelaire changes his attitude from extolling the Satanic posturing found in his early work and begins taking responsibility for his life. Whereas Eliot reflects on a poet who "walked secure in his high vocation"—this, too, alludes to the opening stanza of "Correspondances"—Auden quotes a passage in *Mon coeur mis à nu* where Baudelaire identifies something better than idleness. It is not doing evil but is, rather, sheer work, even when it is "bad," for work always involves and invokes a nexus of responsibility, thus situating the poet in a historical rather than a confabulated context:

> The last few pages of *My Heart Laid Bare* . . . are some of the most terrifying and pathetic passages in literature. They present a man fighting against time to eradicate a lifetime's habits of thought and feeling, and set himself in order and acquire a history.
> The man who wrote:
> Whenever you receive a letter from a creditor write fifty lines upon some extra-terrestrial subject, and you will be saved—
> Now writes:
> Jeanne 300, my mother 200, myself 300—800 francs a month. . . . Immediate work, even when it is bad, is better than day-dreaming. (*Prose* 2:314)

As Auden describes Baudelaire's situation, in his introduction to the *Intimate Journals*, the poet appears as one who desperately struggles to find a way out of the very source of his poetic imagination in "day-dreaming." The "bad" work that emerges from this struggle is the opposite of the—aesthetically good—"flowers of evil." Auden does not discuss the notion of being "saved" from creditors in this context; but he does explain what happens when one keeps an account of one's debts rather than seeking refuge in the realm of the "extraterrestrial": this is what it means to "acquire a history." Despite the brevity of his remarks, Auden sharply outlines a view of history in which it is not something given, nor is it made; rather, it is acquired by giving something of ourselves, where this "something" is what one owes to others—an acknowledgment of the fact that one is indeed indebted in so many ways that they can never be fully or finitely counted. When one has failed to acknowledge and repay one's debts, one is estranged from one's own history.

And this is precisely the condition that Auden describes in the third stanza of "The Fall of Rome," where he again alludes to Baudelaire in a manner that recalls, however faintly, his appropriation by Eliot. Just as Baudelaire opens *Les fleurs du mal* with a dedicatory poem addressed to his "frère" and "semblable," so he begins *Les paradis artificiels* with a preface that compares himself to "those idle, sensitive women who are said to post letters to imaginary friends."[13] This is the situation of historical estrangement *par excellence*: the poet, engaged in opium-mediated daydreaming, is unable to acquire the history that is nevertheless his own. Invoking the image of holy prostitutes—itself a feature of the Baudelairean tradition—Auden adopts the passage from *Les paradis artificiels* to describe the space of the declining Empire as distributed into two versions of privacy, one dominated by erotic investments ("prostitutes") allied with magic, the other devoted to autoerotic attitudes ("literati") in which there is magical unity ("all") in the absence of a public sphere of individual communication and mutual exchange:

> Private rites of magic send
> The temple prostitutes to sleep;
> All the literati keep
> An imaginary friend. (*N* 32)

The retreat of prostitutes into sleep and of literati into communion with imaginary friends runs parallel to the enactment of "rites of magic"—as opposed to religious services—because in both cases there is the absence of a forum in which economic, political, and cultural interactions could take place. The direction of magical activity is toward retreat into a land of dreams, explicitly in the case of the prostitutes, implicitly in the case of the literati, who are associated with daydreamers through the allusion to *Les paradis artificiels*. The famous dictum of Heraclitus is perhaps in the background of this stanza: "Those who are awake share a common world, but those who are asleep retreat into private worlds."[14] But in any case the absence of a "common world" is what literati and prostitutes in the declining Empire paradoxically have in common. It is not that prostitutes and writers both sell parts of themselves—a tired topos that Auden avoids—but, rather, that they desire the same thing, which no one can satisfy because it consists in the absence of everything other than the magical products of their own imagination.

Disciples, Discipline, and Decline: Kipling and Yeats

"Art, as the late Professor R. G. Collingwood pointed out, is not Magic, i.e., a means by which the artist communicates or arouses his feelings in others, but a mirror in which they may become conscious of what their own feelings really are: its proper effects, in fact, are disenchanting" (*Prose* 2:198). Thus Auden begins his 1943 review of Eliot's introduction to a selection of Kipling's verse and therewith articulates a theory of art, expressed throughout his work and developed with fervor in the 1940s, most especially perhaps in *The Sea and the Mirror*. In the 1943 review Auden illustrates this theme in a pointed depiction of two figures drawn from the world of education: the complacent "schoolmaster," who does not find in Kipling's "If" an occasion for self-reflection, but, instead, a confirmation of the necessity of molding his pupils; and the self-righteous "undergraduate" who wants his tiresome parents to read "The Waste Land" so they will finally understand why he cannot be expected to hold a job. Auden begins with these amusing examples of certain tendentious misappropriations of both Kipling's and Eliot's poetry in order to develop an argument about the quandaries of art in which he is able to discern what Eliot missed: namely, the manner in which Kipling's verse is itself implicated in the kinds of magical misreadings Auden identifies. The review seeks to show that appreciation for Kipling's "politics of . . . critical emergency"— enticing though it may be in the midst of a world war—is misplaced and must be guided by a careful analysis of what makes Kipling distinct among "European writers since the fall of the Roman empire" (*Prose* 2:199).

Relinquishing the conviction that civilization is menaced primarily by threats from the inside, Kipling, so Auden argues, "is obsessed by a sense of dangers threatening from *outside*" (*Prose* 2:199). Auden thus identifies the focal point of Kipling's political-aesthetic imagination: "Poem after poem, under different symbolic disguises, presents this same situation of the danger without, the anxiety of encirclement—by inanimate forces, the Picts beyond the Roman Wall" (*Prose* 2:199). It may seem that a shift from the effete concerns of literary interiority to the perils of military assault signals a commensurate shift from illusion to reality and thus a tough-minded insistence on vigilance as opposed to daydreaming. Kipling's remedy for the menacing dangers of encirclement, which consists in the resolute administration of discipline, reinforces such a reading. Discipline must never be relaxed, for every moment is potentially one of encirclement. But this enticing formula—ready discipline in the face of the enemy—is, for Auden, incomplete, because the Pictish tribes that threaten the "civilization" of Roman-controlled Britain are "inanimate forces," no more real for Kipling than any other magical projection of a literary imagination. The danger of mistaking art for magic in the case of Kipling is that it reaffirms the obsession with encirclement, rather than allowing one to become conscious of this very obsession—an obsession that is every bit as detached from existing enemies as Baudelaire's letter writers are disconnected from actual friends. Because Kipling sees civilization encircled, Auden further notes, he conceives of history as circular; the threat from the outside returns again and again. As Auden proceeds to argue, however, any conception of events as circular, governed by the threat of encirclement, betrays the very idea of history: "If by history we mean *irreversible* temporal changes as contrasted with the cyclical and reversible changes of Nature, then Kipling's imaginative treatment of the past is an affirmation of Nature and a denial of History, for his whole concern is to show that the moment of special emergency is everlasting" (*Prose* 2:201).

In response to this review, Auden was himself accused of a lack of discipline in an outraged letter written by the poet William Rose Benét to *The New Republic*, which published it along with Auden's reply.[15] Benét seeks to defend Kipling against the primary claim of Auden's appraisal. In the light of the war in which, as Benét notes, the British and Americans are facing a "disciplined" enemy on all sides, there is every reason to applaud a poet like Kipling who, Benét maintains, instills in his readers the need for a similar discipline. Auden's own lack of discipline—together with the general laziness of the "intellectual poet"—is discernible, for Benét, in the typos he identifies in the review. A "Common Man" poet like Kipling, and presumably himself, would not make such sloppy errors. Acknowledging the mistakes, Auden ironically attributes to Benét a degree of self-control that the letter otherwise belies: "I must thank Mr. Benét for his restraint in pointing out only two of the misprints in my review of Kipling. To my knowledge there were at least four bad ones. For these, since I cannot type and my fist is barely legible, I am entirely to blame. But to generalize my personal failings into a blanket condemnation, to suggest that all intellectual poets are careless and all poets of 'The Common Man' precise, is unworthy of him" (*Prose* 2:531). As for the more general question of what Auden had once called "Kipling and his views" (*AT* 99), Auden allows Benét's letter to speak for itself. After noting that Kipling admired the "Roman code," Benét adds: "He admired discipline in almost any form"—to which Auden responds by underlining the phrase "almost any form" and reiterating the principle on which his own assessment of Kipling rests: "discipline is to be judged by the end to which it is a means ('though I give my body to be burned and have not charity, it profiteth me nothing')" (*Prose* 2:531).

Just as the opposing diagnoses of the source of the threat to civilization—outside or inside—are, for Auden, equally misguided, so is the supposition that there is a unity of discipline from a civilization's military to its cultural forms, such that an emphasis on discipline in one sphere influences the degree of discipline in another. The continuity from military to poetic discipline depends on both the projection of an external threat that is insensitive to the historical reality of actual adversaries, and a certainty about the ability of poetry to neutralize that threat—its magical power to intervene in the historical world. Benét unwittingly indulges in this supposition when he sees a connection between a few typos and a general characteristic of "intellectual poets," whose intellectualism inclines them against discipline in general. He thus shows himself to be an inattentive reader, for in the review, Auden explicitly claims that the weakness of Kipling's poetry can be traced to its false commitment to the unity of military and poetic discipline—the mistaken identification of the orders of words and people and the authoritarian manipulation of each: "It may not be too fanciful, either, to see in the kind of poetry Kipling wrote, the esthetic corollary of his conception of life. His virtuosity with language is not unlike that of one of his sergeants with an awkward squad. . . . Under his will, the vulgarest words learn to wash behind their ears and to execute complicated movements at the word of command, but they can hardly be said to learn to think for themselves" (*Prose* 2:202). With this vividly expressed assertion that discipline, as a means, must be judged on the basis of the ends it serves (not obedience but self-conscious reflection), Auden rejects not only any supposition that there is continuity among the forms of discipline but also that it can be seen as generally beneficent—as salvation from danger rather than a symptom of the "anxiety of encirclement." This is evident in the passage from Paul's letter to the Corinthians that he quotes for corroboration. Discipline, understood as the act of offering one's body "to be burned," is contrasted with love, here called "charity." It is not as though, for Auden, there is no discipline in love, but a belief in the soteriological power of discipline obliterates the very idea of charity.

In reflecting on Kipling's demand for discipline in response to his unacknowledged "anxiety of encirclement," Auden is drawn toward the image of the Picts threatening Hadrian's Wall. Without reference to military threats from the outside, the central stanza of "The Fall of Rome" similarly revolves around the question of discipline—or the lack thereof. And the stanza includes a figure akin to the "intellectual poet" who, according to Benét, cannot appreciate the moral efficacy of discipline for its own sake. But Auden, so to speak, turns the tables on Benét by presenting the intellectual as the—necessarily reactionary—exponent of "Ancient Disciplines." As the intellect is opposed to the body, so the lone intellectual is contrasted with the multitude of the muscular, who correspondingly express the absence of discipline:

> Cerebrotonic Cato may
> Extol the Ancient Disciplines,
> But the muscle-bound Marines
> Mutiny for food and pay. (*N* 32)

The major divisions of classical culture, as outlined in Cochrane, are captured in this stanza. Just as the philosopher is distinguished from the multitude, so is the mind divided from the body and the *vita contemplativa* from the *vita activa*. Unlike the multitude, the philosopher is named, guaranteeing his uniqueness; but the name—specified as neither Cato the Elder nor Cato the Younger—does not so much identify a singular individual as represent the doomed and perhaps even suicidal class to which he belongs. And unlike the body, which is degraded in classical philosophy because of its tendency toward mutinous disorder, the mind is oriented toward "Disciplines," which are not themselves practiced for the purpose of gaining insight into the structure of the heavens, but only "extolled." As for Cato's withdrawal from the world, it is presented as a consequence of his being a behavioral type, not an expression of his insight into the ultimate nature of the universe. The word *cerebrotonic* is itself cerebrotonic, since it belongs to a technical vocabulary from which the multitudes are excluded. The word also accords with the notion of extolling the "Ancient Disciplines," for, despite its Latin root, it is the invention of the modern discipline of psychology. The term clearly contrasts with the one that qualifies the marines: "muscle-bound," which is as full-bodied as cerebrotonic is cerebral. Along with the division between mind and body, intellectual and muscular, there is thus a corresponding division in language, with an esoteric term recently derived from Latin standing against old and blunt Anglo-Saxon expressions. The central stanza of "The Fall of Rome" thus breaks into two parts that are related to each other solely by way of the conjunction, "But," which points toward a contrast but does not specify how the contrasting halves are connected with each other.

Despite the many divisions around which the central stanza of "The Fall of Rome" is structured, Cato and the marines do have a single trait in common: lack of discipline. Cato may not be rebellious or distracted, but this is owing to his characterological type, "cerebrotonic," not to an exertion of his will. His lack of discipline is expressed in his promotion of diverse bygone disciplines, and discipline in the singular is not even a memory, much less a principle of action. Indeed, it seems as though discipline has been forgotten altogether—which could easily lead readers to conclude that this, the total lack of discipline, is the cause of Rome's fall. If only the various classes that make up the Empire, from the intellectual to the military, would simply subject themselves to the requisite discipline in accordance with "Kipling and his views," the Empire could stabilize and its collapse would thus be averted. This suggestion is, in brief, the ruse and temptation of the poem. It responds to a desire on the part of the reader to conceive of "The Fall of Rome" as a description of the symptoms of the so-called decline of civilization and to look, in turn, for the appropriate remedy: threats from the inside can be countered by an imaginary Cato who would practice the "Ancient Disciplines," and threats from the outside would be halted by a masculine and muscular military force. The combination of the phrase "Ancient Disciplines" and the image of mutinous marines in the central stanza makes it almost unavoidable that readers will conclude that discipline is the thing that would keep the Empire—Roman or British—from going under. But to imagine that the Empire could withstand internal and external threats if only discipline were restored in all its social classes mistakes an explicit absence for an implicit one: the absence of "charity," which is even more absent than discipline precisely because it was never present and thus remains unspoken. The reader of "The Fall of Rome" is thus tempted to forget about the absence of love because the lack of discipline is so very apparent.

"Little Birds" and Rapid Reindeer

Despite the intricate texture of its allusions to major works of the modern literary canon, "The Fall of Rome" explicitly references the name of only a single contemporary writer: Cyril Connolly, editor of the journal *Horizon*, to whom the poem is dedicated.[16] According to a story Connolly recounts in his review of the volume in which the poem appeared, he once challenged Auden to write him a poem that would make him cry, which resulted in Auden sending him "The Fall of Rome."[17] There is something decidedly odd about this story of the poem's origin, and Connolly, although its original source, later claimed not to remember the actual occasion of the poem's genesis.[18] The poem as a whole, and its final stanzas in particular, lack the intense emotion generally associated with tear-inducing literature. And in any case, what is there to cry about? It is certainly not the fall of Rome, since the poem gives no indication that the Empire was ever something to be cherished. Auden's attraction to the work of Cochrane indicates that he was skeptical at the very least of the value and viability of classical culture as a whole and Roman imperial virtue in particular. Nevertheless, the story about the genesis of "The Fall of Rome" may not be as dubious as it seems at first, for there is a condition under which the poem could generate the pathos that would make Connolly cry, and that would be if, in recognizing the poem's intra-historical correspondences, he came to feel the collapse of the imperial civilization in which his own life was invested. In 1947, of course, the British Empire was indeed falling apart with the loss of its "Crown Jewel." Connolly may not have had an emotional attachment to the integrity of the British Empire; but there is no question that in his view its disintegration augured the end of the "West" as a whole.[19] Thus, in the last issue of *Horizon*, which closed its offices in 1950, Connolly, making his own Herod-like lament, declares that the borders of Western civilization have been breached, with uncertain and terrifying consequences: "it is closing time in the gardens of the West, and from now on an artist will be judged only by the resonance of his solitude."[20] When Auden, three years earlier, wrote about the same phenomenon—"All the literati / Keep an imaginary friend"—it may have induced tears in Connolly, but that can hardly be read as a principle of artistic achievement.

Connolly was not, of course, the first to lament the "decline of the west," to cite the title of Spengler's lugubrious work, which both captured and contributed to a general atmosphere of cultural pessimism when it was published at the end of the First World War. A similar mood was evident after the Second World War, particularly in Britain, which won the war but "lost" its Empire. Despite its massive size, Spengler's *Decline of the West* is based on a simple schema: a vibrant "culture" gives way to a sprawling "civilization," which collapses as a consequence of its aimless expansion.[21] When Freud begins *The Future of an Illusion* by disdaining to distinguish between culture and civilization, he is directly taking aim at Spengler's work and indirectly registering its immense influence, which can still be perceived in Connolly's lament over the "closing time" of the West.[22] The appeal of Spengler's schema depends in large part on a simplified interpretation of classical civilization, in which ancient Greece, which embodies "culture," gives way to the Hellenistic "civilization" adopted by Rome, as it became an imperial power. The fall of the Roman Empire thus functions as the prototype of declining civilization. But—and this is, of course, an inevitable objection—there is no single "fall of Rome." Because the Empire split apart into an Eastern and a Western side in the late third century, the Roman Empire disintegrated twice: first in the West during the sixth century and then again a thousand years later in the East, where the Empire, still calling itself Roman but with only intermittent control of Rome itself, had developed a new form of civilization that acquired the numinous name of Byzantium.

The thousand-year reign of the Roman-Byzantine Empire requires a revision in the simplified interpretation of the ancient Mediterranean world. An imperial civilization can survive by making decline into the paradoxical principle of its preservation; for as long as it declines, it fails to fall. When Gibbon entitles his massive work *The Decline and Fall of the Roman Empire*, he alludes to the split in the Empire, after which one side declines, while the other falls. By calling his poem "The Fall of Rome" Auden appears to amend Gibbon's broad perspective: only images of the falling Empire of the West emerge; none appear of its declining counterpart in the East. A high degree of semantic tension is thus inscribed into the title. Even as the fall of Rome represents the prototype of all collapsing empires, including the British Empire circa 1947, the name in Auden's title means what it says: the city of Rome, which is the only geographical name in the short poem. Nevertheless, the concluding stanzas of the poem move away from the singularity of Rome, first of all by using the singular of the noun *city* to imply a multiplicity of cities, and secondarily by identifying the multiplicity of cities with a destructive force that is strongly associated with the Byzantine world: "Little birds . . . / Eye each flu-infected city" (*N* 32).[23] Nova Roma, often called "Constantinople," was famously struck by the plague at the pinnacle of Emperor Justinian's power, and in the penultimate stanza of Auden's poem, each city is ravaged by the flu, which is as representative of disease in general as the name "Rome" is representative of *urb* in general. In this respect, subtle though it may be, "The Fall of Rome" moves away from Rome itself. But it does not therefore move in the direction of the "other" side of the Empire by setting sail for a distant and exquisitely decadent civilization. Instead, Auden's introduction of bird imagery moves the poem in the direction of the most important image of the Eastern Empire in modern European literature, Yeats' "Sailing to Byzantium." Eliot associates the question posed by Baudelaire in his *Journaux intimes*, "Quand partons-nous pour le bonheur?" with Laforgue's response: "Oh! Qu'ils sont chers, les trains manqués." But the very same question also finds a response in "Sailing to Byzantium," the title of which can be read as an escape not only from life—one sails to Byzantium only after death—but also from the fall of the Western Empire. Read against the background of Yeats' poem, which was written precisely twenty years earlier, the opening line of Auden's poem, "The piers are pummeled by the waves," reads as a response to Yeats, specifically as a rejection of the magical journey he describes. There will be no setting sail for happiness. Not only is the train abandoned, but there are no ships that could accomplish the transformative task by taking passengers "out of nature." The "outlaws" filling the "mountain caves" at the beginning of Auden's poem thus proceed in the opposite direction from the one Yeats proposes:

> Once out of nature I shall never take
> My bodily form from any natural thing,
> But such a form as Grecian goldsmiths make
> Of hammered gold and gold enamelling
> To keep a drowsy Emperor awake;
> Or set upon a golden bough to sing
> To lords and ladies of Byzantium
> Of what is past, or passing, or to come.[24]

In a section of *The Dyer's Hand* entitled "Two Bestiaries," Auden makes a brief yet illuminating remark about the final stanza of "Sailing to Byzantium": "When Yeats assures me, in a stanza of the utmost magnificence, that after death he wants to become a mechanical bird, I feel that he is telling what my nanny would have called 'a story'" (*DH* 81). In seeking an image of permanence beyond the possibility of decay, Yeats imagines an eternal world of artifice, in which the poet so perfectly accords with the laws of nature that he becomes an artifact himself. For Auden, this is "a story"—not so much a blatant lie as a fictional construct through which one denies responsibility for one's actions and treats any untoward event as a consequence of natural causes. "Sailing to Byzantium" and "The Fall of Rome" are related to each other as story is to history. The opening two stanzas of Auden's poem can be described as journeys to the interior: away from the coast and into "mountain caves" where there are "outlaws," and through the "sewers of provincial towns" where there are tax-evaders. The collapse of the public sphere is coordinated with retreat, as everyone in the decaying Empire seeks a magically private place that will protect them from decay. Whereas the attempt to escape the collapse of the public world by flights into privacy intensifies the disintegration of the Empire, the movement of the poem as a whole into the core of the Empire ends up by transcending its borders—but not in the direction of an imaginary land where emperor and poet mutually enliven each other. In "The Fall of Rome," there are birds, to be sure, but instead of singing for the emperor, they only observe urban sites. An "elsewhere" also emerges; but instead of being beyond the sea, it is a landscape, without cities, that can be related to history only if herds of animals are interpreted as human communities—in this case, as the tribes of marauding Goths, who repeatedly sacked Rome. And, finally, whereas gold in "Sailing to Byzantium" is the substance of cultural completion and the sign of incomparable richness, the gold that appears in the final stanza of "The Fall of Rome" has nothing to do with wealth, belongs to nature alone, and is not really gold after all:

> Unendowed with wealth or pity
> Little birds with scarlet legs,
> Sitting on their speckled eggs,
> Eye each flu-infected city.
>
> Altogether elsewhere, vast
> Herds of reindeer move across
> Miles and miles of golden moss,
> Silently and very fast. (*N* 32–33)

At the end of "The Fall of Rome" city-bound birds are thus set against a wild species of animal. Separated from each other, bird and reindeer stand in double contrast with a pairing of bird with mechanism that Auden uses to begin both a much earlier poem, "Consider," and a contemporaneous poem, "Memorial for the City." The function of the birds in all three poems remains the same: they are dispassionate observers of civilizations in crisis. In the poem from the early 1930s, the bird's-eye view, paired with a perspective made possible by recent technology, becomes a poetic imperative: "Consider this and in our time / As the hawk sees it or the helmeted airman" (*SP* 14). As if it were a repudiation of this dubious perspective, the opening lines of "Memorial for the City" describe a similar bird-mechanism pair; but this one is capable of observing only another time, specifically the beginnings of classical civilization: "The eyes of the crow and the eye of the camera open / Onto Homer's world, not ours" (*N* 39). The first section of "Memorial for the City" proceeds to describe the paradoxical knowledge that distinguishes the world of classical civilization from "ours":

> Our grief is not Greek: As we bury our dead
> We know without knowing there is reason for what we
>   bear,
> That our hurt is not a desertion, that we are to pity
> Neither ourselves nor our city;
> Whoever the searchlights catch, whatever the loudspeakers
>   blare,
> We are not to despair. (*N* 40)

It is not as though classical civilization knows no pity, but its pity does not extend beyond the walls—or, in contemporary terms, the "barbed wire stretches"—by means of which the city is demarcated from both the other as non-citizen and the outside as uncivilized. The end of "The Fall of Rome" is strikingly different from the beginning of both "Consider" and "Memorial for the City," for it presents the sharpest image of pitiless birds that impassively observe human suffering, and yet it refrains from pairing the birds with the apparatuses of modern technology that promote similar effects. This, of course, is not because "The Fall of Rome" keeps itself free of references to modern technology; on the contrary, its first stanza includes an "abandoned train." And there is a noteworthy continuity among the three mechanisms under consideration: the aircraft bearing the "helmeted airman" distances him from the earth; the camera distances the viewer from the object of vision; and the train travels great distances over short periods of time. The abandoned train in "The Fall of Rome" suggests that the project of conquering distance by means of ever-more effective technology has come to a halt. The remainder of the poem, until its final stanza, indicates a reason: with the collapse of the public sphere, the distance among human beings has become so great that no distance-reducing mechanism accomplishes its aim. The abandonment of the train is thus coordinated with the movement of reindeer, which travel great distances in a short time: human beings are the agents of abandonment in the first case; in the second, by contrast, they are altogether absent—which suggests that they, not the trains, are the ones who have been abandoned. But the poem has not thus returned to its point of departure, and the reindeer are not substitutes or replacements for modern technology. Instead of reducing distance by their running, the reindeer expand it; but they do not therefore create a condition that is comparable to the bird's-eye view, where pity would extend only to "ourselves" or "our city." Unlike both human beings and the nesting birds that observe them, the reindeer create no condition for themselves whatsoever. It is for this reason that the space they traverse is not only elsewhere, as judged from a "here" or "there," but "*altogether* elsewhere"—a place that cannot be located in relation to any place of human or avian perches. The reindeer are "elsewhere" wherever they are, for they do not demarcate the place of their existence, not even in the inarticulate expressions of their existence. In being "altogether elsewhere," they are not only outside of civilization but also beyond the distinction between civilization, as represented by the "flu-infected city," and nature, as represented by the "little birds."

Congruent with its reference to an "altogether elsewhere," the final stanza of "The Fall of Rome" breaks off from the previous ones. Some of the undeniably haunting quality of the poem derives from the apparent lack of connection between the image with which it begins, a single abandoned train, and the image with which it ends, a multitude of fast-moving reindeer. One can be seen to represent modern technology, the other nature. They do not move in different directions, causing a conflict that could somehow be resolved by technical means; rather, insofar as the poem is viewed as a whole, the immobility of the one unleashes the hypermobility of the other, such that there is no longer any natural rhythm of motion and stasis. *This* fall of Rome does not therefore run parallel with the collapse of classical civilization; rather, past and present part ways, such that there is no longer any Baudelairean "correspondence." The poem begins with modern technology abandoned unto itself, without "human" governance or conveyance, and it ends with living creatures that are unable to rest, suggesting—but only suggesting, without any definitive connection—that the former is the cause of the latter. This is among Auden's shortest yet most far-reaching visions of the massive transformation of the natural world wrought by modern industrial civilization.[25] At the same time, however, the poem declines to present any relation between its beginning and its end, that is, the falling Empire, on the one hand, and creatures unbound, on the other. The altogether elsewhere-ness of the space in which the reindeer roam wholly removes their movement from the horizons of city life, which certain city-dwelling animals—namely, the "little birds"—relentlessly survey.

And this elsewhere-ness likewise corresponds to an openness in the meaning these roving creatures bear in the poem. The figural character of "reindeer" cannot be determined because their sole defining feature—endless, horizontal movement—is itself indeterminate, that is, without prescribed tracks or terminals. If, however, as the previous stanzas of the poem suggest, the fall of Rome consists in a common movement of human life away from the openness of a public sphere, then the—spatial, temporal, figural—openness of the reindeer acquires a fully ambiguous meaning: it represents both a final confirmation of the fall, since a purely open space, without any borders, can no longer be called "public," and the beginning of a counter-movement to collapse, which is by its very nature borderless. The horizontal movement of the reindeer not only contrasts with the vertical directionality signaled by the word *fall*; it suggests a correction of the other major word in the title of the poem, namely *Rome*: as human life falls, non-human life roams. As for the nature of this roaming life, it can be discerned in the name of those who engage in it: "deer" is a homonym of *dear*, which is a synonym of "love," and "rein" is a homonym of *reign*, which is a synonym of "dominion." Just as *Roma* can be read in reverse as *amor*, so the inversion of *reindeer* allows readers of the poem to see in a word—but not, to be sure, the Word—an image of love's dominion. "The Fall of Rome" points toward such a "dear reign" but refuses to describe its characteristics except by way of negation: Auden's elsewhere is a place without walls, without fronts—and is therefore the very end of history as long as history is understood in terms of securing ever greater expanses of "civilization." The dear-reign of Auden's reindeer is an image of the exact opposite of this imperial vision.

PART II

FOUR

Isotopes of Love

Who Accompanies Eros?

Auden once described the awkwardness of casual encounters such as occur on trains: when he was asked what he does for a living, the answer "writer" invariably elicited a follow-up question about the type of writer; the answer "poet" provoked general embarrassment, since, as he put it, "nobody can earn a living simply by writing poetry." In order to avoid these fumbling, drawn-out conversations Auden determined to cut them off before they began: "The most satisfactory answer I have discovered, satisfactory because it withers curiosity, is to say *Medieval Historian*" (*DH* 74). There's something of the prankster in this description, but it is something more than simply a ruse, for Auden did indeed develop a keen, albeit idiosyncratic interest in medieval history, sparked at least in part by Eugen Rosenstock-Huessy's *Out of Revolution*, which he encountered soon after it first appeared in 1938. In subsequent years—in both prose and poetry— Auden would repeatedly return to Rosenstock-Huessy's central claim, according to which the entire revolutionary tradition in the Western world derives from the Investiture Controversy of the eleventh century, otherwise known as the Papal Revolution, to which all later political-social upheavals, culminating in the October Revolution, remain indebted.[1] Just as

Rosenstock-Huessy's account of the eleventh century gave Auden a point of reference for his understanding of the political-theological character of European modernity, so did another work of the same period, Denis de Rougemont's *Love in the Western World*, give him insight into an equally significant social-historical transformation: the invention of romantic love. As Auden writes in his preface to *The Portable Greek Reader*—this is one of the many passages in his prose and poetry where he summarizes the episodic argument of *Love in the Western World*—"about three-quarters of modern literature is concerned with one subject, the love between a man and a woman, and assumes that falling in love is the most important and valuable experience that can happen to human beings. We are so conditioned to this attitude that we are inclined to forget that it does not go back beyond the twelfth century" (*Prose* 2:355).

Auden's review of de Rougemont's *Love in the Western World*, published under the title, "Eros and Agape," is generally favorable, but it offers two cardinal points of criticism, one subtle, the other explicit. In both cases, Auden indicates that de Rougemont is under a massive yet understandable confusion: he does not comprehend the nature, structure, and elements of erotic love. The subtle point of this criticism is discernible only to readers who are familiar with the work under review. According to de Rougemont, there is only a single, long-standing, and far-reaching myth in which the idea of romantic love expresses itself throughout Western history, from troubadour poetry to modern pulp romances, namely the myth of Tristan. Under the spell of this myth, lovers see themselves as united from time immemorial, with the result that they not only cannot take any action of their own; they should not do so. Instead of acting, they should let destiny take its predetermined course. Auden, for his part, discerns another, more recent myth of romantic love. Presenting his analysis of love as akin to the work of contemporary nuclear physicists, Auden shows that the dynamic agent called "Eros" can be isolated into two related yet distinct "isotopes" (*Prose* 2:138). One is identified with Tristan, the other with Don Juan. *Love in the Western World* is a rather short volume, comprising seven "books," but it is remarkably expansive, covering all of European history from the Middle Ages to recent fascist dictatorships. Within the profusion of topics and figures under discussion, Don Juan is a minor one indeed, largely confined to the opening paragraphs of the thirteenth chapter of the fourth book, wedged between a chapter on "the end of myth" and a polemic against the Marquis de Sade as the representation of the Tristan myth in the age of modern rationalism. De Rougemont concludes his brief discussion of Don Juan by comparing him with Tristan and finding only "one trait in common. Both appear sword in hand."[2] For Auden, the very lack of resemblance—except in this decisive feature—reveals the degree to which one is the "negative mirror image" of the other: "Tristan sees time as something evil to be passively endured; Don Juan sees time as something evil to be aggressively destroyed: the former is a suicide, the latter a murderer. But they have three things in common: both are interesting sinners; both lack all knowledge of the beloved as a person; both 'appear sword in hand'" (*Prose* 2:138).

For de Rougemont, the figure of Don Juan is an expression of a radical rationalism, preparing a space of eroticism that would unfold in de Sade's novels. Auden, however, takes a longer view of this figure and finds the source of the legend of Don Juan in the Middle Ages, specifically in Jean de Meun's "realist" version of the *Roman de la Rose* (*Prose* 2:138). The purpose of Auden's insistence on the medieval origin of the legend consists not so much in a demonstration of the co-originality of the two "isotopes of Eros" as in a critical refutation of the concept of love that governs *Love in the Western World* in general: "My only criticism of Mr de Rougemont's profound and brilliant study is that I find his definition of Eros a little vague" (*Prose* 2:139). Modestly stated though it may be, Auden's critique strikes at the heart of de Rougemont's argument, for it suggests that the author of *Love in the Western World* succumbs to the very Manicheanism that Augustinian and thus "Western" Christianity was supposed to overcome. If de Rougemont misconstrues Eros, how can he recount the history of love, Western or otherwise? In schematic terms, de Rougemont sees the flesh as evil, spirit as good; the Catholic conception of marriage, so he argues, allows for the total domination of the latter over the former, so that Eros may be depreciated and Agape enshrined as the supreme form of love. De Rougemont can sustain such a non-dialectical opposition between Eros and Agape only by making his definition of the former "vague" in the extreme. Auden does not respond with an exact definition of Eros, for there is no such thing; rather, guarded by a hesitant "surely," he translates Dante's *amor* with Eros: "[de Rougemont] sometimes speaks as if he meant, which I am sure he does not, that Eros is of sexual origin and that there is a dualistic division between Agape and Eros rather than—what I am sure he believes—a dialectical relation. For Eros, surely, is '*amor sementa in voi d'ogni vertute, e d'ogni operazion che merta pene*,' the basic will to self-actualization without which no creature can exist" (*Prose* 2:139).[3]

Eros is love, and love is Eros, even if it is not exactly "erotic" in the standard use of the term. The unity and totality of Eros in all its *operazione*—to use Dante's word—means that it can remain unaware of itself; more exactly, it means that Eros can be unaware of itself *as* love, in which case it produces delusions of self-sufficiency that express themselves in the two "isotopes of Eros." Tristan and Isolde are under the delusion that they need only each other; Don Juan that he can be altogether himself, regardless of whom he "loves." Auden's review of *Love in the Western World* thus comes to revolve around a paradox of love: Eros is love in its entirety, and yet, unless Eros is accompanied by a complementary form of love, it produces the illusion of lovers who need either nothing other than themselves or nothing but any random lover, whose very "love" is a replacement for another *ad infinitum*. It may be surprising that Auden uses the lexicon of contemporary physics to describe the forms of Eros, yet it is even more surprising that he presents the relation between Eros and Agape through a term drawn from contemporary biology—that of mutation, in which change is a matter of chance, here associated with "Grace":

> Agape is that Eros mutated by Grace, a conversion, not an addition, the Law fulfilled, not the Law destroyed. That is why the symbol of Agape is not the act of sex but the act of nutrition: just because eating is the one primal act common to all living organisms irrespective of species, race, age, sex, or consciousness, the one act in which, since we demand all and give nothing, we are necessarily completely alone, therefore only this can testify to the utter dependence of all creatures on each other, to the fact that *everyone* is our neighbor. (*Prose* 2:139)

For the purpose of refuting de Rougemont's Manichean dualism, the image of mutation serves Auden perfectly well, for it unmistakably revokes any trace of counter-Augustinian dualism; at the same time, however, Auden's line of argument shows a high degree of hesitation despite its apparent confidence. How, after all, is the image of nutrition connected to the understanding of Agape as a "mutation"? And why, indeed, "mutation" rather than, say, "sublimation"? Auden must have recognized, too, that within the broader terms of a history of love in the Western world, such a quasi-biological rendering suggests that the transition from the classical culture of Eros to its Christian counterpart was akin to a moment in that evolutionary process that governs the course of the natural world. However boldly formulated, this representation of how Eros and Agape are paired with each other leads to the dangerous and wrongheaded supposition that there is, after all, no real difference between history and nature, for so-called history is only a version of natural history, governed as it is by mutations for which no one—other than an allegorical figure called "Grace"—can be held responsible. There is, moreover, another and equally troubling danger in producing formulae through which the exact relation of Eros to Agape would be captured—namely, that it would not only present itself as the last word but would also thereby freeze history in place. Around the time that Auden reviews *Love in the Western World* he writes a poem that appears in the appendix to *The Double Man*, in which the "tired old men" of Renaissance Catholicism, charged with stamping out the recent schism prompted by Luther, found such a "formula" and thus made themselves into the last vehicle of "Spiritus Sanctus":

> The doors swung back: success had been complete.
> The formulae essential to salvation
> Were found for ever, and the true relation
> Of Agape to Eros finally defined:
> The burghers hung out flags in celebration,
> The peasants danced and roasted oxen in the street. (*DM* 132–33)[4]

Despite the absence of a title, readers of *The Double Man* would doubtless know the precise historical event to which the poem refers: the Council of Trent in 1563, which established the terms for the Counter-Reformation and thus set the stage for the Thirty Years' War of the following century. Unlike T. S. Eliot, for instance, who, then barely in his twenties, adopted the persona of an old man—"I grow old . . . I grow old . . ."—Auden did not generally present himself in such solemnly pompous guises; but by formulating the exact relation of Eros to Agape, he nevertheless, willy-nilly, associates himself with the elderly churchmen who, far from concluding the book of history, established the conditions for a particularly violent chapter of European modernity. It is not as though there should be no attempt to understand the relation of Eros to Agape; rather, attempts to capture and formalize their relationship tend to be self-defeating, even hazardous. In a passage of *The Double Man* near the opening of "New Year Letter," Auden pairs the figure of Eros, who represents life, not with Agape but, rather, with Apollo, who represents art. As Auden writes, "each intends a synthesis" (*DM* 17), but every synthesis fails, for "Art is not life, and cannot be / A midwife to society, / For art is a *fait accompli*" (*DM* 17).[5] Art not only is defined but also lives, as it were, only insofar as its process of self-definition comes to completion; Eros, by contrast, is life pure and simple, or life in its entirety, because it always defies accomplishment, hence definition. Who, then, is Eros, such that, while remaining undefinable, he nevertheless again and again solicits a companion—Agape, on the one hand, art, on the other—against whom he is thus somehow defined?

A question of this kind traverses Auden's work of the late 1930s and early 1940s. The pairing of Eros with Agape may have been prompted by the widespread discussion of Anders Nygren's treatise *Agape and Eros*.[6] And the pairing of Eros with Apollo in *The Double Man* represents a suggestive transformation of Nietzsche's famous pairing of Apollo with Dionysus.[7] Two other pairings of Eros with an opposing or complementary figure can be found in Auden's poetry of this period, specifically in the concluding stanzas of the "Occasional Poems" that appear in the final section of *Another Time*. In the closing lines of "September 1, 1939" Auden pairs Eros with the biblical image through which Thanatos is named:

> May I, composed like them
> Of Eros and of dust,
> Beleaguered by the same
> Negation and despair,
> Show an affirming flame. (*AT* 106)

The "and" binding Eros with "dust" recalls the "or" in an earlier line that Auden would later change to "and" before dropping the poem from his collected works altogether: "We must love one another or die" (*AT* 105). Any number of reasons can be adduced for the alteration of the line and the subsequent elimination of the poem, beginning with simple honesty: all of us die, Auden notes, regardless of whether we love. In the same vein, he could have also affirmed the converse: all of us love in some way or another, for, to repeat the lines from Dante's *Commedia*, "*amor sementa in voi d'ogni vertute, / e d'ogni operazion che merta pene*." In describing "Eros" and "dust" as the universal elements of creaturely life—a concept that stealthily unifies the synthesis of life with that of art—Auden recalls the principles Freud first proposed in *Beyond the Pleasure Principle*: the pleasure principle, here associated with Eros, and the death drive, associated with dust. The end of "September 1, 1939" thus combines an affirmation of the principal function of the poet—the affirmation of Being—with a recognition of historical change that takes place because Eros and Thanatos are inextricably combined with each other. And in the climactic last lines of the poem Auden wrote upon learning of Freud's own death in 1939, he assigns a new—equally familiar yet more enigmatic—companion to Eros, namely his mother, who can scarcely be seen as a figure of death or its drive:

> One rational voice is dumb. Over his grave
> the household of impulse mourns one dearly loved:
> sad is Eros, builder of cities,
> and weeping anarchic Aphrodite. (*AT* 111)

Thus ends "In Memory of Sigmund Freud," which begins by alluding to the "low, dishonest decade" of "September 1, 1939," as it asks: "When there are so many we shall have to mourn, / [. . .] of whom shall we speak?" (*AT* 107).⁸ Of the various figures with which Auden pairs Eros in the poems he wrote from 1939 to 1941, none is as striking as the mother of Eros, whose appearance is as unsettling as these memorable lines are moving. Aphrodite is as far removed from Agape as possible, insofar as her name is synonymous with sexual desire; she is similarly distant from Thanatos, since no figure in the Greek pantheon remains as distant from Hades as "laughter-loving Aphrodite," to quote one of Homer's epithets.⁹ And yet here she is neither alluring nor joyful, but "weeping anarchic." Added to the puzzle surrounding these haunting lines in memory of "one rational voice" is the fact that Freud himself is almost entirely silent about Aphrodite and discusses her only once in all of his massive work, namely in his 1913 essay "The Theme of the Three Caskets." Concerned with a famous scene from Shakespeare's *Merchant of Venice*, this essay can be considered Freud's first contribution to English literary criticism. Beginning with a question directed at Bassanio's decision to choose lead over more alluring metals, Freud expands his inquiry to include other examples from literature and myth where a choice is made among three objects, especially "three sisters," one of whom is dull, inarticulate, or silent. According to Freud, the leaden object represents death, and this is true even in the story of Paris making a choice among Helen, Artemis, and Aphrodite. "She went dumb," he quotes from Jacques Offenbach's *La belle Hélène*, and concludes: "If we decide to regard the peculiarities of our 'third one' as concentrated in her 'dumbness', then psycho-analysis will tell us that in dreams dumbness is a common representation of death."¹⁰ Thus does Aphrodite become a "Goddess of Death."¹¹ It is not as though "In Memory of Sigmund Freud" directly responds to Freud's reading of Offenbach, and, indeed, "The Theme of the Three Caskets" may have nothing to do with the figure of Aphrodite at the end of the poem; but the image of Aphrodite weeping is so strikingly memorable precisely because she appears to represent nothing beyond herself—sad for her son, who is himself sad for his "son." Auden's model is perhaps Thetis, weeping for her son Achilles, who mourns the loss of his companion, Patroclus; in any case, Aphrodite acquires the non-Homeric epithet "anarchic," above all, because she represents no principle. What Aphrodite "means" is perhaps only this: there is always another "isotope" of love for history to discover. If Eros, as the "builder of cities," is the source of civilization on the grand scale, his mother is the concretion of history in an "anarchic" and thus savage—yet also free—sense: not weeping for the natural death of the great man but, rather, silently weeping for all those whom this one poem does not name.

Freud, Historian

In the late 1930s, Auden's elegy for Freud captured one particularly intense moment of reflection on the relation between love and history. In the early 1950s, the birth of psychoanalysis became, for Auden, the focal point for an altered analysis of the same relation. As Auden developed his thoughts in the course of four review-essays on the history of psychoanalysis, published between 1952 and 1955, he came to the conclusion that Freud's invention was born from a struggle that the inventor waged against himself: it was not a psychic conflict that could be addressed by the techniques Freud later developed; rather, it was a struggle between the canons of natural-scientific explanation and the demands of historical facticity. The moment in the late nineteenth century when Freud decided in favor of the latter over the former amounted to a revolutionary change: "Freud," Auden writes in the first of the four essays, "is a clear and beautiful example of a revolutionary thinker . . . who is much more revolutionary and in quite another way than he himself realizes" (*Prose* 3:342).[12] Rosenstock-Huessy's *Out of Revolution* argues that the Papal Revolution of the eleventh century was the model of all subsequent revolutions in the West, despite the fact that Gregory VII would not be able to recognize himself as a revolutionary; on the contrary, he saw himself as a traditionalist. A trace of Rosenstock-Huessy's argument gives shape to Auden's exposition of the revolutionary character of Freud's work: just as the Pope sought liberty from the totalizing claims of the Emperor in the eleventh century, so Freud liberated himself from the similarly totalizing claims of the natural sciences some eight hundred years later.

The basic line of argument Auden pursues in his essays on the history of psychoanalysis runs counter to Freud's own presentation of his achievement. Furthermore, when Auden was writing his essays in the early 1950s, the status of psychoanalysis had not yet been subject to waves of withering criticism from proponents of self-described scientific psychology, which would eventually dislocate Freud from the center of both academic and clinical psychology, pushing him further and further into the margins.[13] If Auden's reviews had appeared in the mid-1980s, for instance, they would be easily recognized as a contribution to a growing trend among readers of Freud to rescue his work by claiming that he is better seen as a philosopher, a poet manqué, or—to quote "In Memory of Sigmund Freud"—"an important Jew who died in exile." Auden can be heard to respond in advance to the debates unleashed by Frank Sulloway's *Freud: Biologist of the Mind* and, then again, by Adolf Grünbaum's *Foundations of Psychoanalysis*, both of which put intense pressure on "defenders" of Freud to counter their differently accented accusations that psychoanalysis was conceived as a science but fails to be one.[14] Even under these counter-factual conditions, however, the image of Freud that emerges from Auden's essays is unusual, perhaps even unprecedented. Instead of trying to rescue Freud by formulating a version of Paul Ricoeur's argument, according to which psychoanalysis is at bottom a hermeneutic discipline, Auden reframes the birth of psychoanalysis, so that it becomes a historical event: Freud did want to become a "biologist of the mind," but the intensity of this desire, once it applied to the situation in which he found himself—people talking about their lives—made him into a historian.[15] The four reviews published in the early 1950s correspondingly help Auden redefine the idea of historiography, so that it definitively parts ways with inherited notions of unimpeachable scientificity.

Auden wrote the first of these reviews when W. W. Norton reissued several of Freud's books, and the editors of *The New Republic* asked him to write an essay. Titled simply "Sigmund Freud," this review can be read as a revised version in prose of Auden's elegy in memory of the inventor of psychoanalysis.[16] Beginning with a series of amusing sketches that cover a panoply of "Freudian" phenomena, Auden indicates the degree to which the dissemination of psychoanalysis into everyday life has changed the way in which we see ourselves and our relations with others. Thus, for instance, slight errors are now interpreted as acts of aggression, while apparently straightforward cases of anxiety are recognized as protective screens, behind which unacceptably violent phantasies are acted out: "The letter of apology to the hostess whose dinner invitation you have forgotten is much more difficult to write than it used to be. If an Isolde worries all day lest her absent Tristan should be run over by a bus, the dumbest Brangaene could warn her that her love includes a hope that he will never return" (*Prose* 3:341). It would be easy to imagine Auden continuing in this vein, explaining, for instance, how different schools of Freudian thought help us understand the "isotopes" of Eros he had identified in his review of *Love in the Western World*. But he quickly turns away from the pervasive presence of Freud in the contemporary world toward the origins of psychoanalysis in late nineteenth-century natural science, when, as he notes, there was more or less univocal confidence that "we shall soon be able to describe all mental events in terms of physical events in the brain" (*Prose* 3:342).

After noting the absence of mathematics in Freud's work, Auden lays out the central thesis of his article. What matters is not the body of theories proposed by Freud, but his methods, and his methods are incompatible with the procedures of the natural sciences:

> [I]f every one of his theories should turn out to be false, Freud would still tower up as the genius who perceived that psychological events are not natural events but historical and that, therefore, psychology as distinct from neurology, must be based on the pre-suppositions and methodology, not of the biologist but of the historian. As a child of his age who was consciously in a polemic with the "idealists" he may officially subscribe to the "realist" dogma that human nature and animal nature are the same, but the moment he gets down to work, every thing he says denies it. . . . Freud is not always aware of what he is doing and some of the difficulties he gets into arise from his trying to retain biological notions of development when he is actually thinking historically. (*Prose* 3:343)

When the first volume of Ernest Jones' three-volume biography of the founder of psychoanalysis was published in 1953, Auden found further evidence for the argument he proposed in "Sigmund Freud." Drawing on Jones' admirable if rather hagiographic research, Auden identifies the precise circumstances in which Freud became an apostate from physical reductionism. "Brought up on the firm rock of the Helmholtz faith," Freud, as a young scientist worshipped at the altar of a single, monolithic physical force, and only turned away, reluctantly, when he began to talk to his patients about their illnesses: "to take such a step was to enter a ground forbidden, not by conventional prudery but by his God; for the historical world is a horrid place where, instead of nice clean measurable forces, there are messy things like mixed motives, where classes keep overlapping, where what is believed to have happened is as real as what actually happened, a world, moreover, which cannot be defined by technical terms but only described by analogies" (*Prose* 3:386–87).[17] As for the evidence in the biography that Freud was always at bottom a historian, regardless of how he perceived himself, Auden saves this for the final paragraphs of his review. Piecing together a series of separated remarks, Auden proposes that Freud was able to betray the creed of scientific materialism only because his primary interest was always in singular instances rather than regular cycles: "Freud could hardly have dared or succeeded had he not been endowed by nature with a historian's type of mind rather than an exact scientist's. Dr Jones says of him: 'His great strength, though sometimes also his weakness, was his quite extraordinary respect for the *singular fact* . . . the idea of collecting statistics was quite alien to him . . . he was apt to be careless and imprecise in his use of technical terms'" (*Prose* 3:387).[18]

Respect for the singular fact is thus the *conditio sine qua non* of historiographical research, which immediately distinguishes it from natural science, where the particular instance is either a token of a general law, a mistake in the technique of observation, or a clue to a better theory that would ultimately reduce it to a token. That Freud had such respect to a "quite extraordinary" degree means that, as a historian, he was exemplary. For Jones, such respect can also be a weakness but, not so for Auden. The characteristics described in the other two passages he takes from the biography—aversion to statistics and laxity in the usage of technical terms—follow from the primary strength. Singular facts can be approached only by way of comparison, hence via analogy, not through the subsumptive procedures of causal or statistical explanation. Auden also adds a second source of Freud's greatness beyond his struggle against his own commitment to scientific reductionism: he fell in love. Only because he experienced the phenomenon of erotic love could he become a historian in spite of himself. This, too, is a remarkable claim, which Auden reserves for the very end of his review, where he praises Freud for being uninterested in the question whether he had "cured" any of his patients. A cure has no other source than love, which cannot be forced or even simply effected by means of well-applied rules of the trade: "No one can resist trying to cure by force, no one can allow another his right to himself, even to his misery, who has not learned to love: Dr Jones' chapters on Freud's courtship and marriage leave one in no doubt where he learned it" (*Prose* 3:387–88).

A year after the first volume of Jones' biography appeared, the letters between Freud and Fliess were published in English, along with notes and drafts from the period in Freud's life, from 1887 to 1902, which Auden considered the crucible of Freud's revolutionary discovery. Auden enthusiastically reviews the volume of letters and includes an uncharacteristically large number of long citations. It is as though he wants his readers to follow the path of his own discovery that when Freud invented psychoanalysis, he revealed nothing so important as his own, perhaps unconscious, affirmation of human experience as historical and subject to the research methodologies of the historian. Thus, in the volume's first pages, Freud appears as a scientist: "These letters are, therefore, all the more fascinating as a demonstration that, despite all differences in subject matter and methodology, the process of creative work in the scientist and the artist are strikingly similar" (*Prose* 3:473). By the end of the review, however, everything has changed, as Auden elaborates the claim he made in his earlier essay for *The New Republic*: "Freud's greatest achievement was not the hitherto unsuspected facts about the life of the mind but his discovery of the only method by which they could be found. If every one of his findings should turn out to need modification, he would remain the genius who made real knowledge of the psyche possible by regarding mental events, not as natural events, but as historical events to be approached by the methods of the historian" (*Prose* 3:476). And when, soon after Auden completed the review of the Freud-Fliess letters, the second volume of the Jones biography was published, Auden announced his argument in the very title of his review: "The History of an Historian." Whereas the review of the first volume of the biography is animated by "the life-drama" produced by "a revolutionary discovery" (*Prose* 3:596), the review of the second volume is without drama—not even the obvious and much-discussed drama resulting from the antagonism created by the schisms experienced by the psychoanalytic movement. None of the major revisions that Freud's thought underwent during the twenty years surveyed by the volume enter into Auden's discussion; rather, "The History of a Historian" consists largely of an expansion and distillation of the argument announced in its title, as Auden proceeds to identify the elements of a historiography that understands its task primarily in relation to the singularity and irreducibility of its facts.

The first element of historiography is uncontroversial. In ascertaining the facts of any given situation, the historian must attend to the available evidence: "the difference between the good and the bad historian is a difference between carefulness or honesty and carelessness or dishonesty" (*Prose* 3:598). As Auden quickly adds, however, the virtues of honesty and thoroughness go only so far. This leads him to the second element of historiography, which is slightly more contentious. In contrast to chronologists, historians also ascertain the relations among events, which are represented in terms of causes and influences, that is, the pre- and post-history of the fact in question; indeed, as Auden argues, the pre- and post-history of the fact make it historical in the first place—and not tokens that could be subsumed under general laws: "In assessing the importance of his data, all historians are governed by the same general principle that the importance of an historical event is in proportion to its causal effect upon subsequent historical events which includes its influence upon later interpretations of the past" (*Prose* 3:598). The third element is more controversial still, for it dissociates historical research from its natural-scientific counterparts. Historical facts are generated by previous facts; but since the interpretation of a fact can itself be a fact, the terms *earlier* and *later* acquire a degree of density, in which the post-history, including the later interpretation of the fact, can be understood as the cause of the earlier one, since its significance and thus its very factuality derive from its interpretation. And the final element follows directly from the third: a cause in historiography is not the same as a cause in the natural sciences. Despite its legitimate use in both disciplines, the term is not univocal, for *cause* means necessitation among scientists, motivation among historians. Auden uses algebraic abbreviation to represent the fundamental situation of historians, who are barred in principle from representing causes in mathematical terms: "in history, to say that A causes B does not mean that if A occurs then B has to occur but only that A provides B with a motive for occurring" (*Prose* 3:598).[19]

Auden's use of algebraic terms in "The History of an Historian" is by no means unusual among his prose writings of the period. *The Enchafèd Flood*, for instance, is filled with much more elaborate algebraic formulations. It is nevertheless striking in the context of his reflections on Freud, not only because it is precisely not the language of historiography but also because it is so very anemic. Nowhere does Auden address the raging sexuality associated with Freud—nothing about the polymorphous perversity of little children, for instance, or the castration complex, or even the Oedipus complex, and all of the other so-called hot topics that made Freud such a widely discussed figure. In the same vein, Auden says nothing about Freud's "speculative" writings, especially *Beyond the Pleasure Principle*, where, in the end, the battle between Eros and Thanatos is seen as the matrix of all organic life, hence of all history, both human and non-human, perhaps even geological as well. At the very moment in which Auden published "The History of an Historian" Herbert Marcuse was completing *Eros and Civilization*—about which Auden, for his part, made no public comment. And there is yet another striking absence. Auden says nothing about the primary historical thesis Freud proposes in *Civilization and Its Discontents*, whereby post-classical Western European civilization is afflicted with a sometimes conscious, sometimes unconscious malaise that both expresses and results from its adoption of Christianity, with its impossible demand that everyone love one's neighbor as oneself. Freud adopts a kind of faux naiveté as he lists a variety of reasons for rejecting the demand that he love his neighbor, beginning with an honest reflection on his own limited quantity of love, which he must be careful in expending on others.[20] In "The History of an Historian" Auden suggests that Jones "dismisses the anthropologists' objections to *Totem and Taboo* too cavalierly" (*Prose* 3:600); but he is himself silent about Freud's own reflections on the course of Western European civilization since the fall of Rome.

The absence of any remarks about Freud as a historian in a conventional sense corresponds to another salient feature of the four essays on Freud:

all of them are altogether uncritical. There is neither criticism of Freudian theory nor a critique of civilization from the perspective of psychoanalysis. At the same time, however, the essays do not amount to a pledge of allegiance to Freud as all-knowing sage or, to quote Jacques Lacan, as "le sujet supposé à savoir." Auden's return to Freud is not a return to the authentic theory of psychoanalysis that later practitioners more or less systematically distorted. In the origin of psychoanalysis Auden finds something that he briefly—and unsuccessfully—seeks to grasp in his review of *Love in the Western World*: not the precise relation between the two "isotopes of Eros," about which he is already quite certain, but "the true relation / Of Agape to Eros," which the Council of Trent presumed to define once and for all. The "true relation" does not consist in a formula but, as the phrase indicates, in a relation, including the clinical relation in its original form. Freud's decision to listen to those who gave voice to versions of Eros in all his manifold manifestations not only made Freud himself a historian; it also represents the practice of agape. For this reason, there is nothing about Freud to criticize, only a discovery—missed by the "tired old men" of the schismatic church—to honor.

The Third Sister

In 1957 the third and final volume of Jones' biography of Freud appeared, under the subtitle "The Last Phase, 1919–1939." Auden never reviewed it, and the name "Freud" appears only rarely in his writings after "The History of an Historian." Instead of further following Freud's progress as a historian, Auden writes "Homage to Clio." The poem draws on the insights that he acquired from his four-year-long analysis of Freud; but neither the poem nor the like-named volume is anything like an "application" or "illustration" of his insights. In a crucial sense, prose and poetry are even in conflict with each other. As the author of the reviews, Auden sees Freud wresting himself away from his desire to become a new Helmholtz when he fully recognizes that the stories of childhood "seduction" are rooted in fantasy. This does not make them any less real for the traumatized child, to be sure, yet they remain fantasies all the same. The "seduction" did not really happen; in other words, it was not a historical event that could be publicly attested. This change in perspective is at the core of Auden's Freud. Nothing like it appears in "Homage to Clio." The trauma of history is so unquestionably real that the poet does not for a moment pause to ask himself whether the experiences of the figure to whom he pays homage—experiences, it should be noted, that he cannot identify with any degree of certainty—are a matter of her or anyone else's imagination. Not only, then, does Auden's poetry diverge from the direction adopted in his prose, it also anticipates still *another* debate around Freud that emerged in the 1980s, when his archives were opened, the seduction theory came under renewed scrutiny, and trauma theory emerged as a significant critical field.[21]

Whatever else Clio may be in "Homage to Clio," she is different from her two "Tall Sisters" (*HC* 15), Aphrodite and Artemis, each of whom is thoroughly implicated in all-embracing fantasies of conquest—erotic in one case, violent in the other. As the muse of history, however, Clio has one thing in common with her more conspicuous sisters, namely that she, too, is a mythological figure. But how so? This is not so simple a question as it may at first appear. When, for instance, the noted Whig historian G. M. Trevelyan entitles an essay "Clio, a Muse," he takes no interest in anyone, mythic or otherwise, who bears the name *Clio*; rather, like countless others before and since, he uses the name simply as a "poetic" way of designating either the art or the science—this "either/or" summarizes Trevelyan's dilemma—with which she became associated in Roman antiquity.[22] Auden must have long suspected that there was something strange about the traditional muse named Clio. According to Hesiod's canonical account of the muses at the opening of the *Theogony*, their mother is Mnemosyne.[23] As progeny of "Memory," all nine sisters are thus, in some sense, related to history, broadly speaking, and the question therefore arises: what is to be made of the "memorial" provenance of these sisters, in light of which one of them separates herself from the others, so that she can become associated with the memorialization of what could otherwise be altogether forgotten?

In a variety of essays, including "Mimesis and Allegory" from 1940 and "Nature, History and Poetry" from a decade later, Auden reminds his readers of Hesiod's genealogy of the muses: they are all "daughters of memory" (*Prose* 2:85; *Prose* 3:23). In the later essay, he adds a further note, which leads him to a restatement of Wordsworth's famous definition of poetry as "emotion recollected in tranquility": "but Memory herself is not a muse" (*Prose* 3:23). And shortly after the initial publication of "Homage to Clio" in 1955, he sketches another line of argument, as he begins to emphasize the historical character of memory itself: "The ancient Greeks called the Muses the daughters of Memory, but memory meant something very different to them than it means to us. If we say someone has a good memory, we mean that he can recall the exact particulars of the past as they actually happened; to a Greek, remembering meant re-creating the past in what he would call its real form and we should call an ideal form" (*Prose* 3:581).[24] To some extent, this remark is only an expression of a thesis that Auden had long maintained, namely that the experience of time in ancient Greece is fundamentally different from the experience of time that began to appear during the early years of the Roman Empire; but the remark may also be responsive to a groundbreaking monograph that first appeared in the early 1950s, E. R. Dodds' *The Greeks and the Irrational*, where a provocative footnote sheds light on the standard genealogy of the muses by showing that their common function consists in compensating for the inherent frailty of *kleos*: "The Muses were the daughters of Memory," Dodds writes, "and were themselves in some places called *Mneiai*. . . . But I take it that what the poet [Homer] here prays for is not just an accurate memory—for this, though highly necessary, would be memory only of an inaccurate *kleos*—but an actual vision of the past to supplement the *kleos*. Such visions, welling up from the unknown depths of the mind, must once have been felt as something immediately 'given,' and because of its immediacy more trustworthy than oral tradition."[25]

    E. R. and A. R. Dodds are the first names to appear in *Homage to Clio* after "Clio," for it is to them that the volume is dedicated.[26] As for the name of the muse, it clearly derives from *kleos*, which is related to the word for "hearing," *kluo*, and means "tale," "report," "acclaim," "renown," "fame," and above all, in the epic tradition, "glory," the pursuit and preservation of which govern heroic life.[27] The importance of *kleos* for the ancient Greek bards can scarcely be overstated, for Hesiod indeed names Clio first among the daughters of Mnemosyne and "lord Zeus," even if he concludes his list of muses by placing Calliope above her eight sisters.[28]

A discerning reader of the previously cited passage from *The Greeks and the Irrational* would immediately see, however, that Clio, as a muse, is called upon to repair the defectiveness of *kleos*. She can thus be understood as a mythological figure who is divided against herself: as a muse, Clio grants a lasting vision, whereas *kleos* alone belongs to the fleeting sphere of sound.[29] Because the muses have the power to grant vision, the Memory from which they derive, as Auden claims in his Foreword to *Some Trees*, can be characterized as "ideal," in other words, as impervious to change.[30] By contrast, the Clio to whom Auden turns in the opening, titular poem of *Homage to Clio* remains loyal to the word from which she derives: fragile, vulnerable, elusive, and associated with the sense of hearing rather than that of vision.

Clio in her classical form inherited from the early Roman Empire is generally seen holding icons of writing, for writing is the original technology that makes up for the flaws of mere *kleos*.[31] In the beginning of "Homage to Clio," by contrast, it is the poet who is holding a book, and Clio is nowhere to be found. For the first six stanzas of the poem, thus more than a quarter of its length, she is eclipsed and overshadowed by a pair of her sisters: "Provocative Aphrodite" and "her twin, / Virago Artemis" (*HC* 15). As the goddess of the hunt, Artemis is intimately linked with death, and despite her importance here, she can be found in no other Auden poem. The same is not true of Aphrodite, of course. "Homage to Clio," however, reiterates the slight note of self-criticism that can be discerned in his last essay on Freud, where "the sexual"—and thus the aphrodisiac—is said to be rule-bound, not anarchic. Later in the volume *Homage to Clio*, specifically in "Dichtung und Wahrheit," the identification of Aphrodite with "the sexual" is complete: "It is easy for a poet to hymn the benevolent deeds of Aphrodite (filling his song with charming pictures like the courtship ritual of the Great Crested Grebe or the curious behavior of the male stickleback and then all those jolly nymphs and shepherds loving away like mad while empires rise and fall) provided that he thinks of her as directing the lives of creatures (even human beings) *in general*" (*HC* 44, § 18). Instead of the weeping and therefore mute figure that concludes "In Memory of Sigmund Freud," there appears in both the volume and the poem dedicated to the muse of history an Aphrodite who is highly vocal, hence "provocative." Auden's reimmersion into Freud's work may have prompted this revision, or the alteration in the function of Aphrodite may simply be a function of the familial figure with which she is associated: her son in the earlier poem, her sister in the later one. Aphrodite in "Homage to Clio" is in any case thoroughly erotic, while Artemis is unambiguously thanatotic. And in the opening stanzas of the poem, the "Dual Realm" ruled by the two sisters appears as a battlefield in which they enact their sibling rivalry:

> Our hill has made its submission and the green
> > Swept on into the north: around me,
> From morning to night, flowers duel incessantly,
> > Color against color, in combats
> Which they all win, and at any hour from some point else
> > May come another tribal outcry
> Of a new generation of birds who chirp,
> > Not for effect but because chirping
> Is the thing to do. (*HC* 15)

Whereas the closing line of "In Memory of Sigmund Freud" can be understood as an allusion to one of the stranger moments in "The Theme of the Three Caskets"—where Freud identifies Aphrodite with the "goddess of death" by means of an Offenbach operetta—the very structure of "Homage to Clio" is stamped by the question prompting Freud's essay: how should we interpret the silence of the third sister? For Clio is indeed the third sister, whose unassuming presence alongside her imposing siblings generates the movement of the poem. In its opening stanzas, before the poet encounters Clio, Aphrodite and Artemis are paired as twins; in the central stanzas, they again appear together under the rubric of "Major Powers"; and in the final stanzas, they part ways, as Artemis consorts with princes, and Aphrodite speaks for lovers.[32] In keeping with Freud's argument, the ubiquity of the "Major Powers" in conjunction with the silence of Clio suggests that she, as the third sister, should represent death—but this would be a mistake.[33] Whereas Auden's essays on Freud are almost wholly uncritical, the poem is not; on the contrary, it refutes the argument proposed in "The Theme of the Three Caskets." Clio is no "goddess of death." At the same time, however, Auden does not identify the third sister with the other major term that traverses both his poetry and prose of the period; in other words, he does not write a poem entitled "Homage to Agape," who could be figured, following Auden's reflections in "Eros and Agape," by the act of nourishment, which discloses our universal and total dependence. In honoring Clio in the company of Aphrodite and Artemis, Auden is doing something surprising both from the perspective of psychoanalysis and that of Christianity: against psychoanalysis, the silent sister is not a figuration of death; and in contrast to the doctrinal drift of Christianity, it is history, rather than Agape, that stands apart from the "Major Powers" that otherwise dominate all earthly life.

Historical Sense

From the first moment in which Clio appears, unlike the "Tall Sisters," especially "Provocative Aphrodite," she is said to be silent. This is her most striking and significant feature. The metrical structure of the poem honors Clio's silence, insofar as it, too, is scarcely audible. Adapting the third Asclepiadean strophe as revived by Horace—but modified beyond any assured recognition of its classical origin—Auden composes "Homage to Clio" in the syllabic meter he associates, above all, with Marianne Moore.[34] His twenty-three quatrains alternate between eleven- and nine-syllable lines with remarkable consistency. As he notes in a discussion of Moore's prosodic practice, English readers tend not to hear syllabic verse, attuned as they are to accents, and Auden exploits this tendency in his poem by employing what he calls "the fullest elision," that is, "always eliding between contiguous vowels or through h" (*Prose* 3:650). For example, "any hour," a phrase from the second stanza, is generally heard as three syllables, with the last further elongated by the diphthong, but functions in this stanza as only two. Metrical pattern thus diverges from its audible expression. Even in its smallest units, such as "any hour," there emerges a difference between the temporal measure that structures the poem and the time of its audible expression.[35] And Auden's decision to use only internal rhyme—as opposed to end rhymes, which tend to produce "more static and logical" effects (*Prose* 3:649)—enhances this divergence, with the result that the metrical pattern, like Clio herself, remains silent. As for her silence, it stands in contrast to the noises of nature, which dominate the opening stanzas of the poem, culminating in the array of sound words that frame the sixth stanza—from the earthquake's "roar" through the "whispers of streams" to the rhyme-stop, "loud sound," that Auden suspends in the enjambment of the line and qualifies in the sound chiasm of the next, "**Not a din**." At this precise point, where there is no "din," Auden introduces a caesura that reflects back on his own position, while naming Clio for the first time as the counterpoint to her sisters: "but we, at haphazard // And unseasonably, are brought face to face / By ones, Clio, with your silence" (*HC* 15).[36]

The "we" that encounters Clio, as Auden stresses, is not a collective subject; it happens only "by ones," not as a group. Within the context established by the "Tall Sisters," each of whom is easily legible under Freudian categories, it may seem as though the poem would stage what Auden describes in his essays on Freud: the discovery of history through the techniques of analysis. The use of the phrase "face to face" points in this direction as well, for it suggests that history can be approached only through the kind of face-to-face conversation that one of Freud's early patients famously called "the talking cure."[37] And if Clio's silence is understood as a function of the analytic session, comparable to the silence of the traditional Freudian analyst, the moment in which the poet encounters her can be seen as something akin to a clinical appointment. Beyond the bizarre reversals that would result from this interpretation, whereby Clio would somehow be in service to the poet, seeking to relieve him of his anxieties rather than being the source of his homage, the stanza in which she appears is resistant to any suggestion that her silence is comparable to a psychoanalyst's. The encounter cannot be confused with an appointment, for it is altogether unplanned. Not only is the encounter expressed by means of the passive voice: "we . . . are brought face to face . . . with your silence," but two adverbs specify how it occurs in the absence of any agency: "at haphazard" and "unseasonably." The first emphasizes the unintentional character of the encounter; the second refers back to the scene of nature in which the poem began. Unlike the observational capacities of the animals, which follow the rhythms of nature, beginning with the victory of spring over winter, the poet's ability to sense the presence of Clio does not follow a cyclical pattern. At the same time, the "unseasonable" character of the poet's initial encounter with Clio, combined with the explicit intention of the poem as a whole—to affirm history in a certain sense—indicates that the "prooftext," so to speak, for the initial perception of Clio is those passages in Nietzsche's *Unzeitgemäße Betrachtungen*, generally translated at the time as *Thoughts out of Season*, where he begins to question the value "for life" of the much-vaunted "historical sense."[38]

Historical sense must itself be understood as historical. In order to encounter history, not only must it be distinguished from nature, but different epochs must be distinguished from each other—and the sense for this distinction must be an element of the condition under which Clio can be encountered. For Auden, the crucial difference between historical epochs is the difference between post-medieval civilization and Greco-Roman antiquity. As he argues in an essay in 1954, it is because of Nietzsche's work that nineteenth-century historiography differs from its twentieth-century counterpart: "the chief difference between the attitude of our time towards both Greece and Rome and that of the nineteenth century is that we—Nietzsche is our spiritual father in this respect—are much more conscious of the difference between the Ancients and ourselves, of how strange, almost incomprehensible, their ways of thinking often are to us" (*Prose* 3:418). Not only did Nietzsche teach us to recognize how far removed modern Western culture is from the culture of the ancient Mediterranean basin; at the same time he understood that the much-vaunted "historical sense" of his contemporaries was a burden and, indeed, a disease, which historians seek to assuage by representing the products of their inquiry in a variety of ways. In "Homage to Clio" the poet acknowledges the uneasiness Nietzsche describes at the very moment in which Clio is "unseasonably" encountered: "After that / Nothing is easy" (*HC* 15). And this immediately poses a question to the poet about his own function: how can Clio be represented in language without the verbal image instantly betraying what it seeks to capture?

The beginning of Nietzsche's essay on history in *Thoughts out of Season* and the opening stanzas of "Homage to Clio" are mirror images of each other. Whereas the poem presents the animals as observant, the essay begins by calling on its readers to "observe the herd as it grazes past you."[39]

Nietzsche emphasizes the silence of the happy animal: "A human being might ask the animal: 'Why do you just look at me like that instead of telling me about your happiness?' The animal wanted to answer, 'Because I always immediately forget what I wanted to say'—but it had already forgotten this answer and hence said nothing, so that the human being was left to wonder."[40] Auden's animals are similarly insensitive to history; but their volubility gives their forgetfulness a completely different significance: the "tribal outcry / Of a new generation of birds who chirp" and the cock's garrulous crowing each morning, "pronouncing himself himself," enact a double forgetting: both of the deadly battles of previous generations and of their own impending deaths. While Auden rejects the indifference of the observant creatures who escape the pain of memory—"to chirp like a tearless bird . . . unthinkable"—Nietzsche finds that observation of creaturely life incites unhappiness among human beings: "Over and over a leaf is loosened from the scroll of time, falls out, flutters away—and suddenly flutters back into the human being's lap. The human being says, 'I remember,' and he envies the animal that immediately forgets and that sees how every moment actually dies."[41] The German word that is here translated as *leaf*, namely *Blatt*, also means *page*, and the book that the poet in "Homage to Clio" identifies as his own—perhaps because he owns it, perhaps because he wrote it—is even more sharply distinguished from the ever-observant living things than the meditating poet: "To observation / My book is dead" (*HC* 15).

For Nietzsche, history is the name for a mode of Being that makes human beings uneasy. So, too, for Auden, who recognizes that uneasiness directly results not so much from seeing or hearing as from simply sensing Clio's presence: "After that / Nothing is easy." As Nietzsche explains, moreover, monumentalization responds to this uneasiness by fixing it in place and assigning it to a past that transcends anything in the present. "Homage to Clio" is as hostile to monumentalism as *Thoughts out of Season*, and it captures the desire for imperturbable permanence in the image of granite, which can be used for the figuration of the "Major Powers" but is utterly inappropriate for Clio: "How shall I describe you? They / Can be represented in granite" (*HC* 16). Whereas Nietzsche warns against monumental history, Auden goes even further and deems it impossible: wherever granite figures of greatness emerge, Clio goes missing. And it is in preparation for this question—"How shall I describe you?"—that Auden describes Clio in such a way that she comes as close as ever to the figure of Agape:

> But it is you, who never have spoken up,
>   Madonna of silences, to whom we turn
>
> When we have lost control, your eyes, Clio, into which
>   We look for recognition after
> We have been found out. (*HC* 16)

At the precise point where the poet thus seems to reveal the identity of Clio—she is "Madonna"—he clearly subverts this identification in the very same stroke.[42] For, just as Artemis and Aphrodite can be represented in granite, so, too, can Madonna, insofar as she is the Virgin Mary, rendered in countless icons. The "Madonna of silences" does not take shape as an image that would monumentalize her silence. The critique of monumental history goes so far as to destroy the identification of Clio with any figure who has been or could be preserved in stone, including "Madonna." Love, as ever, is the cure; but if "cure" is understood as the end of a disquieting condition that is—to coin a term—Clionic, then the supposed "cure" is only an intensification of the disease. This is not to say, though, that the poet abandons his attempt to discover a way in which Clio can be fixed into his field of vision. The search continues as an inquiry into the limits of figuration within the history of art:

>   what icon
> Have the arts for you, who look like any
>
> Girl one has not noticed and show no special
> Affinity with a beast? (*HC* 16–17)

The question posed in the poem corresponds to a line of argument Auden develops in a section of *The Dyer's Hand* entitled "Two Bestiaries," the first part of which consists in an amusing critique of D. H. Lawrence, whose ability to represent animals is directly proportional to his inability to live in a human, thus historical world: "Man is a history-making creature who can neither repeat his past nor leave it behind; at every moment he adds to and thereby modifies everything that had previously happened to him. Hence the difficulty of finding a single image which can stand as an adequate symbol for man's kind of existence" (*DH* 278). Auden's other "bestiary" is that of Marianne Moore, who is as delicate in her use of animal images as she is in her deployment of the syllabic line. "Two Bestiaries" concludes with a reflection on Moore's poem, "The Pangolin," in which the outward form of an animal is shown to resemble the appearance of a recent invention in the technology of warfare. Thus does Moore's bestiary expand beyond those traditionally employed, while at the same time identifying the site where comparisons between human and animal traits collapse. Noting that "The Pangolin" was written during the Second World War, Auden quotes only two of its lines—"in fighting, mechanicked / like the pangolin"—and concludes with a paradoxical "moral" that summarizes the disadvantage of animal imagery for poets who want to identify an emblem of history: "men ought to be gentle-natured like pangolins but, if they were, they would cease to look like pangolins, and the pangolin could not be an emblem" (*DH* 305).

Auden undertakes an expansion similar to Moore's. He does not seek to find a generally neglected animal with which Clio can be compared; rather, he looks toward a new medium in which her image could be captured: "I have seen / Your photo, I think, in the papers, nursing / a baby or mourning a corpse" (*HC* 17). The uncertainty expressed in these lines arises from a paradoxical feature of modern technology in which the poet "thinks" he sees an image of the muse.[43] The camera may be able to capture a wider or more minutely detailed field of vision; but because photographs are mechanically reproducible, they are detachable from the singular "face to face" where she resides and cannot unambiguously capture her image.[44] Both traditional and contemporary forms of visual art are all thus rendered suspicious in relation to Clio, who is redescribed yet again, as the poem renews its reflection on the silence that distinguishes her from her sisters. Her image cannot be properly captured in either visual or auditory media;

but for the same reason—with silence now understood as "merciful"—she is able to listen to "screams" that are "superfluous" in an exact sense, since they transcend the endless and cyclical flow of the "Major Powers":

> Muse of the unique
> Historical fact, defending with silence
> Some world of your beholding, a silence
>
> No explosion can conquer but a lover's Yes
> Has been known to fill. So few of the Big
> Ever listen: that is why you have a great host
> Of superfluous screams to care for (*HC* 17)

"Homage to Clio" could end at this point—with the muse of the "unique / Historical fact" distinguished from her sisters, especially Artemis, whose "children" would be honored by the traditional muse of history, and with Clio captured in the image of a silent figure, without any positive features of her own, caring for those who scream. But the poem continues in its last stanzas to distinguish Clio yet again from the "Tall Sisters." The children of Artemis conform to the cyclical motion of nature, either moving up and down "like the Duke of Cumberland" or going "round and round like the Laxey Wheel / The Short, the Bald, the Pious, the Stammerer" (*HC* 17)—all names derived from qualities that subsume the individuality of those to whom they are applied. This, though, is not true of Clio's children: "Not yours," so begins the twentieth stanza. The question to which the rest of the poem is directed thus becomes: who, after all, are her children, now that we have recognized that, as "Madonna of silences," she cannot be identified with the Madonna encountered in commemorative statues? If Clio were a traditional muse of history, her children would presumably coincide with Artemis', for they would be those honored for what they have done, either founding or strengthening political structures. The reader would perhaps expect that her children would rebel or, at least, resist the children of Artemis; but this not the case; the children of Clio are identified by the exact opposite trait, namely their obedience: "Not yours. Lives that obey you move like music, / Becoming now what they only can be once, / Making of silence decisive sound" (*HC* 17). The cardinal characteristic of music is that each of its sounds is motivated by previous ones, not caused by them. For this reason, existence in history is comparable to musical development, which does not lead anywhere but is not therefore static. Because they emerge from an absolute condition, here called "silence," specifically musical sounds acquire a similar absoluteness that Auden associates with a distinguishing characteristic of historical existence, namely the decisiveness in which responsibility is formed: each sound is the negation of silence and contributes to the creation of a reality to which all others are co-indebted. That reality is, of course, the music itself. Auden's emphasis on the significance of historical interpretation in his exposition of Freud as an exemplary historian—each new event can prompt a new interpretation of previous ones—thus emerges as a structuring element of the poem.

"Move like music," the last simile in "Homage to Clio," contrasts with its first one: "to chirp like a cheerless bird." The birds are not Romantic nightingales that make natural music; rather, they emit a "tribal outcry." Recognition of the difference between the two comparisons solicits a retrospective reinterpretation of the opening stanzas, in which the animals are seen to engage in something akin to warfare. In these highly metaphorical stanzas Auden does not avail himself of the time-honored trope most closely associated with impassioned animals, namely the epic simile, which he discusses at length in his essay on Moore's "bestiary." Far from being emblematic of historical existence, animals are incomparable to anything human—except when human beings conform to the cyclicality that governs the generations of animals and the movements of mechanisms as well. The time of historical existence cannot be measured according to the circular movements of a clock or the iterative character of the calendar but is given, rather, only when it is found: "it sounds / Easy, but one must find the time, Clio" (*HC* 17). Alluding to the concept of *kairos* as opposed to that of *chronos*, Auden is also altering the sense of easiness with which he first introduces Clio. The malaise of history is not caused by the lingering presence of memory traces, as Nietzsche proposes in *Thoughts out of Season*; nor can such disquiet be attributed—as Freud famously does in *Civilization and Its Discontents*—to unconscious guilt.[45] Rather, uneasiness comes from an unwillingness to "find the time." And here Clio acquires a new name: she becomes the "Muse of Time" because this—"the time," distinguished from the movement of "the Laxey Wheel"—is precisely what she, as muse, gives to those who seek her out.

Recollection

The final stanzas of "Homage to Clio," like its final simile, correspondingly invite a retrospective reinterpretation of the poem's opening; but they also solicit similar reassessments of Auden's earlier poetic engagements with the concept of history, especially his 1937 poem "Spain."[46] One of the poems in the volume *Homage to Clio* is called "T the Great," where the once terrifying name of Tamburlaine is reduced to a preposterous anagram, and Clio, for her part, returns to her earlier function as the muse who honors the so-called greats: "Though T cannot win Clio's cup again, / From time to time the name crops up again, // E.g., as a crossword anagram: / 11 Down—A NUBILE TRAM" (*HC* 25). A more somber wordplay appears in "Homage to Clio" itself, for the title of the poem pays homage to George Orwell's description of the Spanish Civil War in his *Homage to Catalonia* from 1938: both titles include the phrase *homage to*, and the name *Clio* can be formed from *Catalonia* by a simple subtraction and rearrangement of its letters. In January 1937, Auden traveled to Spain, where he hoped to drive an ambulance for the Republican side. In March, Auden returned to England, where he wrote and published "Spain," in the form of a pamphlet in order to raise money for Medical Aid in Spain; but he was otherwise reluctant to describe his experiences: "I did not wish to talk about Spain when I returned," he said many years later, "because I was upset by many things I saw or heard about. Some of them were described better than I could ever have done by George Orwell, in *Homage to Catalonia*."[47] Spain is also where Auden found himself—to his surprise—dismayed by his discovery that the churches had been closed. Orwell, for his part, disliked Auden from a distance (they had not met at that time) and did not hesitate to write a scathing review of "Spain," first in 1938 and later, and more expansively, in his "Inside the Whale" from 1940.[48] While praising the poem as "one of the few decent things that have been written about the Spanish war," he vehemently rejects one of its concluding lines: "The conscious acceptance of guilt in the necessary murder" (*S* 11). To which Orwell responds: "notice the phrase 'necessary murder.' It could only be written by a person to whom murder is at most a word. Personally I would not speak so lightly of murder. It so happens that I have seen the bodies of numbers of murdered men—I don't mean killed in battle, I mean murdered. Therefore I have some conception of what murder means—the terror, the hatred, the howling relatives, the post-mortems, the blood, the smells. To me murder is something to be avoided."[49]

Auden thought that Orwell misunderstood him but was nevertheless troubled enough by the phrase "necessary murder" to change the line when the poem was republished in *Another Time*.[50] He chose not include the poem in his *Collected Poems*, and in the foreword to the 1966 revision he utterly repudiated the poem's final lines. Describing his reasons for "throw[ing] out a number of poems from the volume," Auden writes of "Spain": "Again, and much more shamefully, I once wrote: 'History to the defeated / May say alas but cannot help nor pardon.' To say this is to equate goodness with success. It would have been bad enough if I had ever held this wicked doctrine, but that I should have stated it simply because it sounded to me rhetorically effective is quite inexcusable" (*CP* xxvi). In the conclusion to his scathing review of Albert Camus' *The Rebel*, Auden recollects the phrase "necessary murder," which troubled him as much as Orwell, and notes that the wickedness and equivocation implicit in this phrase do not seem to trouble Camus:

> As a model for political action he offers us the Russian martyr-assassins like [Ivan] Kaliayev who "kill and die so that it shall be clear that murder is impossible." It is certainly admirable about these brave men and women that they accepted responsibility for their acts, though both the wisdom and the morality of killing another not because you disapprove of him personally but because you disapprove of his function is questionable. Then why must Mr Camus rob their act of all significance by saying: "The sole but invincible hope of the rebel is incarnated, in the final analysis, in innocent murderers," which is precisely what they refused to be? The only innocent murderer in peace time is the public executioner. (*Prose* 3:501–2)

Auden's repudiation of the lines from "Spain, 1937"—with its ambiguous apologia for political assassination—is one of the starting points for "Homage to Clio." At the end of the earlier poem Auden describes a condition that is the very opposite of the situation with which the later poem opens: "the animals will not look: / We are left alone with our day, and the time is short" (*S* 12). In "Homage to Clio" the animals not only look but are keenly observant; human beings are singular but not solitary, and the time is there to be found for those who are willing. Most importantly, though, the poem both elaborates and retracts the phrase "necessary murder" by expanding it. In a sense, Auden explains what he meant to say without making the explanation into an excuse for what he recognized in hindsight as an error: "Muse of Time, but for whose merciful silence / Only the first step would count and that / Would always be murder" (*HC* 17). This oddly hyperbolic pronouncement—who would have expected the word "murder" at this moment in the poem?—discloses the horror inherent in the "Laxey Wheel," and by extension, the confusion of historical time with natural or mechanical processes. Whenever motive is confused with cause, the events that follow from any given "step" are necessary—including "the fact of murder." The opposite of "necessary murder" is forgiveness, which always begins anew and must be freely given. Near the end of "Homage to Clio," a conclusive distinction is made between the "Major Powers" and Clio, the silent third sister. Turning to her alone, he makes a request: "forgive our noises." The possibility of forgiveness distinguishes her from Aphrodite; the "noise" for which we are to be forgiven goes beyond the rumblings of Artemis' children and even beyond the poem itself, insofar as it, too, is "noise," and includes the "youthful noise" (*CSP* 16) that, in Auden's view, characterized the rhetoric of "Spain."[51] In the act of forgiveness the past is not forgotten; but remembrance does not require a "one-eye-for-one" recompense and is therefore free—again, not free to make up what actually happened but free to connect singular facts with singular facts in an "obedient," thus responsible, manner. Auden thus adds a second appeal to Clio consistent with his request for forgiveness: "And teach us our recollections."

According to the scenario proposed by Nietzsche at the beginning of his essay on history in *Thoughts out of Season*, a "leaf" of memory flits by, causing us to lose the happiness that characterizes the non-historical lives of animals. Auden appropriately changes the leaf to a book, which does not read itself but must always be interpreted. In Auden's concluding essay on Freud, he is emphatic about the essential historiographical distinction between motive and cause. In "Homage to Clio" he goes so far as to suggest that the source of this distinction lies in the interpretable character of memory, which expresses itself in the concept of recollection: if the past metamorphosized into a leaf that somehow remains in the present, then the nexus of cause and effect would be unbreakable. At stake in the final stanzas of "Homage to Clio" is the temporal structure as a whole. It is for this reason that the poet ultimately identifies Clio, against a long tradition, with the "Muse of Time." Obedience to the newly named muse is a music-like finding of the time—not compliance with supposed laws of historical movement. As he writes in his review of Camus, "since history is something man *makes*, it is meaningless to talk of *obeying* it" (*Prose* 3:501). Clio is asked to "teach us our recollections" so that these recollections are understood to be teachable in the first place, that is, we learn that the backward perspective of memory, which interprets past events as causes, tends to forget that each action could have been otherwise. And to the extent that we can learn from our recollections, the past is not a closed book, but open, as is the book the poet holds in his hand at the beginning of the poem. The word *recollection* contains the word *collection* and may be read as the volumes of collected poetry through which Auden "re-collects," "forgives," and "throws away" his earlier poems. The book the poet holds at the opening of "Homage to Clio" is thus presumably his own book, a book of poems he has written, which, however, he must still learn to re-collect.[52] In the section of *The Faber Book of Aphorisms* devoted to "History," Auden quotes one of Nietzsche's very last reflections: "By seeking after origins, one becomes a crab. The historian looks backwards; eventually he also *believes* backwards" (*FBA* 238).[53] The final appeal to Clio in the poem Auden wrote in her honor can be understood accordingly: make me a historian but keep me from this dreadful "eventually."

FIVE

From Poem to Volume

Three Clios, Each Radically Different from the Others

Even as "Homage to Clio" represents a poetic summation of Auden's long and intensive reflections on history, its final lines express a palpable sense of hesitation. The poet and the muse do not, so to speak, see eye to eye: "I dare not ask you if you bless the poets, / For you do not look as if you ever read them / Nor can I see a reason why you should." Every aspect of this conclusion is puzzling, including its flattened tone. Auden declines to ask for her blessing because Clio does not appear to him to be a reader of poetry. Yet the function of the traditional muses in relation to the artists whom they inspire does not require that they be acquainted with the works those artists have hitherto produced. Even the reference to reading is puzzling, since reading the work of those they inspire is not a role conventionally associated with the muses. By projecting in the final lines of the poem a Clio who is disinclined to read his work, Auden paradoxically links her to the animals whom he describes in the opening, for whom "My book is dead" (*HC* 15). Stranger still is the premise of the final lines of "Homage to Clio": the poet seems at last to have grasped an image of the elusive muse, but instead of presenting it in positive terms, he draws only a negative conclusion, which is itself shrouded in doubt. Are there reasons for Clio to read poetry, even if the poet cannot see them? Could a historian discover a reason? And how do things stand with respect to Auden and the muse of history? There is a comic quality to such questions, of course, which derives from the fictive status of Clio, whose uncertain regard for poets is a product of the poet's imagination. Clio's character is as enigmatic at the end of the poem as it was in its beginning. Who is she, after all?

The name *Clio* first appears in Auden's poetry in his previous volume, *The Shield of Achilles*, specifically in "Plains," where, contrary to her appearance in "Homage to Clio," she consorts with a Napoleon-like emperor: "Born as a rule in some small place (an island, / Quite often, where a smart lad can spot the bluff / Whence cannon would put the harbor at his mercy), / Though it is here they chamber with Clio" (*SA* 26). Beyond the two designations conferred on Clio in "Homage to Clio"—"Muse of the unique / Historical fact" and "Muse of time"—she acquires a number of other roles throughout the like-named volume. A Clio akin to the one named in "Plains" reappears in a poem included in Part 1 of *Homage to Clio*, "T the Great," which concerns the fourteenth-century warrior, Timur or Tamburlaine, whose name, having fallen into oblivion, "cannot win Clio's cup again" (*HC* 33). And the final stanza of the poem immediately preceding "T the Great," "The Makers of History," presents Clio as an altogether different muse:

> Clio loves those who bred them better horses,
> Found answers to their questions, made their things,
> Even those fulsome
> Bards they boarded: but these mere commanders
> Like boys in pimple-time, like girls at awkward ages,
> What did they do but wish? (*HC* 31).

The volume entitled *Homage to Clio* thus contains three versions of the muse, each of whom is the very opposite of the other two: first, there is a Clio who, while distinct from her sisters, the "Major Powers," appears to be uninterested in poetry ("Homage to Clio"); then, in reverse, there emerges a Clio who, scorning military leaders, loves only "poets" in the original Greek sense of the word *poiēsis* ("The Makers of History");[1] finally, in yet another reversal, there is now a Clio who would honor military conquest if only it would be repeated ("T the Great"). This is a strange situation that directly affects the sense of the title Auden assigned his volume of poetry. To which of the three Clios does he pay homage? In "Homage to Clio" there is doubtless some obscurity, insofar as the representation of Clio cannot be secured in the form of a monument; but there is no ambiguity concerning the muse whom the poem honors. In the volume, by contrast, the diversity of Clios makes the object of homage ambiguous in the extreme, for each of the figurations of the muse contradicts the others. The complex of contradictions reaches a crescendo in "The Makers of History," the last stanza of which self-reflectively rescinds the final, flattened lines of "Homage to Clio" insofar as it makes the muse of history into the lover of "poets" in general and "fulsome / Bards" in particular.

The ambiguity of the muse's functions comes to characterize the figure of the poet as well: does the "even" in these lines indicate that Clio loves all makers, "even" poets, who would be the last and perhaps the least of the makers, or does the "even" suggest that it is *precisely* "fulsome / Bards" who gain her favor, while other kinds of poets, understood as "makers" do not? This question immediately raises another: where does Auden stand in relation to the fulsomeness of the bards? One sense of the word, namely smelliness, recalls the opening of "Homage to Clio," where the poet recognizes that, from the perspective of animals, he is "an inedible patch / Of unsatisfactory smell." The Clio of "The Makers of History" would be the opposite of the animals, for she would find his malodorous "fulsomeness" satisfying. *Fulsomeness*, however, also means "extravagance," above all extravagance in praise, including presumably praise of Clio herself—at which point the density of self-reflexive contradictions becomes vertiginous, as the second Clio of the volume would then be said to love the poet for the extravagance of the homage he pays to the first Clio, who is as little interested in him as are noisy insects. If it were permitted to give stage directions for a volume of poetry, at the point where Auden writes "even those fulsome / Bards," one might add in bracketed italics, "peals of laughter," for it is here that the tense relation of poet to muse in the final lines of "Homage to Clio" bursts into comic absurdity. Instead of stage directions, Auden adds "T the Great," itself structured as a joke, wherein Clio returns full circle to her original function, attested to in "Plains," of consorting with military commanders. After this, the name *Clio* is never mentioned again in *Homage to Clio*—nor indeed in any of Auden's subsequent poetry.

The tension between the figure of Clio in "The Makers of History" and in "T the Great" is reflected in the structure of *Homage to Clio* as a whole, where the first poem, "Homage to Clio," stands in contrast to the poems in its appendix, "Academic Graffiti." To the seriousness and pathos of the former, which refers by name to no historical figure, there stands the playful, often stinging clerihews about famous historical figures arranged in alphabetical order. The laughter generated by some of the poems in *Homage to Clio* does not make the figure of Clio in the title poem any less compelling; rather, their boisterous humor—in combination with the variety of contradictory Clios—indicates that, for Auden, the absence of any resolution of the problematic relation between history and poetry is not a source of lament. By naming the volume after its first poem, Auden stresses that the title poem is only a beginning, not a conclusion, much less a solution to the problem to which the title alludes: poetry, for Auden, affirms Being and is thus always an homage in a certain sense; Clio at once belongs to Being, since history is distinguished from fantasy by virtue of its facticity; yet as a version of Becoming, historical facts cannot simply be affirmed, since such affirmation would suggest that "all is well with the world" or even "all's for the best in this best of all possible worlds."[2] The specter of *Candide* haunts the very idea of an "homage to Clio." The poet who wrote "Voltaire at Ferney" is aware of this danger—but also does not shy away from it. "Homage to Clio" reveals a poet who recognizes that, by remaining a poet, his relation to history is always tenuous; *Homage to Clio* displays versions of this tension from beginning to end.

Another Kind of Silence

Just as "Homage to Clio" begins with the noises of animals, so does "Reflections in a Forest." In both poems, noise is contrasted with stillness: Auden's own stillness, in the first poem; the immobility of the trees, in the second. It is as though Auden returns to the setting with which "Homage to Clio" begins, altering the landscape from meadow to woods, repeating his disapproval of animal language, and reflecting on the mimetic impulse that makes him wish that he were even stiller than before:

> Within a shadowland of trees
> Whose lives are so uprightly led
> In nude august communities,
> To move about seems underbred
>
> And common any taste for words;
> When, thoughtlessly, they took to song,
> Whatever one may think of birds,
> The example that they set was wrong. (*HC* 7)

Auden is perhaps playing with the etymological connection between *tree* and *truth*, which is presumably rooted in an archaic conviction that truth is like trees because both are unyielding, steadfast, and thus trustworthy. The truthful character of trees is reinforced by their combination of nudity and uprightness, which Auden also emphasizes in the first stanza, as he distinguishes their "august communities" from human societies, like the Roman Empire, where an Augustus is, as Octavian designated himself, "princeps." But "Reflections in a Forest" does not become an homage to arboreal majesty. Nor does the poem celebrate natural steadfastness as opposed to human wandering. The four-by-four regularity of rhyming iambic tetrameter quatrains both suggests a straightforward honesty and, at the same time, reveals the limits to that honesty; the poem is, after all, written in one of the hymn meters, which associates it with a bird's song. And in using the term "reflections," Auden moves in two directions at once. The natural world is seen as a mirror, from whose perspective he sees himself; instead of yielding to a mimetic impulse that would make him as still as the trees, however, he breaks free in reflections that are characterized by negation and, indeed, by a negation of his own disapproval of song in the midst of the forest. This is, in a sense, the drama of this quiet poem. The opening lines allude to the beginning of the *Inferno*, but the subsequent poem moves in a different direction. Whereas Dante finds himself in a forest "because the straight path had been lost," Auden celebrates the very possibility of deviousness, thereby suggesting that the opposite, a life dedicated solely to "la diritta via," opens onto hell.³

If "Reflections in a Forest" acquired a subtitle, it would perhaps read: "On Conditions Encouraging Quietism." Auden is hiding nothing in this regard, for he goes in search of what makes it possible for the trees to maintain their "posture" and "social ease" and discovers that it derives from their particular language, which includes no terms for negation and thus affords no possibility of standing against the status quo:

> In keeping still, in staying slow,
> For posture and for social ease,
> How much these living statues owe
> Their scent-and-color languages.
>
> For who can quarrel without terms
> For Not or Never, who can raise
> Objections when what one affirms
> Is necessarily the case? (*HC* 7)

According to the famous first proposition of Wittgenstein's *Tractatus Logico-Philosophicus*, "The world is all that is the case."⁴ Whenever Auden invokes the *Tractatus* and its associated notebooks in his late prose writings, hell is never far away. Under the subtitle "Infernal Science" in a section of *The Dyer's Hand* entitled "The Shakespearean City," Auden begins with a passage from Wittgenstein's early notebooks and directs attention to one of the last propositions in the *Tractatus*: "Ethics does not treat of the world. Ethics must be a condition of the world, like logic," to which Auden immediately adds, "On this God and the Evil One are agreed" (*Prose* 4:643).⁵ The same proposition begins the section of Auden's "autobiography," *A Certain World*, bearing the title "Hell."⁶ And, then again, in a discussion of anger, which culminates in the following statement about the Wrath of God: "If there are any souls in Hell, it is not because they have been sent there, but because Hell is where they insist upon being" (*Prose* 4:390; cf. *CW* 180). In the same vein, Auden quotes Walter Savage Landor's observation about the *Inferno*: "its inhabitants do not want to get out" (*Prose* 3:154). In "Reflections in a Forest" Auden draws a direct consequence from the absence of "no" in the language of trees and their upstanding comportment. Not only are they where want to be; but they are each paradoxically incapable of growth, here understood as historical change:

> My chance of growing would be slim,
> Were I with wooden honesty
> To show my hand or heart to Him
> Who will, if I should lose, be Me. (*HC* 8)

A situation akin to the Cretan Liar's paradox thus arises, as the poet distinguishes himself from the trees to whose silence he was initially attracted. It is not as though "Reflections in a Forest" simply declares its falseness along the lines of the Cretan who says of Cretans that they are all liars; but the poet presents deceptiveness as a condition for the possibility of a "growth" that is different from natural growth, above all, because it cannot be measured in "tree" terms—that is, in terms of demonstrable straightness and uprightness. Here, then, is the poem's center of gravity: in reflecting on the tall trees, which are reminiscent of the "Tall Sisters," Auden discovers that the "chance for growth" outweighs whatever counts as perceptible progress—and this chance depends on a language of negation, opposition, duplicity, and ultimately "bluff":

> Our race would not have gotten far,
> Had we not learned to bluff it out
> And look more certain than we are
> Of what our motion is about (*HC* 8)

Just as "Homage to Clio" represents a summation of Auden's reflections on history, so "Reflections in a Forest" can be viewed as a recapitulation of his often-formulated affirmation of the value and even the virtue of crookedness.[7] For Dante, the departure from the straight path leads him to the "obscure woods" where he discovers the entrance to hell. Auden, by contrast, discovers that the "shadowland of darkness" derives from a condition of unreflective straightness in which unquestioned self-identity reinforces communal conformity: "trees are trees, an elm or oak / Already both outside and in." Unlike Dante, Auden does not explicitly come across the entrance to hell; instead, without any warning, the specter of police interrogation suddenly enters the poet's consciousness at the precise point when his thoughts on the value of bluffing give way to a reflection on finding himself in the "buff":

> Nor need one be a cop to find
> Undressing before others rude:
> The most ascetic of our kind
> Look naked in the buff, not nude. (*HC* 8)

The "cop" appears, of course, under the characteristic sign of negation; but in this case, negation suggests the Freudian concept of denegation: one "need" not be a cop, but the police nevertheless present themselves to consciousness as soon as reflection turns to a version of nakedness that extends beyond the "face to face" encounter described in the previous poem of the volume. "Crook" was one of Auden's names for queerness, and "Reflections in a Forest" is an affirmation of the double sense of "crook(ed)-ness" that corresponds to the poem's double consciousness, which itself recalls the allegorical character of the "selva oscura" where Dante discovers the entrance to the inferno. To be sure, the poet simply finds himself in a forest, where trees are just trees, wholly identical to themselves, regardless of what they are called; but for the same reason, upon reflection, the poet also finds himself in a social situation, marked by the specter of police interrogation, and the trees represent an un-reflective conformity that serves a definite purpose, namely "For posture and social ease."[8]

From Makers to Epigoni

As with "Homage to Clio," "Reflections in a Forest" makes no mention of actual historical events. Within the context of *Homage to Clio*, this happens first with "Hands," the poem that follows "Reflections in a Forest." "Hands," however, makes such mentions only in negative terms, as "busybodies" show no sign of regret for "the Fall of the Roman Empire" or the arguments voiced by "Trinitarian, Arian, Gnostic lips" (*HC* 20). Four successive poems in the first part of the volume then specifically revolve around discrete historical figures and events: "Makers of History," "T the Great," "Secondary Epic," and "The Epigoni." These poems are organized in pairs, with "Makers of History" and "T the Great" disagreeing about Clio's character, and "Secondary Epic" and "The Epigoni" interrogating the first and last poets of the Roman Empire in the West. "Makers of History" initiates this ensemble of poems by negating the final stanza of "Homage to Clio," where the poet expresses doubt about his relation to the muse he honors. According to "Makers of History," all those who stand under the aegis of "Greatness" become indistinguishable from one another, insofar they are all "re-iterations of one self-importance." History is here contrasted with legend: whereas the former is dedicated toward the articulation of distinction, the latter "melts" would-be conquerors "into one / Composite demi-god." And just as "serious historians care for coins and weapons"—this is the opening line of the poem—so Clio, as their muse, is unconcerned with "mere commanders," who do not themselves make things, least of all the coins and weapons that are issued under their names. The end of the poem thus traces back to its beginning, contrasting the commanders of history with the makers of history and summarizing the dubious achievements of the so-called greats with a question: "What did they do but wish?"

The apparently rhetorical question that concludes "Makers of History" is pointedly answered by the following poem, "T the Great." For the "T" in question, Tamburlaine, is a "mere commander," who, far from making anything, subtracts from the world: eliminating the lives of all who stand in his way and the very blades of grass on which they stood. And this subtraction is ironically expressed in the "T" that stands for his name: "A synonym in a whole armful / Of languages for what is harmful" (*HC* 32). As a synonym, "T" is interchangeable with other commanders defined by their "military success"; thus "T," who comes from the East, can then be replaced by an "N," who comes from the North, who is then "replaced by S." And like the terrifying "T" before him nevertheless assumes over time the "ineffective" function or "job" of scaring children: "And T was pushed off to the nursery / Before his hundredth anniversary // To play the bogey man who comes / To naughty boys who suck their thumbs" (*HC* 33). Subtracted in this way from history—with the exception of "Some scholars," who hesitate to discuss obscure figures for fear such arcana will be "unpopular"—"T" is further diminished into a random arrangement of letters without relevance, thus an entry into a dictionary or encyclopedia that is useful to know only when one does anagrammatic crossword puzzles: "11 Down—A NUBILE TRAM" (*HC* 33). "T the Great" is especially remarkable because the grimness of T's destructiveness contrasts so sharply with the intricately constructed gleefulness of the verse, where lilting couplets often rhyme two and even three syllables. Reminiscent of some earlier poems with a similar contrast between gruesome content and comic form, such as "Victor," "Miss Gee," and "James Honeyman," "T the Great" remains distinct from these Brechtian-inflected ballads insofar as it declines to say anything about the autobiography of "T" beyond its opening lines: "Begot like other children, he / Was known among his kin as T" (*HC* 32).

Whereas the temporal situation of "T the Great" reflects on a historical figure from a perspective in which the circumstances of his putative greatness have largely been forgotten, "Secondary Epic" issues a plea to a well-remembered poet (it is Virgil, of course) that he reconsider those lines of his epic that eternalize the greatness of the emperor whom he serves. For this reason, the first and last stanzas of Auden's poem begin with the injunction, "No, Virgil, no."[9] Thus does "Secondary Epic" practice what Auden praises in "Reflections in a Forest": negation. It is not that Auden denies the extraordinary achievement of the *Aeneid*, but its value is tainted by Virgil's betrayal of the very sense for history that he helped initiate. Auden recognizes that the most renowned of Latin poets achieved something unknown to his Greek predecessors. In his review of Rolfe Humphries' translation of the *Aeneid*, Auden describes the immense debt owed to its author in disclosing the concept of history as shaped by the decisions that individuals make, thus creating a new reality for which they themselves—not the gods, not nature, not fate— are responsible:

If . . . we are not completely pessimistic about the human enterprise, if we have any faith that historical decisions are meaningful, that we are not merely the puppets of chance and immediate self-interest, that a just and peaceful world is a possibility, admittedly remote, which it is our duty to try to realize, we owe that faith as much to Virgil as to anyone or anything else. To imagine a world in which that hope has not yet been born, one has only to go back to Homer and hear, for instance, Achilles speaking to Priam, who has come to beg the body of Hector. "Here, far from home, I sit in Troy, afflicting you and your children." Why? For no reason. That is how things are. (*Prose* 3:243)

In contrast to Homer, Virgil wants heroic action to mean something beyond the tautological affirmation of its own heroism. Nevertheless, as Auden further explains—and this is the source of the repeated negation with which "Secondary Epic" begins—a grave flaw traverses Virgil's understanding of history, in which hindsight can be transformed into foresight.

Virgil's *Aeneid*, for Auden, is doubly "secondary": it is modeled on the Homeric epics, and it makes itself accessory to the imperial regime it intends to glorify. As soon becomes apparent, moreover, the double secondariness of Virgil's epic is crystallized in its depiction of Aeneas' shield, which is, of course, modeled on Homer's description of the shield of Achilles, but which has an altogether different intentional structure.[10] The shield of Aeneas is different from its model—but not different enough. Hence, the imploring, almost personal quality of "No, Virgil, no," which presents Virgil as a contemporary of Auden's at the very moment in which he is being chastened for misunderstanding the nature of historical time. The urgency of the poetic voice that sets "Secondary Epic" into motion derives from the realization that Virgil has detached himself from his Greek predecessor and is therefore prepared to do something new. More precisely, heroic action is on the verge of being directed toward a goal beyond its own self-assertion. In this way, the epic could have become equal with its author's "faith" in history. Auden's review of the translation of the *Aeneid* is not ultimately in conflict with "Secondary Epic," even if the latter plunges its readers *in medias res*—where the *res* in this case is the eighth book of the *Aeneid*—while the former rejects the widespread depiction of its author as "State Bard," a depiction summarized, as Auden notes, in Ezra Pound's malicious epithet: "a Tennysonized Homer" (*Prose* 3:242). But Virgil forecloses the novelty of his ekphrasis by enclosing the history displayed on the shield of Aeneas within a teleological framework that repeats in the figuration of his own civilization what Homer reserves for exceptional individuals. For Homer, heroic action only reaffirms the superlative quality of the hero whom the poet glorifies; for Virgil, to Auden's dismay, the heroic action similarly reaffirms the superlative quality of "an Age of Gold" in which the poet produces his epic:

> No, Virgil, no:
> Not even the first of the Romans can learn
> His Roman history in the future tense,
> Not even to serve your political turn:
> Hindsight as foresight makes no sense. (*HC* 26)

These opening lines of "Secondary Epic" resonate with the untitled, four-line poem that prefaces the first part of *Homage to Clio*, which can be understood to refer to an event contemporaneous with the founding of the Roman Empire:

> Between those happenings that prefigure it
> And those that happen in its anamnesis
> Occurs the Event, but that no human wit
> Can recognize until all happening ceases. (*HC* 13)

Virgil can justify his glorification of the Empire founded by Augustus only under the condition that it represents the cessation of all "happening," at which point hindsight and foresight finally converge. In the absence of this eschatological moment, hindsight functions as foresight only when foresight is massively shortsighted. Virgil can see nothing beyond the present moment, which Auden designates as "31 B.C." (*HC* 26). Without indicating what distinguishes the abbreviation "B.C." from those like "T" and "N" in the previous poem—here is the place for a form of silence that is not marked as such—Auden admonishes Virgil for failing to create an Aeneas who has sufficient "human wit" to ask the question that governs all narrative: "What next?" (*HC* 34).

In the final stanza of "Secondary Epic," which begins with the repetition of its opening line, Auden recapitulates his reflections on history. The last appearance of the name "Clio" in *Homage to Clio*—and all of Auden's collected poetry—occurs near the end of "T the Great." But a weak figuration of the muse whose name first emerged in late antiquity is perhaps palpable one last time in the final stanza of "Secondary Epic," where an unnamed Muse does not speak through a poet but is, rather, overheard by a "we" whom the poet similarly declines to identify. The perception of the precise moment in which a muse is betrayed becomes an integral—both disturbing and amusing—element of Auden's collection of poems in honor of the muse of history. The moment of betrayal occurs when the poet introduces a "shade" who foretells the future that stops with the poet's glorification of the present. Here, responsive to a muse who has fallen silent, Auden correspondingly implores the poet to stop:

> No, Virgil, no:
> Behind your verse so masterfully made
> We hear the weeping of a Muse betrayed.
> Your Anchises isn't convincing at all;
> It's asking too much of us to be told
> A shade so long-sighted, a father who knows
> That Romulus will build a wall,
> Augustus found an Age of Gold,
> And is trying to teach a dutiful son
> The love of what will be in the long run,
> Would mention them both but not disclose
> (Surely, no prophet could afford to miss
> No man of destiny fail to enjoy
> So clear a proof of Providence as this)
> The names predestined for the Catholic boy
> Whom Arian Odovacer will depose. (*HC* 27–28)

Just as "T the Great" concludes with reference to a crossword puzzle, so "Secondary Epic" ends with a question best suited for connoisseurs of trivia: What is the name of the last, pitiful ruler of the Western Roman Empire? In hindsight, the missing name, "Romulus Augustus," is obviously ironic, for it combines the legendary name of the founder of Rome with the acquired name of the founder of the Empire. Equally ironic is the absence of the word *Christian* in a description of the violent struggle between Catholicism and Arianism for ideological supremacy. To the extent that he exists in the poem, "the Christ" is there only in the historical abbreviation, "B.C." The comic character of "Secondary Epic" does not so much stem from the smug delight a reader may experience in knowing the name of the last Western Roman emperor, as from the concluding suggestion that a "man of destiny" would enjoy hearing about the collapse of the regime he is in the process of founding. Providence—as the Latinate version of *foresight*, implicitly combined with hindsight—has the quality of a cosmic joke, for heroic action is pointless.

In the radio broadcast from 1955 that would become the basis for *The Dyer's Hand*, Auden offered an interpretation of the legend that Virgil himself said may have betrayed the muse who inspired Homer: "the pathos of Hector's death is simple; the noble character is slain: the pathos of Turnus' death is ironic; he is a more sympathetic character than Aeneas, but he is slain defending the wrong cause. It is better for the future of the world that Aeneas should win. Perhaps it is just this historical element which prompted Virgil's supposed remark that he was working against the Muse" (*Prose* 3:540). "Secondary Epic" expands and transforms this same remark by showing how Virgil betrays, instead, the muse of history. Homer, for his part, could not have betrayed her, since she was never his muse in the first place. The greatness of his Roman successor, as Auden explains in his review of the Humphries translation, lies in his transformation of the epic tradition to a point where it no longer precludes the idea of hope. Hope is directly opposed to providence—not because hope is blind but because it does not blur the distinction between hindsight and foresight. At the decisive moment in which the Latin poet revises the image of the heroic shield and is thus in a position to produce not a secondary epic but a genuinely historical one—inspired perhaps by Clio rather than Calliope—he denies his own insight, opening the space for a never-ending "interpolation" that begins and ends with ellipses marking endless cycles of war.

"The Epigoni" follows "Secondary Epic" in *Homage to Clio* for two corresponding reasons: the epigoni are the successors to Virgil, who are either unable or disinclined to write major poems about their experience in the late days of the Western Roman Empire; and "The Epigoni" begins with a further negation—beyond "No, Virgil, no"—in which the absence of the gods is the condition of their poetic productivity: "No use invoking Apollo in a case like theirs; / The pleasure-loving gods had died in their chairs" (*HC* 36). The absence of the Apollonian realm, in turn, can be understood in two alternative ways, for it is both the absence of inspiration, which expresses itself in the aesthetic poverty of epigonic poetry, and the absence of the ancient Latin pantheon without the presence of the new Christian one. Along with adopting the Wittgenstein-inflected term "case" from "Reflections in a Forest," the opening lines of "The Epigoni" represent the counterpoint to the final line of "Homage to Clio." In the first poem of the volume, the muse of history has no reason to read poetry, whereas in "The Epigoni" only a historian—more exactly, a historian of the late Western Empire who is concerned with its literary culture—bothers with the poetry in question.[11] If any poetry can be called purely historical, it is that of the epigoni, for it means even less to the contemporary world than it did to the decaying civilization in which the last poets of the Western Roman Empire lived:

> It would have been an excusable failing
> Had they broken out into womanish wailing
> Or, dramatizing their doom, held forth
> In sonorous clap-trap about death;
> To their credit, a reader will only perceive
> That the language they loved was coming to grief,
> Expiring in preposterous mechanical tricks,
> Epanaleptics, rhopalics, anacyclic acrostics:
> To their lasting honor, the stuff they wrote
> Can safely be spanked in a scholar's footnote,
> Called shallow by a mechanized generation to whom
> Haphazard oracular grunts are profound wisdom. (*HC* 29)

"The Epigoni" is an homage to a purely historical poetry, which ironically acquires topicality by the manner in which it turns away from the events of its own times. Without repudiating Virgil, his successors nevertheless do not reiterate the closed conception of history that expresses itself in the description of the shield of Aeneas. Beyond the pleasure principle associated with Apollo lies, according to Freud, the "repetition compulsion" that ambiguously signals the operation of the death drive.[12] And the epigoni, whose name already indicates a repetitive quality, are fully under the sway of the compulsion to repeat. It finds expression in epanaleptics, in which a word or phrase at the beginning of a clause or line is repeated at the end of the line after an intervening word or succession of words. The palindromic repetition of anacyclic verse testifies to the same compulsion, and the idea of living spirit can be said to expire in acrostics, where the bare letter, devoid of independent meaning, provides the primary principle of composition. But instead of treating the theme of death, whether it be their own or that of their civilization, the Latin poets of the late Western Empire grant insight into the death of their language and thus indirectly into their own deaths as poets and the demise of classical civilization in general.

It is not, however, as though the epigoni engage in a strategy of indirection, nor do they attempt to show the death drive rather than say something about it; rather, the death of their language becomes perceptible to the "reader," who, unlike the "scholar," does not evaluate the cultural position of the epigoni but, instead, as the designation suggests, only reads their poems. The act of reading requires the identification of the poems' formal features, which consist in highly regularized and endlessly repeatable "mechanical tricks." The untimely character of these "tricks" is already apparent in the term by which Auden qualifies them: "preposterous," which means "before-behind." Like the "Laxey Wheel," mechanical language marks the time. A rhopalic, for instance, is a series of words built on a principle of systematic sequential accretion (either by a single letter or single syllable in each successive word): every line thus tells the time without saying anything about the times. The result is "stuff," a synonym for *matter*, which exhibits formalism for its own sake. Thus, in accordance with the schema of dialectical reversal, form becomes matter.

But Auden decisively rejects a similar dialectical formulation, in which the epigoni would themselves become as thoroughly mechanized as their language. It is not the poets who are mechanized but, rather, the members of a "generation" that is incapable of distinguishing between the highly articulated language of poetry and inarticulate grunts. The language of the epigoni, although doomed to die, keeps their work from the shallowness of "profound wisdom." Even if the poetry of the epigoni does not advance beyond the impasse Auden identifies in "Secondary Epic," which sees the Roman Empire as the unsurpassable horizon of civilization, the fact that they celebrate language distinguishes them directly from the "mechanized generation" and more distantly from the trees, whose "scent-and-color languages" allow for variation but reserve no place for the "No" with which this poem, like its predecessor in the volume, begins.

From a Complaint About Goethe to an Unwritten Poem

Of the three major parts of *Homage to Clio* (Part 1, Interlude, and Part 2), only the Interlude has a title and subtitle: "Dichtung und Wahrheit (An Unwritten Poem)." Auden borrows the title from Goethe, who subtitled his own autobiographical reflections "Dichtung und Wahrheit." A certain secondary, even epigonic quality thus appears in the title—as though the relation between Goethe and Auden were akin to the relation between Homer and Virgil, or perhaps Virgil and later Latin poets. But there is a difference—perhaps even a "profound" difference—between Goethe's and Auden's "Dichtung und Wahrheit." It is not simply that the latter is a relatively brief set of numbered reflections, whereas the former is a long, rather disjointed complex of self-referential narratives. No, the essential difference between the two versions of "Dichtung und Wahrheit" is that Auden's is not concerned with the poet's past but is, instead, oriented primarily toward his future: "Expecting your arrival tomorrow," Auden writes in the first of the fifty aphorisms, or fragments, "I find myself thinking *I love You:* then comes the thought:—*I should like to write a poem which would express exactly what I mean when I think these words*" (*HC* 41). As Auden proceeds to explain, he does not want his poem simply to be good and genuine: "if it is to satisfy me, it must also be true." Hence the title of the Interlude, which can be translated into English as "poetry and truth" or, perhaps better, "fictionality and truth."

A more precise relation between Goethe's and Auden's versions of "Dichtung und Wahrheit"—and thus the appearance of a German-language title in a book of English-language poetry—would require a study of its own; but a brief description can still outline the manner in which Auden conceives of his German predecessor. An index of Auden's appreciation of Goethe's achievements can be found in the following lines from "The Cave of Making" from the early 1960s: "I should like to become, if possible, / a minor atlantic Goethe, / With his passion for weather and stones, but without his silliness / re the Cross" (*CP*, 692).[13] As for an example of his critical attitude toward Goethe, one of the clerihews in "Academic Graffiti," the section that concludes *Homage to Clio*, is perhaps sufficient:

> The Geheimrat in Goethe
> Made him all the curter
> With Leute who were leery
> Of his Color Theory. (*HC* 86)

Goethe did not simply happen to become a Geheimrat ("privy council") in a small German state; as the clerihew notes, the Geheimrat function lies "in" him, making it impossible for him to accept criticism of any kind, even if it concerns matters of natural science.[14] And this criticism of Goethe's inability to abide criticism is complemented by a complaint Auden expresses succinctly in a later poem, fittingly entitled "To Goethe: A Complaint":

> How wonderfully your songs begin
> With praise of Nature and her beauty,
> But then, as if it were a duty,
> You drag some god-damned sweetheart in.
> Did you imagine she'd be flattered?
> They never sound as if they mattered. (*CP* 718)[15]

The poem Auden proposes to write in "Dichtung und Wahrheit" is exactly the opposite of the love poems criticized in "To Goethe." Auden's intended poem is oriented solely toward the "you" whom the "I" loves. The project of writing a poem that would perfectly capture the thought and feeling of one's own "I" loving a singular "you" can be understood, in part, as an outcome and extension of the last poem in Part 1 of *Homage to Clio*, which immediately precedes the Interlude, "The More Loving One." Set in a cosmic order, the poem explores the relation of poetic artifice to the absence of love. Auden draws on a common trope of love's magnificence—the eternal splendor and perfection of heavenly bodies—but recasts the readily identifiable hyperbole in colloquial language that arrives at the precise opposite of celestial love: "Looking up at the stars I know quite well / That for all they care, I can go to hell" (*HC* 38). The poet's knowledge is not, however, a hard-earned truth born of poetic disenchantment, but the projection of a perfectly poetic and poetizing imagination that grants subjectivity to stellar beings. Although the conditional mood of the subsequent verse makes it clear that the poet recognizes the irreality of representing stars as conscious subjects capable of love, the reversal that occurs in the next stanza—where the poet becomes the subject rather than the object of love—registers an awareness of how expressions of love can falter. Nevertheless, the reversal accomplishes nothing beyond this bleak awareness: "Admirer as I think I am / Of stars that do not give a damn / I cannot, now I see them, say, / I missed one terribly all day" (*HC* 38). However much the colloquial turns of phrase may suggest a rejection of the grand exaggerations of love poetry; and however much the recognition of the indifference of stars as both subjects and objects of love (they neither care nor matter) may seem a sober assessment of the "true" dynamics of affection, "The More Loving One" is still a self-consciously poetic artifact, unable to move any closer to the truth of love where the "I" and the "you" are both singular individuals who enter into an equally singular relation. Even as its four-by-four stanzas of rhyming couplets suggest a resounding linkage, the question remains whether such a harmonious relationship of total uniqueness can become a linguistic construct.

Just as the title of "Dichtung und Wahrheit" is borrowed, so, too, is its form. Speaking of *The Enchafèd Flood*, Auden once said that he wanted to create a work of reflection that rivaled Heidegger's in terms of its difficulty.[16] Auden's "Dichtung und Wahrheit" goes in the opposite direction: eminently readable, though indisputably indebted to philosophical grammar, its model is not *Sein und Zeit*, nor even the *Tractatus*, which is even denser than Heidegger's philosophical works, but rather Wittgenstein's *Philosophische Untersuchungen* (*Philosophical Investigations*), especially as they were reflected in the work of the mid-twentieth century "Ordinary Language Philosophers" in Oxford and Cambridge. Like *Homage to Clio*, *Philosophical Investigations* is divided into two sections, likewise called Part I and Part II. The opening pages of the former describe a "language game" that Wittgenstein—without any explicit autobiographical or, indeed, historical intention—derives from Augustine's *Confessions*: "Let us imagine a language for which the description given by Augustine [of language learning in the first book of his *Confessions*] is right. The language is meant to serve for communication between a builder A and an assistant B. A is building with building-stones: there are blocks, pillars, slabs and beams. . . . For this purpose they use a language consisting of the words 'block', 'pillar', 'slab', beam.' A calls them out;—B brings the stone which he has learnt to bring at such-and-such a call."[17] The scenario Wittgenstein imagines is different in many respects from the one with which Auden begins "Dichtung und Wahrheit," but they have one essential point in common: both the poet and "A" are seeking to construct something—a building in the first case, a poem in the second. There is failure, too, in each of the two scenarios: Augustine's account of language learning is shown to be insufficient, insofar as it accounts for only one "language game," and Auden's poem, for its part, remains unwritten.

Auden's path in the reflections that comprise "Dichtung und Wahrheit" expands Wittgenstein's critique of modern thought. As explained in the fourth paragraph, Auden can achieve his goal of expressing precisely what he means by "I love you" only under the condition that the utterance attain the same epistemic status as the Cartesian cogito: "It would not be enough that I should believe that what I had written was true: to satisfy me, the truth of the poem must be self-evident. It would have to be written, for example, in such a way that no reader could misread *I love You* as 'I love you'" (*HC* 35–36). Auden, in other words, is seeking a double truth of poetry: not only must it be true in the conventional sense that it accurately represent reality, but it must be true in the same sense that the famous Cartesian utterance "Ego sum, ego existo" as the foundation of modern thought is held to be true: the formulation of the utterance in the privacy of one's own mind, regardless of what it supposedly represents, makes it true; it verifies itself. And so Auden's project consists in creating a poetic equivalent to "Ego sum" but includes an object—the irreplaceable "you" whom he loves—that remains in principle and in fact irreducible to his state of consciousness. To this end, Auden distinguishes among cogito states, each of which has its own intentional structure, depending on its internal object:

> The I-feeling: a feeling of being-responsible-for. (It cannot accompany a verb in the passive.) I wake in the morning with a violent headache and cry *Ouch*! This cry is involuntary and devoid of I-feeling. Then I think: "I have a hangover"; some I-feeling accompanies this thought—the act of locating and identifying the headache is mine—but very little. Then I think: "I drank too much last night." Now the I-feeling is much stronger: I could have drunk less. A headache has become my headache, an incident in my personal history. (I cannot identify my hangover by pointing to my head and groaning, for what makes it mine is my past act and I cannot point to myself yesterday.) (*HC* 46)

Cognizant of Wittgenstein's critique of the pretense that an "I" could invent its own language of pain—this is the now-famous "private language argument"—Auden undertakes an investigation into the possibility of writing a poem that would be as self-evidently true as the utterance "Ouch!" but would also connect an "I" with a "you." In this way, the "feeling of being-responsible-for" would be bound with the "feeling of attributing-responsibility-to" (*HC* 43). Solving this problem requires him to identify the precise characteristic shared by the "I-feeling" and the "you-feeling." It lies in the affect underlying narrative: "a feeling of being-in-the-middle-of-a-story" (*HC* 43). The narrative character of both "I-feelings" and "you-feelings," however, runs counter to the task Auden assigns himself in "Dichtung und Wahrheit," since it is characteristic of narrative—its "grammar" in the Wittgensteinian sense—that it not be self-evident. The intention of a narrative can be non-veridical: such is the case with fiction. Or it can be veridical, as in the case of history, broadly speaking, including biography and autobiography, but in none of these cases is the narrative self-evident. Goethe recounts an incident in his own *Dichtung und Wahrheit* where he doubts his memory, and Freud, following suit, subjects Goethe's self-reflection on true and false memory in "A Childhood Recollection from *Dichtung und Wahrheit*" to critical examination.[18] The self who recounts its own story is doubtless in a different position from someone who seeks to capture someone else's feelings; but as Wittgenstein emphasizes, the differences cannot be explained by saying that the self "knows" what the other only surmises. Auden accordingly uses the term "personal knowledge" in such a way that it can be applied both to self-awareness and awareness of others. In neither case is "knowledge" interchangeable with the results of scientific inquiry: "The most difficult problem in personal knowledge, whether of oneself or of others, is the problem of guessing when to think as a historian and when to think as an anthropologist" (*HC* 43). Auden is, as usual, exact in his formulation: the "problem in personal knowledge" is whether the object of one's awareness is a unique fact, in which case it is historical, or an instantiation of a type, in which case it is anthropological. The problem is not solved in accordance with a mathematical procedure; rather, it can only be "guessed," and each guess is itself subject to the same dilemma—whether it is to be regarded as a unique historical fact or the instance of an anthropological type.

The poem Auden attempts to write is predicated on the expectation of the imminent arrival of the one whom he loves. In the middle of *Philosophical Investigations* Wittgenstein begins a series of reflections by claiming that "an 'inner process' stands in need of outward criteria" with particular attention to the experience of expectation: "An expectation is imbedded in a situation, from which it arises."[19] As often occurs in the course of his investigations, Wittgenstein gives voice to an interlocutor who objects to the consequences of his claims:

> "But you talk as if I weren't really expecting, hoping, now—as though I thought I was. As if what were happening now had not

deep significance."—What does it mean to say "What is happening *now* has significance" or "has deep significance"? What is a *deep* feeling? Could someone have a feeling of ardent love or hope for the space of one second—no matter what preceded or followed this second?—What is happening now has significance—in these surroundings. The surroundings give it its importance. The word "hope" refers to a phenomenon in human life.[20]

As if he were expanding on Wittgenstein's response to his interlocutor, which retains the word "hope" but drops all interest in "ardent love"—Auden writes in paragraph 48: "'I will love you for ever,' swears the poet. I find this easy to swear to. *I will love You at 4:15 p.m. next Tuesday*: is that still as easy?" (*HC* 50). Wittgenstein suggests that it is absurd to speak of an "ardent love" unless it exhibits certain outward criteria, one of which would presumably be a time-span beyond a single second. Here, though, the absurdity of "outward criteria" becomes evident—and this is true even if the promise of love takes the form of a good and genuine poem. Thus Auden's project fails, as he acknowledges in the concluding paragraph: "This poem I wished to write was to have expressed exactly what I mean when I think the words *I love You*, but I cannot exactly know what I mean; it was to have been self-evidently true, but words cannot verify themselves" (*HC* 51).

Failure, however, is no cause for lament; on the contrary, to borrow a famous image from the *Philosophical Investigations*, failure rooted in a mistaken conception of the relation between language, thought, and life, shows "the fly the way out of the fly-bottle."[21] Auden's "Dichtung und Wahrheit" appropriately ends on a celebratory note, as if he were finally released from an enclosure created by the mistaken premise that language could somehow verify itself. Upon acknowledging his failure to write the requisite poem, he momentarily sees himself as a character in a novel; but once again, the desire for truth expresses itself, and he replaces the ever-so-brief fictive scenario with a reality that remains, of course, unknowable. And he turns to a goddess of nature who, as such, appears to be the very opposite of the muse to whom the volume as a whole is dedicated:

> So this poem will remain unwritten. That doesn't matter. Tomorrow You will be arriving; if I were writing a novel in which both of us were characters, I know exactly how I should greet You at the station: *adoration in the eye; on the tongue banter and bawdry*. But who knows exactly how I *shall* greet You? Dame Kind? Now, that's an idea. Couldn't one write a poem (slightly unpleasant, perhaps) about Her? (*HC* 48–49)

With this question, Auden concludes "Dichtung und Wahrheit" and prepares the way for Part 2 of *Homage to Clio*, the first poem of which is the very poem in question: "Dame Kind." Just as "The More Loving One" gives rise to the project that Auden undertakes in "Dichtung und Wahrheit," so "Dame Kind" emerges from its failure: the early poem is concerned with a unique person, whereas the latter one indulges in the lavishness of both nature and language. The major elements of *Homage to Clio* are thus tightly bound together: a "you"-less love poem leads to a reflection on the possibility of creating a love poem about a singular and unmistakable "you" that, upon recognition of its failure, yields a poem that is equally "you"- and "I"-less. In saying it "doesn't matter" that the perfectly veridical poem will remain unwritten, Auden can be heard to repeat in altered form one of his most famous lines: "Poetry makes nothing happen." The event in question, the arrival of the lover, will happen whether the poem can be written or not. Though couched in a fiction of jovial language corresponding to the expectation of his lover's arrival, the question ("who knows?") and its tentative answer ("Dame Kind?") is more than "slightly unpleasant," for it signals a naturalist reduction. If nature knows everything in advance with perfect exactitude, then the arrival of the singular "you" is no event at all but simply a more or less arbitrarily isolated moment in a process. And this is true of all events: they disappear under the optic of an omniscient Dame Kind, who recognizes not single individuals, but only kinds. The last words of "Dichtung und Wahrheit" exactly respond to this collapse: the poet sees himself not as an "I" but as a "one," and he personifies nature, so that she is someone, too.

SIX

Anthropology, Hell, "Good-bye"

Exercises in Exorcism

Homage to Clio is marked by a series of jarring contrasts, beginning with the incongruency between its first part, with three contrasting figurations of Clio, and its second part, where the muse of history is nowhere to be found. One of the clearest expressions of the variance traversing the volume lies in the stylistic difference between the gravity of the titular poem with which it begins and the comic clerihews of "Academic Graffiti" with which it ends. Between the first and last poems are those that comprise wildly disparate formal elements. Levels of prosodic complexity range from highly wrought forms like epanaleptics and rhopalics to simple prose sentences; shifts in tone veer from the high abstraction of "a sentence uttered makes a world appear" to the derisive silliness of "Martin Buber / Never said 'Thou' to a tuber"; registers of diction likewise proceed from the ostentatiously erudite ("steatopygous," or "anacyclic") to the casually colloquial ("for all they care, I can go to hell"); and from beginning to end, a wide variety of subjects course through the volume, from the imagined thoughts of someone in a bathtub to the execution of an anti-Nazi theologian. In the same bewildering vein, some poems follow others in accordance with readily discernible connections, as in the transition from

"Secondary Epic" to "The Epigoni," while others stand in direct contradiction with each other, as with "The Makers of History" and "T the Great." Still others, however—perhaps the majority—appear to have no direct connection with their predecessors, prompting reflection on whether there may be indirect connections or, indeed, none at all.

Regardless of their subject matter and formal characteristics, all the poems in Part 2 participate in the failure Auden recounts in "Dichtung und Wahrheit": the failure to write a poem in the first-person "I" that is absolutely and irrevocably about a second-person singular "you" whom he loves; a poem, moreover, where the "I" cannot be "first" but must, rather, be the last and lesser of the two. Congruent with the goddess after whom it is named, "Dame Kind" can do without both "I" and "you" because it is concerned solely with the doings of natural kinds. Extravagantly boisterous, "Dame Kind" is punctuated by Anglo-Saxon expressions, including a phrase set entirely in capital letters, as well as by words of Greek and Latin origin that are rarely used outside of specialized disciplines or crossword puzzles—beginning with the first word of the poem, "Steatopygous" (*HC* 55), which means, incidentally, the condition of having a large amount of flesh around the buttocks. At this point, indeed in this very word, "Dame Kind" detaches from the Clio honored in "Homage to Clio" and joins with the muse described in the final lines of "The Makers of History," whose affections extend to "even the fulsome / Bards." Because Dame Kind is another name for Aphrodite—only a few pages earlier "Dichtung und Wahrheit" had explicitly identified the two—she is altogether different from the Clio who is herself defined as different from the "Tall Sisters"; but in her fulsomeness she is very much the product of a "maker" whom the other Clio loves. The volume is thus split not only by the "Unwritten Poem" but also by the poem Auden successfully completed in its stead. Because the absolutely veridical poem about persons cannot be made, the poet experiments with a poem purely about nature, which is composed, however, in a very "unnatural" language. Without a dictionary at hand, "Dame Kind" is writable; but it is almost unreadable.

Along with the disappearance of the name "Clio" and the reappearance of Aphrodite under the Anglo-Saxon rubric of Dame Kind, Part 2 of *Homage to Clio* displays a decrease in the frequency of the word "you." A stanza from "Limbo Culture" describes the linguistic conditions in which personal pronouns are replaced by terms for quantitative approximation:

> The language spoken by the tribes of Limbo
> Has many words far subtler than our own
> To indicate how much, how little, something
> Is pretty closely or not quite the case,
> But none you could translate by *Yes* or *No*,
> Nor do its pronouns distinguish between Persons. (*HC* 75)

Despite the imprecision of Limbo Culture itself, it can be described precisely—although only negatively—as the threshold of hell. In "Reflections in a Forest" Auden considers a language in which there is no possibility of negation and therefore no opportunity for quarrel or argument: "who can raise / Objections when what one affirms / Is necessarily the case?" For this reason, the "shadowland of trees" in which he finds himself is reminiscent of the "obscure wood" with which the *Inferno* begins. In keeping with Auden's own introduction to Hell in *A Certain World* (where he quotes Wittgenstein's proposition that ethics and logic are one and the same), the absence of the logical categories of affirmation and negation in "Limbo Culture" corresponds to the absence of ethical categories required for the recognition of difference among persons. In addition to extending the line of reflection Auden began in the forest, "Limbo Culture" also completes the process that begins in "Dame Kind," whereby "you" and "I" become representative kinds, not distinguishable persons.

The field of reflection and study that stands half-way between the singularity of the historical fact and the generality of natural kinds is anthropology, which is concerned with the typicality of cultural kinds. And with "Limbo Culture"—this is already signaled by the second word in the title—*Homage to Clio* undertakes something like an anthropological turn in response to a problem that "Dichtung und Wahrheit" identifies with characteristic concision: "The most difficult problem in personal knowledge, whether of oneself or of others, is the problem of guessing when to think as a historian and when to think as an anthropologist" (*HC* 43). In Part 1 of the volume, broadly stated, Auden thinks of himself as a historian, whereas in the second part, especially the final poems of Part 2, he is closer to an anthropologist. "Limbo Culture," which reports on the far-away "tribe" to which readers of the volume would in large part belong, shows why this turn has been taken.[1] "You" and "I" disappear from the language of this culture because the self-love of its members enamors them of inexactitude, making it impossible for them to draw distinctions between first- and second-person singularities who cannot be reduced to the representation of a type: "For that [namely, self-love], we know, cannot be done exactly" (*HC* 75).

Auden does not conceal the alteration in question. A "You," initially bound to the poet's "I," introduces the following self-negating lines of verse, which stand as an epigraph under the heading Part 2:

> Although you be, as I am, one of those
> Who feel a Christian ought to write in Prose
> For Poetry is Magic—born in sin, you
> May read it to exorcise the Gentile in you. (*HC* 53)

Expressing in abbreviated form Auden's long-standing opposition between art and magic, these lines clearly outline the dynamics of a new poetic project, which is different from, yet parallel to, the one that failed in "Dichtung und Wahrheit."[2] Auden abandons an "I"-centered project, whereby the poet would produce a self-verifying work of art, and creates, instead, a "you"-directed counterpart. The transformation, here described as exorcism, yields precisely a "you" that is no longer defined in terms of its ("your") *gens* or *genus*, that is, its affiliations or generic qualities. The self-negating lines that begin Part 2 of *Homage to Clio* also indicate why "Dichtung und Wahrheit" was bound to fail: because of its magical character, poetry cannot be truth. The office of poetry would consist in the self-negating disclosure of its non-veracity. But in purely schematic terms, this, too, cannot be true. Or at least it cannot be true in a collection of poems dedicated to Clio.

Insofar as history—unlike legend, myth, or propaganda—is inextricably bound up with truth, poems in honor of its muse cannot simply say, again and again, "we are not true." Under these impossible conditions, a comic situation arises, as "Dichtung" is at once drawn toward and pushed away from "Wahrheit." To borrow a now-famous term from Gregory Bateson, the poems are caught in a *double bind*: committed to truth and yet also, for this reason, bound to disclose falseness, indeed, a vertiginous "bluff."³ The situation explodes into comic absurdity in the appendix to the volume, "Academic Graffiti," as the thirty-four clerihews, which reiterate the aabb rhyme scheme of the poem introducing Part 2, pay mock homage to major historical figures through clever deflation of their greatness: Goethe being curt with those who dispute the truth of his theory of color, for instance, or Nietzsche "cracking his joints / To make a point" (*HC* 88). As compact biographical poems—more whimsical and less reverent than Auden's major elegies—these clerihews focus on a single salient feature or moment of achievement, while gleefully, drily, relieving it of any grandiosity:

> When Karl Marx
> Found the phrase "financial sharks,"
> He sang a Te Deum
> In the British Museum. (*HC* 88)

Or—to give a final example—the philosophers whose mode of argumentation provides the model for "Dichtung und Wahrheit" solicit the following tribute:

> Oxbridge philosophers, to be cursory,
> Are products of a middle-class nursery:
> Their arguments are anent
> What Nanny really meant. (*HC* 88)

The poems comprising the second part of the volume respond to its constitutive double bind in a variety of ways. The shorter ones—"Bathtub Thoughts (c. 500–c. 1950)," "History of the Boudoir," and "From an Aesthetic Point of View"—are similarly comic, and are continuations of the final stanza of "Reflections in a Forest" insofar as they are concerned with truth in the form of nakedness. And at the center of the second part of the volume is a sequence of four poems that are themselves explicitly historiographical, beginning with a poem that directly relates truth to history, namely "The History of Truth."[4] At the end of "The Epigoni" Auden honors the poets of the late Western Roman Empire by comparing them to contemporary critics of their work, who supposedly have no time for their games: "Called shallow by a mechanized generation to whom / Haphazard oracular grunts are profound wisdom" (*HC* 36). What would be more "profound" than a "history of truth" or perhaps, to cite the title of the succeeding poem, "The History of Science"? In *Götzendämmerung* (*Twilight of the Idols*) Nietzsche presented his own history of truth under the comic title, "The History of an Error: How the 'True World' Finally Became a Fable."[5] Shortly before the publication of *Homage to Clio* Heidegger published "Die Frage nach der Technik" ("The Question Concerning Technology"), which, without the slightest comic intention, revises and updates Nietzsche's "history of an error." In Heidegger's essay, pronouncements like the following abound: "the hydroelectric plant was not built into the Rhine River as was the old wooden bridge that joined bank with bank for hundreds of years. Rather, the river is dammed up into the power plant. What the river is now, namely, a water-power supplier, derives from out of the essence of the power station."[6] Thus Heidegger, which Auden converts into a much more compact and memorable line in the final stanza of "The History of Truth": "Truth is convertible to kilowatts" (*HC* 66).

Beyond following Nietzsche and Heidegger in their exposition of the history of truth, the poem recalls the historical situation of the epigonic poets who are neither members of the Christian faith nor believers in the Olympian gods. It would be a mistake to say that Auden's poem, mirroring what he says of the epigoni, consists solely in "mechanical tricks, / Epanaleptics, rhopalics, anacyclic acrostics," but the poem's highly rhetorized lines clearly display their own artifice. Thus, for instance, "The History of Truth" includes the multi-element chiasm of "A fish-tailed dog or eagle-headed fish"; the clunkily obvious simile, "practical like paper plates," which insists on its own ornate construction through the multiple sound repetitions of alliteration and assonance that characterize the rest of the poem as well. The poem even contains elements of the very epigonic "tricks" Auden names. The opening letters of the lines in the central stanza of "The History of Truth" are indeed anacyclic: T-A-W-A-T. And the poem repeatedly suggests the repetition of epanalepsis through the use of "truth" terms and their close relatives: from the barely legible, "Truth was the most of many credibles," through the almost tautological, "The Truth was there already to be true," to the scarcely intelligible, "Some untruth anyone can give the lie to."

The exercise of reading "The History of Truth" includes considering the question of its basic intention: is it a history of truth or an epigonic parody of a history of truth, which abjures the profundity it seemingly expresses? The two subsequent "history" poems pose corresponding questions, as they contrast their own narrative character first with fable, then with legend. In "The History of Science" Auden presents a fable of knowledge as wealth-productive error. Personified as the fourth son who has been overlooked by "All fables of adventure" (*HC* 67), science in the end proves "That one can err his way to riches, / Win glory by mistake, his dear / Through sheer wrong-headedness" (*HC* 68). Finally, in "History of the Boudoir," as the nadir of counter-profundity, Auden recounts the "legend" of "the most beautiful wrists," which outlives the momentary "scandal" of a "Young Person" (*HC* 69) caught in a compromising place. The term "history" is similarly compromised here, insofar as it is precisely the legend—not the singular event, much less the particular young person allegorized as "Young Person"—that informs and determines the so-called history. The absence of the definite article in the title points in the same direction: the double bind in which poems must and cannot be related to truth does not explode into comedy, as in "Academic Graffiti," but dissolves into an uneventful "scandal."

It is perhaps for this reason that the title of the subsequent poem in the volume, "Metalogue to the Magic Flute," does not include the word *history*, even if it is concerned with nothing less than the history of music and music theory from Mozart's time to "Piano in a Post-Atomic Age / Prepared by some contemporary *Cage*" (*HC* 71). By invoking "magic" prominently in its title, Auden indicates that the poem will resume the critique of poetry briefly formulated at the beginning of Part 2. With respect to the other major term in the title, *metalogue*, it may be Auden's own invention, or—this is more likely—he may have borrowed it from

Gregory Bateson, inventor of the phrase *double bind*. Auden, for his part, does not define the genre, remarking only that it is a "Form acceptable to us, although / Unclassed by *Aristotle* or *Boileau*" (*HC* 70). According to Bateson, whom Auden could have easily encountered at Oxford or Cambridge, "a metalogue is a conversation about some problematic subject. This conversation should be such that not only do the participants discuss the problem but the structure of the conversation as a whole is also relevant to the same subject."[7] Thus does Bateson define the term at the beginning of *Steps to an Ecology of Mind*, which was first published in 1972, long after Auden wrote "Metalogue to the Magic Flute" with Chester Kallman in 1955. Much of *Steps*, however, appeared in print as early as the mid-1930s, including a paper written in conjunction with the publication of Margaret Mead's famous study of cross-cultural gender relations, *Sex and Temperament*.[8] Bateson was at the time married to Mead, who enters into Auden's "Metalogue" as the source of what has come to be common knowledge: "Even *Macaulay's* schoolboy knows to-day / What *Robert Graves* or *Margaret Mead* would say / About the status of the sexes in this play" (*HC* 71).[9]

The double bind that characterizes all the poems of *Homage to Clio*, but especially those of its second part, is this: as poetry, they are magical and thus untrue; but insofar as they still honor the muse of history, they cannot simply renounce all allegiance to truth and candidly declare their falsity. Each of the poems express the bind in its own way, some more inclined toward comic discharge, some toward parodic repetition, while, still, the last three intensify the bind, refusing release. As for "Metalogue" itself, it stages both sides of the bind and can be called a metalogue for this reason. Bateson admits that some of his own metalogues do not live up to his definition of the term: "Only some of the conversations here presented achieve this double format"—where not only the conversation about a problem, but its structure is "relevant" to the subject matter under discussion.[10] Auden's "Metalogue," by contrast, does justice to its title by precariously maintaining the double character of its format, while at the same time respecting both sides of the bind that defines the poetic-veridical problem of the volume as a whole. Spoken by Sarastro, it assumes the form of parabasis; but it is *only* the voice of Sarastro. In contrast to the figure of Caliban in *The Sea and the Mirror* who reflects on the situation of his own speech before the audience, Sarastro is a pure spokesperson—or perhaps spokespriest—who concludes his conversation by introducing Mozart's opera as the combination of "Reason & Love" (*HC* 73). The "Metalogue" includes, moreover, a precise term through which history can be negatively characterized: there is no going backward; in musical terms, no cancrizans. Instead of presenting the obligation to Clio in comparison with the movement of music, Auden presents—almost in reverse—the history of music as a prototype for the irreversibility of historical experience in general:

> The History of Music as of Man
> Will not go cancrizans, and no ear can
> Recall what, when the Archduke *Francis* reigned,
> Was heard by ears whose treasure-hoard contained
> A *Flute* already but as yet no *Ring*;
> Each age has its own mode of listening. (*HC* 70)

Just as those who have been present for a performance of the *Ring* cycle experience a different *Magic Flute* than those for whom that opera was originally performed, so those who read "Metalogue to the Magic Flute" experience a different "Homage to Clio" than those who encounter it in the absence of its meta-logique presentation of human history in its musical manifestation. In the context of "Homage to Clio" alone, the thought of a life obedient to the muse of history is as abstract as the term "music," which functions solely as an enigmatic point lying between the silence of the muse and "our noises" (*HC* 17). With the "Metalogue to the Magic Flute," however, the abstract term "music" gains historical concretion; it becomes closer to a fact, irreversible yet never the same—so much so that the same work of art will still be heard, differently, two hundred years from now. Thus speaks Auden's Sarastro, who is unlike both Mozart's high priest and Nietzsche's harbinger of the overman. The life of Mozart's creation can now be understood as that which obeys Clio, the "Muse of Time." Because the history of music includes no "cancrizans," every version of *The Magic Flute* will necessarily differ from its predecessors; its timelessness, however, has nothing to do with either the transcendence of the world in the direction of heavenly salvation or the Nietzschean overcoming of humanity in the person of the Zarathustrian-inspired overman. Rather, the timelessness of the music, concretized as a work, testifies to the ability of art to transform the sensibility of the times and thus become topical ever again.

A Second Unwritten Poem

In "Dichtung und Wahrheit" Auden briefly turns away from considering the love poem he would like to write and examines, for a moment, the feeling of hate. The initial reason for his brief reflection on hate is the broad problem of self-deception: "could I imagine that I hated when in fact I did not? Under what circumstances could I have a motive for deceiving myself about this?" (*HC* 49). In the subsequent aphorism, he suggests an answer to his questions:

> Romantic Love:—I do not need to have experienced this myself to give a fairly accurate description, since for centuries the notion has been one of the main obsessions of Western Culture. Could I imagine its counter-notion—Romantic Hate? What would be its conventions? Its vocabulary? What would a culture be like in which this notion was as much an obsession as that of Romantic Love is in our own? Supposing I were to experience it myself, should I be able to recognize it as Romantic Hate? (*HC* 49).[11]

It is possible to deceive oneself in matters of feeling, so Auden indicates, as long as one can speak and act in such a way that one's speech and conduct could be willfully misrecognized not only by others, but also by oneself. The motivation for self-deception in this case is clear: a desire to conform to cultural norms. In the next aphorism of "Dichtung und Wahrheit," Auden notes a crucial asymmetry between love and hate: "Hatred tends to exclude from consciousness every thought except that of the Hated One; but love tends to enlarge consciousness; the thought of the Beloved acts like a magnet, surrounding itself with other thoughts" (*HC* 49). The object of hate is tautologically defined as the "Hated One" whose unity is itself a function of the elicited hatred. "Dichtung und Wahrheit" immediately returns to the question of love after its description of the tendency of hate to exclude everything but the "Hated One" from consciousness. There is no further discussion of what it would be like to live in a hate-obsessed culture, where one could fool oneself into thinking one hated someone, regardless of how one actually felt. Nevertheless, the specter of an infernal culture does not disappear from *Homage to Clio*.

In "Limbo Culture" the poet represents himself as an anthropologist reporting on a culture in which romantic love is unrecognizable because the pervasiveness of self-love makes it impossible to say "I love you," where "I" means I and "you" you. In the subsequent poem, the pronoun "you" decisively re-enters the vocabulary of the volume, but this is no triumphant return. The "you" in this case is now wholly defined as the "Hated One," and the poet, relinquishing his self-presentation as neutral anthropologist, announces—this is the title of the poem—"There Will Be No Peace." In the opening stanza, the poet first appears as a natural historian, for he describes the change in weather: "mild clear weather" has returned after a destructive storm. The apparent naturalness of this cycle is punctured, however, by the ever-present memory of a catastrophic discontinuity that defines the "you" to whom the poem is addressed: "the storm has changed you: / You will not forget, ever, / The darkness blotting out hope, the gale / Prophesying your downfall" (*HC* 76). The poem proceeds as a continuous undoing of its original figural structure, which represents historical events as natural ones. The persecutors who perpetuated the so-called storm are removed from lunar cycles: "You must live with your knowledge: / Way back, beyond, outside of you are others / In moonless absences you never hear of" (*HC* 76). As the poet repeats the self-knowledge that defines the existence of those to whom the poem is addressed, repetition—rather than cyclical motions—becomes a decisive element of its structure: "What have you done to them? / Nothing? Nothing is not an answer: / You will come to believe—how can you help it?— / That you did, you did do something" (*HC* 76). The strange repetition of terms, first "nothing" and then "you did," recapitulates the problem of history as it is posed in the poem: the disaster happens twice, first in the figure of a natural calamity, and then, without any figuration, as an inexplicable event that is nevertheless known by the "you"—if not by the poet. And by the end of the poem, the events figured in the opening stanza by such deceptive terms as "storm" and "gale" are no longer described at all. Even as he addresses a "you," it is the poet who learns something from the poem, namely that "the darkness blotting out hope" is not a natural disaster. Altered by the knowledge that the event will be remembered differently than he had originally conceived, the poet concludes the poem by returning to its very beginning, that is, its title:

> There will be no peace.
> Fight back, then, with such courage as you have
> And every unchivalrous dodge you know of,
>   Clear in your conscience on this:
> Their cause, if they had one, is nothing to them now;
>   They hate for hate's sake. (*HC* 76)

It is inconceivable that the original readers of *Homage to Clio* would not recognize that "There Will Be No Peace" describes the hatred-obsessed culture of Nazi Germany, where a notion like Romantic Hatred was indeed valid, insofar as the regime had created conventions and vocabularies that encouraged and rewarded both vituperative speech and murderous action, regardless of any "personal feeling." Following immediately upon "Limbo Culture," the poem describes a descent into the further reaches of hell from which there is no return. For any reader who fails to recognize the perpetuator of Nazi atrocities among those who "hate for hate's sake," the next poem in *Homage to Clio* serves as a reminder, for it is dedicated to the memory of Dietrich Bonhoeffer, "martyred at [the] Flossenbürg [concentration camp], April 9th, 1945" (*HC* 77). With "There Will be No Peace" in mind, readers cannot view the destruction of the Nazi regime less than a month later, with Hitler's suicide on May 1st, as the passing of a storm and the return of "mild clear weather."

In a letter to Monroe Spears, Auden describes "There Will Be No Peace" as "one of the most purely personal poems I have ever written."[12] It was written in 1956 after an uncharacteristically long period in which he had written no poetry at all. Thekla Clark, who was with Auden and Kallman on Ischia during the winter of 1956–1957, said this "was the only time [she] heard him express any doubts about his work, not a single piece, but the whole thing."[13] As Edward Mendelson notes, Auden began a reading of "There Will Be No Peace" on BBC radio in the early 1960s with remarks about "the theme of paranoia."[14] This can certainly be identified in the poem, especially in those lines where the enemy of the "you" to whom it is addressed loses all specificity and thus attains almost mythic status: "Beings of unknown number and gender." In the letter to Spears, written some seven years later, Auden remembers the poem as the representation of a crisis in which he felt besieged: "It was an attempt to describe a very unpleasant dark-night-of-the-soul sort of experience which had for several months in 1956 attacked me."[15] It is not out of place to remember, however, that a bout of paranoia can heighten one's awareness of what it means to be the object of hate. And nothing in "There Will Be No Peace" demands of the reader that the "you" to whom it is addressed be understood as the poet himself. On the contrary, as it appears within the structure and sequence of *Homage to Clio*, there are good reasons to resist such a reading, beginning with the final lines of the previous poem, "Limbo Culture," where the poet as quasi-anthropologist addresses a seemingly rhetorical question to the readers of his report: "Could it be / A Limbo tribesman only loves himself? / For that, we know, cannot be done exactly" (*HC* 75).

The exactness of "There Will Be No Peace" suggests that the poet is not simply, and certainly not exclusively, sympathizing with himself. One dimension of its exactness lies in its poetic form; another, more specific dimension can be found in the grammatical indeterminacy of the line mentioned above, which describes a radical inexactness: "Beings of unknown number and gender." To be sure, the line can refer to the inchoate character of phantasmagoric enmity and thus solidify the theme of paranoia; but it can equally well refer to the manner in which the persecutors of the "you" see them—as depersonalized, de-individuated, de- or even anti-sexualized things. The same line can also be understood in a third way that combines both of the previous interpretations: the indeterminate character of the persecutors fosters an image of the persecuted as similarly indeterminate. An aphorism Auden published in *The Dyer's Hand* is instructive in this regard: "A mob is active; it smashes, kills and sacrifices itself. The public is passive or, at most, curious. It neither murders nor sacrifices itself; it looks on, or looks away, while the mob beats up a Negro or the police round up Jews for the gas ovens" (*Prose* 4:512). Similarly instructive are the remarks with which Auden ends an earlier essay on Kafka entitled "The Wandering Jew": "It was fit and proper that Kafka should have been a Jew, for the Jews have for a long time been placed in the position in which we are now all to be, of having no home.... What the contemporary anti-Semite sees in the Jew is an image of his own destiny; of which he is terrified; accordingly he tries to run to the same refuge, Race" (*Prose* 2:113). Understood in this context, the line in question—"Beings of unknown number and gender"—acquires a different sense than one generated by reading the poem as an expression of the poet's own crisis: the number and gender of the persecuted beings are unknown; but nothing is said of race, which presumably *can* be known, for it is what makes them into objects of hatred.

As it appears in the second part of *Homage to Clio*, regardless of its genesis in Auden's own experiences, "There Will No Peace" testifies to a descent from the outer sphere of hell, circumscribed by the self-love of "Limbo Culture," to its central preoccupation: "hate for hate's sake." In "Friday's Child," which immediately follows, Auden places himself and his reader—that is, the "you" and "I" of the brief poem with which the second part of the volume begins—before the scene of the crucifixion. The question posed by "Friday's Child" is the meaning of this event, which each of us is free to determine only under two stringent conditions: no help is sought in "guessing" what is meant, and no appeal can be made to a salvatory Sunday that would retrospectively make this Friday "good." In the first stanza of "There Will Be No Peace" Auden describes the disaster as a "storm" and a "gale"—but also as "the darkness blotting out hope" (*HC* 76). This phrase resonates with his letter to Monroe Spears, where Auden speaks of his personal experience; but it also serves as an apt translation of the Hebrew word *shoah* (darkness), which, since the 1930s, had been used to refer to German persecution of the Jews and in the 1950s was recognized at the Yad Vashem Memorial in Israel as the name for the destruction of European Jewry under the Nazi regime.[16] It is not known for certain whether Auden knew about the Hebrew word *shoah*; but the concluding lines of "There Will Be No Peace" describe the accelerated pace of mass murder that characterized the final years or the "Final Solution": "Their cause, if they had one, is nothing to them now; / They hate for hate's sake."

Auden would not write a Shoah poem. Nevertheless, *Homage to Clio* leaves a trace of another "unwritten poem" beyond the one that prominently divides its two parts. This second "unwritten poem" is the inverse of the one first one: not about love but about hate; not dedicated to the arrival of a single individual but to the departure—more exactly, the industrialized murder—of those who are altogether deprived of individuality. It seems as though Auden did indeed begin to write a poem of this kind. After several attempts, each of which includes an image of a gale blowing "on a certain day," he arrived at the following lines: "No peace offering you can render will be acceptable / Nothing less than your deaths will content them"—after which he immediately adds a line that will become the title of a poem he eventually completes: "There will be no peace." The drafted stanzas include a disturbing line that, perhaps because it says too much, does not enter into the final poem: "Nothing less than your deaths"—in the plural—"will content them." The corresponding line in "There Will Be No Peace" is far milder, as though it wanted to shield the poem from the storm with which it begins: "they do not like you" (*HC* 76). By changing the attitude of those who make peace impossible from genocidal murder to casual dislike, Auden alters the movement of the poem ever so slightly, but still enough to guarantee that the "darkness blotting out hope"— reconfigured as "the gale"—will not be unequivocally associated with the Shoah.[17] As Auden writes at the end of "Infernal Science," which includes one of the very few references to Auschwitz in his published work, "in Hell, as in prison and the army, its inhabitants are identified not by name but by number. They do not *have* numbers, they *are* numbers" (*Prose* 4:644).

Divorce

In 1967, Auden was invited to give the inaugural T. S. Eliot Memorial Lecture established by the (newly named) Eliot College at the University of Kent in honor of the recently deceased poet. In the first lecture— eventually published under the title *Secondary Worlds*—Auden includes a brief discussion of Eliot's dramas; but in the following, more substantial lecture he turns his attention to the relation of poetry to history, as an introduction to the problem to which the lecture series as a whole is directed:

how a "secondary world"—the term stems from J.R.R. Tolkien—stands in relation to the historical world from which it derives, even when, as in some cases, the relation consists in outright negation?[18] This apparently straightforward question develops into Auden's final and most fully articulated reflection on the relation of history to poetry. The historian is the one who is primarily concerned with the primary world, while the defining task of a poet is the creation of a secondary world. By distinguishing between two worlds in terms of a unidirectional succession from first to second, Auden is abbreviating a line of argument that he had elaborated for some thirty years: the world created by a poet is derivative on the primary world, which proceeds on its own. The argument implies that poets are incapable of creating *ex nihilo*; the material of their creation is identical to the world to which historians refer when they pose such questions as "Is this true or false?—Fact or fiction?—Did this occur or did it not?" (*Prose* 5:266). The primacy of the primary world does not imply, however, that historians stand higher than poets in some sort of axiomatic order; on the contrary, their relationship—Auden here calls it a "marriage"—is one of equals, which generates the ensuing conflicts: "The Historian cannot function without some assistance from the Poet, nor the Poet without some assistance from the Historian but, as in any marriage, the question who is to command and who to obey, is the source of constant quarrels" (*Prose* 5:266).

The metaphor of marriage is exact, insofar as marriage is at once a formal arrangement, sanctioned by social conventions, and a union created by separate parties who enter into the relationship under the presumption that each promises the highest degree of fidelity to the other. The formal arrangement in the case of the marriage between the historian and the poet derives from the fact that each side cannot perform its task without some help from the other. The relationship is not a pre-established harmony; but it is nevertheless arranged insofar as every historian becomes a poet of sorts, and every poet inhabits a world not of his or her own making. In the case of the historian, the "arranged marriage" results from the fact that historical research produces a secondary world: "For us, as for all living things, certain beings are of more concern to us than others, because our survival depends upon them, objects which must be watched out for, fled from or fought. But also—and this, so far as we know, is peculiar to man—certain beings and events appeal, as we say, to our imagination, that is to say, irrespective of any practical importance they may have, they are felt to be sacred, enchanting, valuable in themselves. No historian, however dispassionate he may try to be, can omit this fact without falsifying his picture of the human past" (*Prose* 5:267). Conversely, poets must have experienced something in the primary world that not only appeals to their imagination but also prompts them to create secondary ones in its honor: "if [the poet] did not experience such feelings of awe, wonder, enchantment, in the primary world, I very much doubt if the Poet would desire or believe it possible to create secondary worlds. Being a man, not God, a poet cannot create *ex nihilo*. If our desire to create secondary worlds arises at least in part from our dissatisfaction with the primary world, the latter must first be there before we can be dissatisfied with it" (*Prose* 5:267).

As Auden moves toward the end of his argument concerning the relation between poet and historian, in what become the final, devastating paragraphs of "The World of the Sagas," the second section of *Secondary Worlds*, he first describes how the two become separated from each other. Much of the section is concerned with thirteenth-century Icelandic sagas, a few of which he describes in detail, emphasizing the degree to which they revolve around minute legal glitches.[19] Even as Auden evidently delights in retelling these stories, the point of his reflections on "The World of the Sagas" lies in showing that the bards who created the sagas look back on the primary world of the previous century when the events they depict occurred as though it were already a secondary world. From this perspective, which shows the precariousness of the marriage between poet and historian, even during a little-recognized moment when their relationship seems at first glance to have been unclouded by any conflict, Auden examines the situation of contemporary poets and readers of poetry. And what he sees is the unraveling of the relationship under the conditions of industrialization: "The marriage in each of us, whether as writers or readers, between the Historian and the Poet, first began to run into serious difficulties in the seventeenth century, but it is only in the industrialized societies of the last hundred and fifty years, that, by the time most of us are twenty, the two have divorced" (*Prose* 5:288).

Nothing in the opening paragraphs of this section of Auden's inaugural lectures in honor of T. S Eliot would lead its auditors to suspect that, far from being an account of the marriage between the poet and historian, it will recount their eventual divorce. The lecture offers no description of the precise terms of this divorce. It is simply there—a pervasive yet scarcely perceived element of his own primary world, recognizable in reflection on the fragile conditions in which the marriage of historian and poet could once have taken place: precarious in even the best of situations, such as the "rural democracy" (*Prose* 5:275) of twelfth-century Iceland. Just as Auden makes only a few off-hand remarks about the events that led to the separation of the world depicted in the sagas from the primary world of its bards, so he says almost nothing about what led to his own historical condition, in which the poet is not only divorced from the historian, but the historian wants as little do with the poet as possible. Instead, Auden simply and concisely summarizes what befalls poet and historian as a result of a divorce at once acrimonious and scarcely noted:

> The consequences are only too obvious. The primary world as perceived by the divorced Historian is a desacralized, depersonalized world where all facts are equally profane. Human history becomes a matter of statistics, in which individual human beings are represented as faceless and anonymous puppets of impersonal forces. The characteristic virtue of the Historian, his impartiality, which refrains from intruding his own moral values upon events, leaving that duty to the reader, becomes meaningless. . . . The divorced Poet, on the other hand, can find materials for building his secondary worlds only in his private subjectivity. His characteristic virtue, a sense of the sacred, the personal, becomes concentrated upon himself. The narcissism which is right and proper to every individual, for no one can or should think of himself as profane, an impersonal puppet of fate, but as a child of God, turns into self-idolatry. (*Prose* 5:288)

Owing to the double character of the marriage between poet and historian, their divorce cannot occur without unhappy consequences. Each still needs the other: the historian still creates a secondary world, and the poet is still related to the primary world, even when this relation transforms from a certain "dissatisfaction" (*Prose* 5:267) to outright negation. A marriage of convenience thus lives on, with each partner finding a substitute for the other. In the case of historians, the substitute for the poet-function is statistics, which presupposes the absence of individuality; in the case of poets, the absence of any historian-function makes poets redouble on themselves, so that their own subjectivity is the remnant of the primary world to which they remain related.

The full consequences of the divorce emerge only for the poet. Auden's procedure in these concluding remarks is algebraic in its compactness and uncompromising in its demand. The demand concerns the role of the historian, which extends far beyond the disciplines of academic and popular historiography: "it is necessary that we know about evil in the world, about past evil that we may know what man is capable of, and be on the watch for it in ourselves, and about present evil so that we may take political action to eradicate it" (*Prose* 5:288). For the historian, then, the marriage to the poet must be reaffirmed. At the same time, however, the poet cannot remain in the same relationship with the historian as before—where "before" means, first of all, before modern industrialization and, above all, before the recent industrialization of murder. If poets seek to retain the role of historian that, outside their poetic role, they must nevertheless adopt—for all of us must "know about evil in the world, about past evil"—then they enter into a parody of marriage, here called a "business":

> This knowledge [of evil] it is one of the duties of the historian to impart. But the poet cannot get into this business without defiling himself and his audience. To write a play, that is to construct a secondary world, about Auschwitz, for example, is wicked: author and audience may try to pretend that they are morally horrified, but in fact they are passing an entertaining evening together, in the aesthetic enjoyment of horrors. (*Prose* 5:288–89)

Not every historian is obligated to make Auschwitz into an object of research, but some must, and those who do cannot play the part of the "Evil One" and treat it as a "banal fact," no different from the Battle of Hastings (*Prose* 4:643).[20] The same is not true of the poet, however, and this, the shattering conclusion of the second section of *Secondary Worlds*, not only represents the culmination of its reflections on the difficult relationship between poet and historian but is also the fulcrum of the four lectures Auden delivered—ironically, it seems—in honor of a poet who in the 1930s worried about the overabundance of Jews in Christendom.[21] As long as historians resist the temptation of statistics, they create secondary worlds that require, in broad outline, the same poetic functions as the ones that characterized historiography before the advent of modern industrialization. The marriage of the historian with the poet proceeds apace, even if it is ever more anxiety-ridden because of the ever-more pervasive atmosphere of statistical reasoning. Not so in the case of the marriage of the poet with the historian, which must reckon with the full consequences of the divorce.[22] What then, are poets to do? Auden suggests no dictum like the one Adorno famously produced about "poetry after Auschwitz."[23] As a poet, though, he does do two things: he continues to write poetry, while declining to write poetry about the Shoah. And in his Eliot lectures, he poses a question that directly responds to the thought of an audience enjoying themselves at a play set in a camp dedicated to industrialized murder: under the conditions that obtain as a consequence of the divorce between poetry and history, what are poets for?

Returning to "Guilt Culture"

With extreme brevity, *Secondary Worlds* suggests a way for the poet to reckon with the divorce from the historian and therein find a function for poetry. The primary world from which poets create secondary worlds can be none other than their own history, the story of their own subjectivity. And each act of creation can be preserved from "self-idolatry" (*Prose* 5:288) under a sobering condition: the primary world to which their constructions refer is not *theirs*—not a world to which they can be said to belong, but, rather, another's world, like the island home Auden rented in Ischia during the summers from 1949 to 1957.[24] As Auden prepared to leave the sunshine of southern Italy for good and return year-round to the northern climes of New York, Oxford, and Kirchstetten, he wrote a poem of farewell to conclude Part 2 of *Homage to Clio*, "Good-bye to the Mezzogiorno." Though the lectures in *Secondary Worlds* were written almost a decade later, they can be seen in retrospect as a self-clarification of what allowed Auden to complete *Homage to Clio* with a poem of gratitude—both for the place he left, and for the poetic turn he took to complete the volume. The "sunburnt otherwhere" (*HC* 79), to quote from its first stanza, is the otherness of a different culture, far from his own. And although the phrase bears a trace of traditional depictions of hell, that disappears in light of the prior directional sign: "Southward," rather than downward. Under this optic—and others as well—"Good-bye to the Mezzogiorno" represents a step out of the descent into hell and appears as a poem of convalescence. In it, Auden recounts his recovery following his divorce from the muse of history, whom he nevertheless continues to honor.

The opening stanza of "Good-bye to the Mezzogiorno" is unmistakably anthropological. The poet sees himself as a type, and he identifies this type with a kind of culture that is widely discussed among anthropologists and historians alike.[25] It is not the culture in which he had recently immersed himself—that of southern Italy—but, rather, the one from which he comes and from which he had sought to separate himself for a time:

> Out of a gothic North, the pallid children
> Of a potato, beer-or-whisky
> Guilt culture, we behave like our fathers and come
> Southward into a sunburnt otherwhere (*HC* 79)

Even as the opening stanza describes a movement away from his first primary world in northern Europe, it marks a return to his original secondary world—a return, specifically, to the poetic form with which *Homage to Clio* begins. For "Good-bye to the Mezzogiorno" exactly reproduces "Homage to Clio" in terms of its poetic form, down to its precise number of stanzas. The two poems thus function as bookends in a literal sense, holding the volume together, each a mirror image of the other. Whereas the earlier poem begins by situating the poet alone, seated in the midst of bustling nature, the later poem presents the poet as a member of a mobile clan; and whereas the earlier poem revolves around the difference between nature and history, the later one moves through a difference between cultures. This accords with an anthropological turn Auden undertakes in the second part of *Homage to Clio*. Thus, in the first poem of Part 1, "Homage to Clio," he is a single individual, alone in a northern European garden surrounded by nature in battle with itself; in the final poem of Part 2, "Good-bye to the Mezzogiorno," by contrast, he is a representative type, one of a long line of Germanic-speaking northerners who invade southern Italy.

Everything in "Good-bye to the Mezzogiorno" is an inversion of "Homage to Clio," from the first word of its title onward: the word *good-bye* comes from an English phrase invoking God, *homage* from a modification of Latin *hominis*. In the first poem of the volume natural life moves northward in accordance with seasonal causation; in the last poem a certain type of human being travels southward for a variety of motives; in the first poem there is a burst of green, in the last poem no color at all; and, correspondingly, in the first poem there are signs of health, in the last symptoms of sickness. The bond that ties the first and last poems of *Homage to Clio* together thus lies in sickness and in health, with the health of the natural world coming first, followed by signs of sickness—"pallid children"—that are linked with a certain kind of agriculture in combination with "guilt culture." The name of the culture "down South" (*HC* 79) is not stated as such but is simply implied by way of its opposition to the poet's own, since the very meaning of the term "guilt culture" derives from its distinction from "shame culture," a term Auden uses throughout his notes and drafts.[26] In the poem itself, however, the other culture is not positively identified in terms of shame. *Homage to Clio* is dedicated to E. R. Dodds, whose 1951 monograph *The Greeks and the Irrational* is among the early attempts to use the distinction between guilt and shame cultures as an essential element of historiographical investigation.[27] In various prose writings of the late 1950s, including a review of Werner Jaeger's *Paideia*, Auden presents the change from shame to guilt culture as an epochal transition that Greek tragedy both reflects and enacts. Though the implicit distinction between the two cultures traverses "Good-bye to the Mezzogiorno," the poem speaks of shame only in relation to "us," not to "them": "Their dining / Puts us to shame" (*HC* 80). And with regard to the great drama of transition from one culture to another, it is so completely absent that Auden presents it as an illusion, in which the members of the other culture are seen as nothing more than blank slates—literally, in the paradigmatic case of Goethe—by means of which the goods of the guilt culture are produced:

> As pupils
> We are not bad, but hopeless as tutors: Goethe,
> Tapping homeric hexameters
> On the shoulder-blade of a Roman girl, is
> (I wish it were someone else) the figure
>
> Of all our stamp (*HC* 81)

Judging by Auden's notes and drafts, the image around which this stanza revolves—Goethe reproducing ancient culture in modern form on the back of an unconscious lover—seems to be the germ from which "Good-bye to the Mezzogiorno" emerged. At the top of the notebook page in which Auden first describes "Goethe tapping hexameters" as "typical," he lists several elements of a "guilt culture" and a "shame culture."[28] Among the elements of the former are Protestantism, high taxes, and rain; among those of the latter, light-heartedness, *amore*, cheap wine, and sunny afternoons. Lower on the same page, on its left-hand side, he jots down "middle class," which presumably refers to another element of "guilt culture" but does not enter into the dynamics of the resulting poem. And then, on the right-hand side, he writes "Mediterranean despair"—which strikes both sides of the cultural divide.[29] As he reads the faces of those he encounters in this sunny region, Auden surmises that their culture is "without hope." But in the progression of poetic self-reflection, he also comes to see that in a specific situation, members of his own kind are similarly hopeless, namely when they see themselves as "tutors," who would instruct members of the other culture into the ways of "higher" culture, here represented by Goethe's modern restitution of an element of classical culture in his *Roman Elegies*. In brute terms, culture, understood as "a power to resist a blind all-or-none reaction to the immediate stimulus" (*Prose* 2:73), is exercised on the unconscious backs of subalterns, figured by the woman upon whose back Goethe taps out the hexameters of the elegies he is writing in his re-creation of classicism.[30]

Auden's "Complaint" about Goethe could find a no more appropriate image, drawn as it is from Goethe's own poetry: the "sweetheart" Goethe "drags" into his poems "never seems to matter" (*CP* 718). In "Good-bye to the Mezzogiorno," however, a complaint of this kind expands across an entire culture, here figured as a "stamp"—as much Auden's as Goethe's. At issue is the use of other's bodies, specifically others who are on the other side of a "gulf" that "Embraces cannot bridge' (*HC* 81).[31] Although none of Auden's prose writings contributed to the widespread debates about *collective guilt*, there is no question that he was aware of its implications. Carl Jung, who introduced the term in 1945, described it as a "dark cloud" enveloping Germany.[32] Just as the movement Auden describes at the beginning of the poem is collective, so is the guilt that clouds the like-named culture. Far from his being exempted from this collective guilt by virtue of his particular nationality—whether British or American—it engulfs him as well. A general sense of guilt thus pervades "Good-bye to the Mezzogiorno" from beginning to end, as though it is only a short step from tapping on the back of subaltern subjects to trampling them underfoot *en masse*. However the anthropological term *guilt culture* may be understood and evaluated, it means something different in light of what Karl Jaspers famously calls the "Question of German Guilt."[33] "Good-bye to the Mezzogiorno" cautiously explores the perplexities and hazards of that difference.

At the beginning of the poem, Auden identifies himself with the "gothic North," a phrase that recalls ancient and modern forms of collective rampage: the sacking of Rome by Germanic tribes and the Nazi incursion into Italy to prop up Mussolini's fiasco. The poem is not simply an autobiographical recollection by Auden; on the contrary, it presents the poet as a member of an invading army, akin to the invasive forces of nature that set "Homage to Clio" into motion, except, of course, for the fact that the innocence of nature is assured, whereas his is not. But Auden's travels in Italy do not properly belong to the collective guilt described by Jung and Jaspers, and the suggestion of this darker, more terrible guilt is therefore suddenly—and mercifully—transformed into a guilt that Auden freely admits: it becomes the guilt of the collector, whose "loot" is leavened by the fact that it is "spiritual" rather than material. The transformation of collective guilt into the collector's guilt, shared by a "we" that binds him with Goethe but not with all the crimes of the "gothic North," generates a spirit of levity that lightens the concluding lines of the poem and, with it, *Homage to Clio* as a whole:

>   for all
>   The spiritual loot we tuck away,
>   We do them no harm—and entitles us, I think
>   To one little scream at *A piacere*,
>
> Not two. Go I must, but I go grateful (even
>   To a certain *Monte*) and invoking
>   My sacred meridian names, *Pirandello*,
>   *Croce, Vico, Verga, Bellini*,
>
> To bless this region, its vendages, and those
>   Who call it home: though one cannot always
>   Remember exactly why one has been happy,
>   There is no forgetting that one was. (*HC* 82)

As he prepares to leave, Auden is relieved to acknowledge that his collected and recollected plunder "do[es] them no harm." The words "spiritual loot," exist on a linguistic plane that may bear the traces of historical wrongdoing, but also modulate both the sense of actual harm and any claim of cultural achievement to their proper scale. Auden's "Good-bye to the Mezzogiorno" has none of the grandiose aspirations—even "self-idolatry"—of Goethe's *Roman Elegies*. Still, something is achieved. The realization that the culture that has fed his spirit has detracted nothing from those to whom it belongs results in a small exaltation—a "little scream"—that is itself a minimal bridge across the gulf separating southern Italy from northern Europe. The customs of the latter do not allow members of an audience to make noises during artistic performances, whereas the customs of the former are laxer in this regard. In the previous stanzas Auden gently derided those who had "gone southern"—a phrase placed in quotation marks as an indication of its foreignness from his own diction; but he nevertheless admits a "scream at *A piacere*." The Italian phrase refers to those moments in an opera when performers are permitted to sing "at their pleasure." Freedom from the codes of a guilt culture coincides with freedom from the directions of the score. Thus, instead of descending along the path prepared by the previous poems in the volume, from "Limbo Culture" through "There Will Be No Peace" to "Friday's Child," the last poem in *Homage to Clio* reverses direction and concludes with its opposite: a paradisal condition in which everyone, whether northern or southern, performer or audience, can exult.

This condition is unsustainable, as Auden emphasizes, when he quickly, almost pedantically determines its limitation: "one little scream at *A piacere*, / Not two." The singularity of the scream means it is destined to remain incomprehensible: it is a bridge across cultures and beyond the proscenium, but it collapses the instant it emerges. The ever-present possibility of something bridge-like remains, however, and here that something acquires a name: *meridian*. All of Auden's poem is, in a sense, a preparation for the translation of "Mezzogiorno" into "meridian," one of the "great circles" that goes to the very opposite side of the world and returns to its starting point. As Paul Celan wrote in a speech delivered in the same year that *Homage to Clio* was published, a meridian is "something circular that returns to itself across the poles while—cheerfully—even crossing the tropics."[34] The Mezzogiorno names a place where Auden lived and from which he departs; the "same" word, however, as a meridian, names a counter-gulf that does not deny the reality of insuperable divisions and unbridgeable separation.

In the End, "No Forgetting"

The end of "Good-bye to the Mezzogiorno" yields a cascade of names—not only the "sacred meridian" ones, which themselves change from one version of the poem to another, but also the parenthetical "Monte," whose comic role in the poet's departure is left unstated. The profusion of names accompanies a dizzying alteration in the designation of the subject of enunciation.[35] Despite the poem's autobiographical character, the subject has been hitherto a collective "we" travelling from north to south. "I" emerges for the first time in its own right only to disappear once again.

Only in the penultimate stanza does an "I" appear outside of parentheses. The individual who steps outside both a collective "we" and a parenthesized "I" is doubtless reminiscent of the Cartesian subject, for its action consists in thinking, but the "I think" in the relevant phrase—"entitles us, I think"—proceeds in precisely the opposite direction: "I think" is not a stance of security but of its opposite, hesitation. Instead of providing a foundation upon which to construct a home in thought, the emergent "I" is sure only of the necessity of its departure: "Go I must." And this is precisely what the "I" does, for it disappears from the poem immediately after it announces itself, ceding its place to a third subject, neither an autobiographical "I," nor an anthropological "we," nor yet a singular or plural "you," but rather a neutral "one" and, in the same vein, an altogether impersonal subject, "there is," which encloses this "one" and closes the poem.

Everything about the concluding stanzas of the poem is abbreviated, as though the poet were rushing to say good-bye. A hint of collective guilt remains in the collection of "spiritual" goods; the resulting release leads to the emergence of an "I" out of the collective subject; this "I," however, instantly disappears into a "one" that, in a sense, belies the ordering pattern of the poem, which distinguishes "us" from "them," North from South. The appearance of this unexpected subject, neutral with regard to these unbridgeable distinctions, expresses in the present the very happiness it— "one," in other words, everyone—once experienced: a happiness whose conditions and motivations may withdraw from the sphere of historical inquiry, including autobiographical reflection, but which is nevertheless, or perhaps for this reason, as certain as the Cartesian "I think." Auden ends the poem with something like a foundational experience. If one's happiness ever happens, it is unforgettable. And it remains unforgettable, even if its conditions and motivations are inaccessible to the historian. What Auden calls the divorce between poet and historian in his later Eliot lectures is at once decisively prefigured and tentatively reversed in the final stanza of "Good-bye to the Mezzogiorno": it is prefigured in the distance between the impossibility of forgetting something and the possibility that its sources and motivations will always remain unfathomable; it is reversed because this "something," namely one's and therefore everyone's happiness, is the very opposite of the catastrophic "evil" around which Auden's reflections in the second Eliot lecture revolve and toward which the previous poems in *Homage to Clio* are directed.

Deprived of all autobiographical content, without any anthropological tendencies—both are evident from the neutral subject of enunciation—the final line of "Good-bye to the Mezzogiorno" enacts a tenuous reconciliation of poet and historian. Historical research into sources and motivations may have its limits, as the penultimate line indicates, but the poet can nevertheless be assured that a certain portion of the past can always be recovered: "There is no forgetting that one was." Something seems to be missing from this last line: *what* one was. Readers will doubtless close the elision by supplying for themselves the omitted element. Thus does "Good-bye to the Mezzogiorno" extend beyond its leave-taking. But this also means that the poem does not, properly speaking, ever end. Its last word—"happy"—is unwritten, like the poem that divides one part of *Homage to Clio* from the other. For the sake of their own satisfaction—and thus, in some minimal sense, their own happiness—readers are gently forced to complete the poem on their own.

CODA

One of the shorter poems in *Homage to Clio*, "Bathtub Thoughts (c. 500–c.1950)," captures in miniature one of the major lines of thought that traverse Auden's lifelong engagement with the relation of history to poetry. The poem is composed of two parts, the first, in italics, is explained by the second, a couplet that situates the poet in relation to the poem: "So thought, I thought, the last Romano-Briton / To take his last hot bath" (*HC* 61). Two times of imperial collapse are thus entangled with each other, as a poet who is experiencing the dismantling of the British Empire circa 1950 CE imagines the voice of a poet who, while experiencing the collapse of the Western Roman Empire circa 500 CE, prophesizes the presence of a "future friend." What is remarkable about the thought of a thought that makes up this brief poem is its blithely cheerful tone. The earlier poet is seen to greet the later poet—but gives no warning, no advice, no admonition, no words of encouragement, least of all a colloquial, "soldier on." And the accent of the later poet's thoughts falls on the word "last," which would presumably prompt an eschatological vision. But there is nothing of the kind. Nor is there any lamentation, much less any trace of end-times imagery. Nor, finally, is there either a consoling or nihilistic—cyclical view of time, such that the end of one era leads to another, which ushers in still others, until the first era returns, whereby the poet rediscovers himself in his earlier incarnation.

Even as the poet of "Bathtub Thoughts" sees himself in the image of the "last Romano-Briton," he does not represent the institution of public bathing as a trope for either civilized life in general or social hygiene in particular. The very intensity of the poet's identification with his Roman imperial counterpart makes this silence about such oppositions as civilization versus barbarism or social health versus social decay into the unspoken crux of his thoughts. To adopt the title of Foucault's initial inquiry into the ways of modern biopolitics, "Bathtub Thoughts" does not derive from the imperative that "society must be defended." And there is one more "not" to add to this account of Auden's remarkably rich poem about such a seemingly minor historical matter: poetry does not present itself as a cleansing agent that would make the writer or reader purer. If there is an understanding of poetry in general in this small poem, it is that poetry is responsive to history by letting its open-ended contingency—"Chance only knows / The length of our respective rows"—be recognized without selfish lamentations.

Some twenty years after *Homage to Clio* first appeared, Grace Nichols published a volume of poetry that includes a poem that similarly captures certain bathtub thoughts. Unlike Auden's poem, "Thoughts drifting through the fat black woman's head while having a full bubble bath" does not have a bipartite structure in which the poet thinks another's thoughts; rather, the poet pursues and returns to her own thoughts, as the following stanza, which begins the poem, is repeated as the sixth and final one as well:

> Steatopygous sky
> Steatopygous sea
> Steatopygous waves
> Steatopygous me[1]

Rather than assuming the perspective of a privileged citizen of an empire, reflecting on a similarly privileged ancient predecessor, this poet signals her awareness of the mechanisms of power and privilege that sustain imperial perspectives. For this is what the term *steatopygous* evokes: being seen and named in accordance with Romano-British imperial categories. Thus does the word with which Auden begins "Dame Kind" reverberate in the work of a later poet, in a poem which names by turns the principal concerns of *Homage to Clio* in each of its four successive stanzas: "anthropology," "history," "theology," and finally—this is the lodestone—for-profit "industry." "Bathtub Thoughts" is a closed loop that gives a negative insight into the relation of poetry to the reality of history. "Dame Kind" and "Thoughts drifting through the fat black woman's head while having a full bubble bath" constitute an open loop in which this relation is reconfigured, transformed, and thus refreshed.

As Auden himself notes in "Dichtung und Wahrheit," "Dame Kind" was written in lieu of his failed effort to write a love poem that would have been altogether true. The first word of this replacement poem, "steatopygous," is a falsehood, and its mendacity becomes clearer over the course of the poem. Crudely appetitive and "dirty," Dame Kind's kingdom is one of "bloody misrule." An apocalyptic impulse that traverses the poem finds its most emphatic expression in a phrase that would soon be associated with the likes of a Dr. Strangelove: "ONE BOMB WOULD BE ENOUGH" (*HC* 55)—enough, that is, to destroy the entire natural habitat, so that the messy, unclean, uncontrollable sexual goings-on would finally stop. Another voice responds to the desire to launch atomic bombs in the name of societal health by locating the source of this impulse in the abhorrence of "the Primal Scene," as expressed "in medical Latin" (*HC* 56). "Primal Scene" refers, of course, both to the scene of procreation, and the scenery of supposedly "primitive peoples" outside so-called civilized norms. As for "medical Latin," this is nothing other than a precise designation of the first word of the poem, the one Nichols reconfigures and transforms. The root terms of *steatopygous* are Greek; but it is a neo-Latin formulation that was invented in the early nineteenth century by William John Burchell during his journey into the "heart of darkness"—that is, in Burchell's words, the "interior of Southern Africa"—and was quickly adopted as a medical term as well. Its aim in both cases is to make an abnormalizing term falsely objective.[2] Saying someone has a fat backside is an insult; to say of someone—or of certain races, as Burchell does—that they are "steatopygous" is to sound "scientific," as though the speaker somehow inhabits a purely objective or divinely sanctioned realm. Far removed from any personal judgment or prejudicial assessment, the user of "medical Latin" is thus supposedly an exponent of a universal mode of thinking that has sanitized language to such an extent that it states simply the bare facts. This is the falsehood with which Auden knowingly begins "Dame Kind." The identification of "kinds" is anything but kind, and the poem could just as well begin with *steatopseudos*, or "big lie."

However the Romano-British imperial term with which each of these two poems begins may be redescribed, it was created to serve a colonial enterprise and a medical science that wanted to identify the abnormal within a presumably dominant race and the abnormal norm of presumably subordinate races. Auden's poem shows the falsehood of its apparent objectivity by presenting the unkindness of a "Dame Kind" who is first understood in this manner. Nichols' poem goes still further by enwrapping anthropology, history, theology, and capitalist industry around a capacious vision in which sky, sea, wave, and poet are each enlarged by this engrossing word. Though not intended as a commentary on *Homage to Clio* in the same manner that *The Sea and the Mirror* is a commentary on *The Tempest*, the middle four stanzas of "Thoughts drifting through the fat black woman's head while having a full bubble bath" are just that:

> O how I long to place my foot
> on the head of anthropology
>
> to swig my breasts
> in the face of history
>
> to scrub my back
> with the dogma of theology
>
> to put my soap
> in the slimming industry's
> profitsome spoke

The last line before the return of the stanza that begins the poem—"profitsome spoke"—bubbles up beyond the stanza in which it appears, as the soap begins to do its work. Nichols' bathtub thoughts do not, like Auden's, expressly adopt the voice of prophecy across a vast expanse of time; but the speech of a certain prophecy, slightly displaced and a little distorted, can still be heard.

NOTES

All quotations from Auden's manuscripts and typescripts are printed with the permission of the Estate of W. H. Auden.

Introduction

1. An exemplary form of a condition that must be changed, as Auden notes in an essay from the 1940s titled "Mimesis and Allegory," can be found among sharecroppers in the American South, Black workers who are systematically denied what justice demands (*Prose* 2:85). That he is attentive to an especially oppressive mode of production like sharecropping demonstrates a certain continuity with Marxism; that this mode of production plays at most a marginal role in formulations of revolutionary change among then-current forms of Marxism indicates a degree of distance from his earlier commitment. And his reference to the condition signaled by the term "sharecropping" brings the perplexity of his own situation as a poet to a boiling point. He can identify the value of a scientific inquiry into sharecropping—it is proportionate to "its power to change conditions"—and the aesthetic value of a book about sharecropping—proportionate to "its power to help sharecroppers endure with understanding these conditions until they are changed" (*Prose* 2:85)—but he immediately adds a caveat that suggests that endurance-with-added-understanding is not enough: "Naturally enough, these two values often do not coincide" (*Prose* 2:85).

2. See the remarks about Harold Laski at the beginning of Chapter 3.

3. The canonical place in Marx's writings where the topicality of history

comes under discussion is the opening section of *The Eighteenth Brumaire of Louis Bonaparte* (New York: International Publishers, 1963).

4. See especially Carlo Ginzburg, "Microhistory: Two or Three Things That I Know About It," trans. John and Anne Tedeschi, *Critical Inquiry* 20 (1993): 10–35.

5. Undated letter (except for the single word "Tuesday") to Elizabeth Mayer (Manuscript box: To Goethe: a complaint. Typescript draft of poem n.d. With his: 69 ALS [autographed letter signed], etc. to Elizabeth Mayer [Berg Collection, New York Public Library Archives and Manuscripts]).

6. For further elucidation of Auden's ambivalence about Toynbee, see Carolyn Steedman's *Poetry for Historians; or, Auden and History* (Manchester: Manchester University Press, 2018), 164–67. Steedman's study has a wealth of information on Auden's relation to a variety of historians, as well as reflections on the value of Auden's work for historiographical research.

7. See the opening paragraph of Auden's review of Arendt (*Prose* 4:184), which I discuss extensively in Susannah Young-ah Gottlieb, *Regions of Sorrow: Anxiety and Messianism in Hannah Arendt and W. H. Auden* (Stanford: Stanford University Press, 2003).

8. Quoted in Humphrey Carpenter, *W. H. Auden: A Biography* (Boston: Houghton Mifflin, 1981), 207.

9. For a detailed analysis of the operations of the Morale Division, including its questionnaire, see Claire Seiler, *Midcentury Suspension: Literature and Feeling in the Wake of World War II* (New York: Columbia University Press, 2020), 104–10.

10. James Stern, "The Indispensable Presence," in *Auden: A Tribute* (London: Weidenfeld and Nicolson), 126. For a copy of the letter, see W. H. Auden, *"In Solitude for Company": W. H. Auden after 1940* (Auden Studies 3), ed. Katherine Bucknell and Nicholas Jenkins (Oxford: Clarendon Press, 1996), 94.

11. Christopher Isherwood, *Christopher and His Kind: A Memoir, 1929–1939* (New York: Farrar, Straus and Giroux, 1979), 289.

12. Gayatri Spivak, "Can the Subaltern Speak?," in *Colonial Discourse and Post-Colonial Theory: A Reader*, ed. Patrick Williams and Laura Chrisman (New York: Columbia University Press, 1993), 66–111.

13. Jean-François Lyotard, *The Postmodern Condition: A Report on Knowledge*, trans. Geoff Bennington and Brian Massumi (Minneapolis: University of Minnesota Press, 1984), xxiv.

14. See Walter Benjamin, "On the Concept of History," in *Selected Writings*, ed. Michael Jennings and Howard Eiland (Cambridge, MA: Harvard University Press, 1996–2003), 4:395.

15. Because Foucault left the final volume of *The History of Sexuality* only in a

draft version, it is impossible to say precisely how, or indeed whether, Foucault would have ultimately formulated the relation between the transformations described in the last three volumes and the starting point of his research.

16. With respect to "emplotment," see esp. Hayden White, *Metahistory: The Historical Imagination in Nineteenth-Century Europe* (Baltimore: Johns Hopkins University Press, 1975), 27–29; with respect to perspective, see esp. 37–41.

17. Giorgio Agamben, *The Time That Remains: A Commentary on the Letter to the Romans*, trans. Patricia Daily (Stanford: Stanford University Press, 2005).

18. I argue this point in my previous book, *Regions of Sorrow*.

19. See especially Kelly Sultzbach, *Ecocriticism in the Modernist Imagination: Forster, Woolf, and Auden* (Cambridge: Cambridge University Press, 2016); see also the recent volume of Ladislav Vít, *The Landscapes of W. H. Auden's Interwar Years: Roots and Routes* (London: Routledge, 2021).

20. Judith Butler, *Parting Ways: Jewishness and the Critique of Zionism* (New York: Columbia University Press, 2014), 130.

21. Lauren Berlant, *Cruel Optimism* (Durham, NC: Duke University Press, 2011).

22. The debates around Freud and the abandonment of the seduction theory are too complicated to circumscribe in a brief note; but the core of the controversy, as it concerns Freud's texts and practices, is well described in Mikkel Borch-Jacobsen, "Neurotica: Freud and the Seduction Theory," trans. Douglas Brink, *October* 76 (1996): 15–43.

23. The initial critique of Mead's first book, *Coming of Age in Samoa* (1928), can be found in Derek Freeman, *Margaret Mead and Samoa: The Making and Unmaking of an Anthropological Myth* (New York: Penguin, 1986); see also, Marshall Sahlins, *How "Natives" Think: About Captain Cook, for Example* (Chicago: University of Chicago Press, 1995).

24. See Jyotsna Singh, "Post-colonial Reading of *The Tempest*," https://www.bl.uk/shakespeare/articles/post-colonial-reading-of-the-tempest.

25. See Chapter 3, esp. the section titled "The Colonial Administrator."

26. Auden claimed that he modelled Caliban's speech on the novelistic voice of Henry James; see the section of Chapter 3 titled "The Colonial Subject."

27. Derek Walcott, "The Muse of History," in *What the Twilight Says: Essays* (New York: Farrar, Straus and Giroux, 1998); essay originally published in 1974. On the hybridity of "the native muse" in Walcott's *Omeros*, see Jahan Ramazani, *The Hybrid Muse: Postcolonial Poetry in English* (Chicago: University of Chicago Press, 2001), 49–71.

28. Walcott, "The Muse of History," 38–39.

29. Walcott, "The Muse of History," 64.

Chapter 1: States of Marriage

An earlier version of parts of Chapter 1 appeared in Susannah Young-ah Gottlieb, "'With Conscious Artifice': Auden's Defense of Marriage," *Diacritics*, 35:4 (Winter 2005): 23–41.

1. Mitch Albom, *Tuesdays with Morrie: An Old Man, A Young Man, and Life's Greatest Lesson* (New York: Broadway, 1997), 192; hereafter, Albom.

2. See Mendelson, *Early Auden* (Cambridge, MA: Harvard University Press, 1983), 326.

3. For a judicious analysis of Auden's broader practice of revision, see Edward Mendelson, "Revision and Power: The Example of W. H. Auden," *Yale French Studies* 89 (1996): 103–12; on "September 1" in particular, see 110–12. For a sensitive reflection on the question, "Why that poem above all others?" (534), see Stephen (later Stephanie) Burt, "'September 1, 1939' Revisited: Or, Poetry, Politics, and the Idea of the Public," *American Literary History* 15 (2003): 533–59. For a wide-ranging, historically situated reading of revisions to this poem, see Nicholas Jenkins, "Either *Or* or *And*: An Enigmatic Moment in the History of 'September 1, 1939,'" *Yale Review* 90:3 (2008): 22–39. Recently, Ian Sansom has recognized the value of trying to capture the life and afterlife of the poem; see Sansom, *September 1, 1939: A Biography of a Poem* (New York: Harper Collins, 2019).

4. B. C. Bloomfield, *W. H. Auden: A Bibliography. The Early Years Through 1955* (Charlottesville: University Press of Virginia, 1964), viii.

5. This, as it happens, is only one of several moments in 1990s popular culture where Auden's poetry functions as something like pre-marital counseling. Other examples include the 1995 romantic comedy *Before Sunrise*, and the 1998 pilot episode of the television series *Felicity*. In the 2021 film adaptation of Elena Ferrante's *The Lost Daughter*, by contrast, Auden scholarship leads to marital collapse.

6. In the preface to that volume, Mendelson emphasizes that "Auden did not write in one manner for an elite learned audience and another style for a larger popular audience" (*AS* ix).

7. For an excellent discussion of the intersection of private sexual dynamics and the industrial landscape of Britain that also touches on the funeral scene in *Four Weddings*, see Marsha Bryant, *Auden and Documentary in the 1930s* (Charlottesville: University Press of Virginia, 1997), esp. 55–56.

8. For an analysis of the reception of "Funeral Blues" through and beyond the film, see Alan Jacobs, "Auden and the Dream of Public Poetry," in *Literature and the Renewal of the Public Sphere*, ed. Susan VanZanten Gallagher and M. D. Walhout (New York: St. Martin's Press), 83–104.

9. Ann Pointon and Chris Davies, eds. *Framed: Interrogating Disability in the Media* (London: British Film Institute, 1997), 48–49.

10. Jim Obergefell, "Love, Loss and Steadfast Commitment Lead a Nation Forward," *Variety* (June 29, 2015); available at https://variety.com/2015/biz/news/gay-activist-jim-obergefell-love-loss-commitment-lead-nation-forward-1201529672/ (accessed June 9, 2020); further citations of this article refer to this webpage.

11. *Obergefell v. Hodges*, no. 14–556, at 1–2 (U.S. June 26, 2015).

12. See Christopher Isherwood, *Christopher and His Kind: A Memoir, 1929–1939* (New York: Farrar, Straus and Giroux, 1976), 206–8. The marriage certificate describes Auden as a "School Master" by profession, whereas his father-in-law, Thomas Mann, is listed as a "professional writer," and Erika Mann is not accorded a profession (Manuscript box [Auden]: Marriage certificate of Wystan Hugh Auden and Erika Mann 1935 June 15 [Berg]).

13. For a discussion of this and kindred questions, see Richard Bozorth's study, *Auden's Games of Knowledge: Poetry and the Meanings of Homosexuality* (New York: Columbia University Press, 2001), 174–76. See also Raymond-Jean Frontain, "Hiding in Plain Sight: W. H. Auden in Popular Gay Culture," *ANQ* 26 (2013): 63–70.

14. For an account of this marital project, see Charles Osborne, *W. H. Auden: The Life of a Poet* (New York: Harcourt Brace Jovanovich, 1979), 119.

15. For an extensive and informative discussion of the complex relationship between LGBTQ advocacy and the fight for marriage equality in which the idea of dialogue is effectively developed, see Douglas NeJaime, "Before Marriage: The Unexplored History of Nonmarital Recognition and Its Relationship to Marriage," *California Law Review* 102:1 (February 2014): 87–172.

16. There are numerous accounts of this fateful moment in Auden's life; see, for instance, Richard Davenport-Hines, *Auden* (New York: Pantheon, 1996), 187–88.

17. Harold Norse, *Memoirs of a Bastard Angel* (London: Bloomsbury, 1990), 78.

18. See the account in Humphrey Carpenter, *W. H. Auden: A Biography* (Boston: Houghton Mifflin, 1981), 280–81 and 339.

19. Quoted in Davenport-Hines, *Auden*, 188.

20. For an incisive discussion of these two epithalamia in relation to both a broader range of Auden's marriage poems from 1920s to the 1960s and the epithalamium tradition in English literature (with particular attention to Spenser), see Bonnie Costello, *The Plural of Us: Poetry and Community in Auden and Others* (Princeton: Princeton University Press, 2017), 79–93. Taking her

point of departure from speech act theory, Costello emphasizes the future-oriented character of the vow as a specific form of promising and shows how the two epithalamia—"In Sickness and in Health" with greater success than "Epithalamium"—disclose a community (a "we") that gently transcends the sphere of the married couple through the suggestion of an ethical responsibility that is not fundamentally limitless (thus associated not so much with Eros as with Agape). The analyses proposed here, consonant with the theme of this study as a whole, examine how the two poems recall a certain history, such that a "now" of the "vow" can still be celebrated.

21. Edward Mendelson, *Later Auden* (New York: Farrar, Straus and Giroux, 1999), 155; a note on the Mandelbaums' marriage can be found on the same page. As Mendelson further emphasizes, "Auden perfected his gnomic style in writing this poem" (156)—and developed this style in "darker lyrics" in the months following its composition. For a discussion of Auden's earlier, unpublished Epithalamion of 1931, see Lucy McDiarmid, "Auden's 1931 Epithalamion and Other Generous Hours," *Modern Language Quarterly* 46 (1985): 407–28.

22. This is a persistent theme of the young Marx, whose *Economic and Philosophical Manuscripts* were first published in 1932.

23. For a discussion of the structure of *Another Time* as a Shakespearean comedy and of "Epithalamion" as its ambivalently redemptive conclusion, see Lucy McDiarmid, *Auden's Apologies for Poetry* (Princeton: Princeton University Press, 1990), 62–67. The autographed typescript, entitled "September:1939," includes a subtitle, very heavily crossed out, "To Dr. Thomas Mann" (Manuscript box: September: 1939. Typescript draft of poem with the author's ms. corrections and deletions n.d. [Berg]).

24. Many years later Auden made the following comment, which should be quoted in this context: "Most nineteenth-century anti-Semites would have been genuinely horrified by Auschwitz, but one has the uncomfortable suspicion that Wagner would have wholeheartedly approved. His vocabulary in *Know Thyself*, written in 1881, is hair-raisingly prophetic: 'Only when his [Wagner's] countrymen awakened and ceased party bickering would there be no more Jews, a "great solution" (*grosse Lösung*) he foresaw as uniquely within the reach of the Germans if they could conquer false shame and not shrink from ultimate knowledge (*nach der Überwindung aller falschen Scham die letzte Erkenntnis nicht zu scheuen*)'" (*Prose* 5: 391–92). Despite the fact that this passage appears in a review of a biography of Wagner from the late 1960s, Wagner's anti-Semitism may have been an element of at least one draft of "In Sickness and in Health." Soon after drafting a stanza that would ultimately become the second one of the published version of "In Sickness and in Health," Auden refers to the situation of the Jews (see Auden's Commonplace book, p. 17: In sickness and in

health. Holograph poem n.d. [Berg]). The draft of the original version of the fifth stanza, which begins "Nature by nature in nature ends," soon follows and with it, the first reference to Wagner via *Tristan and Isolde* (Commonplace book, p. 21, with several pages almost blank).

25. Nietzsche's critique of Wagner, which Auden adopted, can be understood as the exposition of this unresolvable ambiguity, where "cry" is at once sublimation and histrionics; see Nietzsche, *Der Fall Wagner*, in *Sämtliche Werke*, ed. Giorgio Colli and Mazzino Montinari (Berlin: de Gruyter, 1967–1977), 6:11–53; and Auden, "The Greatest of the Monsters" (*Prose* 5:389–98).

26. See Alan Jacobs, *What Became of Wystan: Change and Continuity in Auden's Poetry* (Fayetteville: University of Arkansas Press, 1998), 79–80.

27. See Genesis 1:2 ("formless void"); *tohu-bohu* is also an important term in the *Zohar*, which Auden was studying and later incorporated into "The Seven Stages" of *The Age of Anxiety*; for a detailed discussion, see Susannah Young-ah Gottlieb, *Regions of Sorrow: Anxiety and Messianism in Hannah Arendt and W. H. Auden* (Stanford: Stanford University Press, 2003), 103–14.

28. In the version in *Collected Poems*, the "O" becomes "So" (*CP* 319).

29. See the reimagining of *Don Giovanni* in the section of *Either/Or* entitled "The Intermediary Erotic Stages." Søren Kierkegaard, *Either/Or*, trans. Howard and Edna Hong (Princeton: Princeton University Press, 1987), 1:84–135.

30. See Søren Kierkegaard, *Fear and Trembling, Repetition*, trans. Howard and Edna Hong (Princeton: Princeton University Press, 1983), 38–39. At the end of *Love in the Western World*, de Rougemont appeals to the figure of the knight of infinite faith as the moment "Beyond Tragedy"; see Denis de Rougemont, *Love in the Western World*, trans. Montgomery Belgion (New York: Harper Colophon, 1974), 321.

31. The interplay between completion and supplementation that informs Auden's reflections on marriage is remarkably similar to the "logic of the supplement" that Derrida pursues in numerous texts, including his decisive reading of Rousseau in Jacques Derrida, *De la grammatologie* (Paris: Minuit, 1967), esp. 203–34.

32. See Auden's discussion of the analogous—but not identical—relation of poetic to divine creation in *DH* 70–71.

Chapter 2: Poetry, Prose, and a Forgotten Practice
An earlier version of parts of Chapter 2 appeared in Susannah Young-ah Gottlieb, "Two Versions of Voltaire: W. H. Auden and the Dialectic of Enlightenment," *PMLA* 120:2 (March 2005): 388–403, © Modern Language Association of America, 2005, published by Cambridge University Press, reproduced with permission.

1. Max Horkheimer and Theodor W. Adorno, *Dialektik der Aufklärung: Philosophische Fragmente* (Frankfurt am Main: Fischer, 1984), 7; and Max Horkheimer and Theodor W. Adorno, *Dialectic of Enlightenment: Philosophical Fragments*, ed. Gunzelin Schmid Noerr, trans. Edmund Jephcott (Stanford: Stanford University Press, 2002), 1. For the sake of convenience, I refer throughout to the single-volume German edition cited here (which corresponds to the recent critical edition in Max Horkheimer, *Gesammelte Schriften*, ed. Alfred Schmidt and Gunzelin Schmid Noerr [Frankfurt am Main: Fischer, 1987], 5:11–290). I also include page references for the new English edition cited here. Hereafter *DA*, German edition page numbers, English edition page numbers. However, owing to the presence of significant mistakes in the new, corrected translation, all translations given here from *Dialektik der Aufklärung* are my own.

2. In one of Auden's most extensive essays for *The Nation*, he makes a remark about Bacon that strongly resembles the opening paragraph of *The Dialectic of Enlightenment*: "During the last four hundred years a third heresy ... has appeared, an empiricism which denies the necessity of any metaphysics. Bacon's description of science as putting nature to the torture is a good [example]" (*Prose* 2:101).

3. See Humphrey Carpenter, *W. H. Auden: A Biography* (Boston: Houghton Mifflin, 1981), 273–302.

4. A broader inquiry into this matter cannot be accommodated in the space of a note, but such an inquiry would include an examination of the relation between Auden's reflections on "new music" (Benjamin Britten's, for example) and Theodor W. Adorno's *Philosophy of New Music*, ed. and trans. Robert Hullot-Kentor (Minneapolis: University of Minnesota Press, 2006), as well as their common interest in Wagner, which can be found throughout Auden's work and in Adorno's case appeared in a book-length essay, translated as Theodor Adorno, *In Search of Wagner* (London: New Left Books, 1981). Similarly illuminating would be a comparison of Auden's early essay, "Psychology and Art Today" (*Prose* 1:93–105) and Horkheimer's early essay "History and Psychology," reprinted in Max Horkheimer, *Between Philosophy and Social Science* (Cambridge, MA: MIT Press, 1993). Longer discussions of Auden in the context of critical theory, which move in a different direction than the one sketched here, can be found in Rainer Emig, *Towards a Postmodern Poetics* (London: Palgrave MacMillan, 2000); and Stan Smith, *W. H. Auden* (Oxford: Blackwell, 1985).

5. See Auden's letters and Kathleen Bell's thoughtful analysis in *MY* 95–115.

6. Auden finds advertising to be among the techniques of "black magic" (*Prose* 5:314–15), which enchants for the purpose of domination. In *The Age of Anxiety*, he shows how the language of commercial advertising can be enlisted

as an instrument of terror; a totally ordered regime uses the language of advertising: "*Has that democratic / Extra elegance*" (*CP* 462); see also Susannah Young-ah Gottlieb, *Regions of Sorrow: Anxiety and Messianism in Hannah Arendt and W. H. Auden* (Stanford: Stanford University Press, 2003), 77–81.

7. The original fragment includes five dashes, which, according to standard German practice, mark the alteration from one voice to another. The first English translation does not reproduce the dashes, whereas the recent translation includes only one set of dashes. Both translations make additional errors, one of which completely misconstrues the text; for further details about errors in translation, see Susannah Young-ah Gottlieb "Two Versions of Voltaire: W. H. Auden and the Dialectic of Enlightenment," *PMLA* 120 (2005): 388–403; esp. notes 9 and 14 (402).

8. See Alfred Noyes, *Voltaire* (London: Sheed, 1936), 480–91; and Norman Torrey, *The Spirit of Voltaire* (New York: Columbia University Press, 1938), 261–84.

9. Georg Wilhelm Friedrich Hegel, *Phenomenology of Spirit*, trans. A. V. Miller (Oxford: Oxford University Press, 1981), 9.

10. In relation to Voltaire's happiness, Auden is doubtless attending to the opening pages of Torrey's biography: "[Voltaire] was sincere when he wrote to one of his friends, 'I am so happy, I am ashamed of it,' at a time when old age and infirmities would have thoroughly depressed any ordinary mortal" (Torrey, *The Spirit of Voltaire*, 8)—that is, the time, late in his life, when he founded a community of workers on his estate at Ferney.

11. Such a concept of happiness can doubtless lend support to arguments for the creation of a welfare state, as the final remark of "A Great Democrat" itself attests; but it is neutral with respect to policy choices. Auden concludes his review with an endorsement of welfare policies: "it is only by removing the obvious causes of misery, poverty and social injustice, that a democracy like the United States can protect itself against the specious appeals of the enemies of freedom" (*Prose* 2:10–11).

12. Auden's most thorough exposition and examination of this thesis can be found in an essay, the very title of which corresponds to the contemporaneous studies undertaken by the dislocated Frankfurt Institute, namely "Criticism in Mass Society": "When we use the word democracy we do not or should not mean any particular form of political structure; such matters are secondary. What we mean or ought to mean is the completely open society. . . . The ideal open society [in contrast to closed societies] would know no physical, economic or cultural frontiers" (*Prose* 2:90–91).

13. Torrey, *The Spirit of Voltaire*, 18.

14. Auden's work of this period can be seen to revolve around the two poles

signaled by the names "Voltaire" and "Pascal": the first a "great democrat" who seeks to foster conditions in which human beings can generally be happy, the second a "great enemy" whose greatness derives at least in part from his recognition of unhappiness as an ineluctable element of human life. The relation between Pascal and Voltaire finds concrete expression in the pages of *Another Time*, where "Pascal" immediately precedes "Voltaire at Ferney," as though the latter responds to the former. Pascal, in Auden's difficult poem, is misery incarnate—so much so that his misery begins even before he is born: "How could he doubt the evidence he had / Of Paris and the earth? His misery was real" (*AT* 26). And at the beginning of the second section of Auden's own "pensées," which he wrote under the title *The Prolific and the Devourer*, he says that Pascal "exaggerated the unhappiness" that human beings in general experience, but that he is nevertheless correct in his "assumption" that they are "more often unhappy" (*Prose* 2:424).

15. See Joseph Warren Beach, *The Making of the Auden Canon* (Minneapolis: University of Minnesota Press, 1957), 58.

16. Ever since Peter's Gay study of the French Enlightenment, Voltaire's anti-Semitism has been a continual source of scholarly controversy; see Peter Gay, *The Party of Humanity: Essays in the French Enlightenment* (New York: Knopf, 1964), 97–108. For a judicious treatment, see Harvey Chisick, "Ethics and History in Voltaire's Attitude Toward the Jews," *Eighteenth-Century Studies* 35 (2002): 577–600. An authoritative account of Voltaire's reception can be found in Owen Aldridge, "Voltaire Then and Now: Paradoxes and Contrasts in His Reputation," *Enlightenment Studies in Honor of Lester G. Crocker*, ed. Alfred J. Bingham and Virgil W. Topazio (Oxford: Voltaire Foundation at the Taylor Institute, 1970). 1–17.

17. Pound is himself revising Voltaire's 1742 poem "Stances VIII: À Madame du Châtelet," which can be found in Voltaire, *Complete Works of Voltaire* (Oxford: Voltaire Foundation, 1968–), 20A:563–65; see in this context Hugh Witemeyer, *The Poetry of Ezra Pound, 1908–1920* (Berkeley: University of California Press, 1969),143–44.

18. On Pound and Voltaire, see Richard Sieburth, "Ideas into Action: Pound and Voltaire," *Paideuma* 6 (1977): 365–90.

19. Auden's measured evaluation of Pound in 1945 can be found in a review of a collection titled *War and Poet*: "In the recent case of Ezra Pound, it is distressing, I think, to find how many people fall into one of two errors: one party, admiring, and quite rightly, his work, seem to think his political conduct should be excused; the other party, abhorring, and, if he is guilty quite rightly, his political conduct, seem to think his work should be barred, a wicked folly which is poisoning the whole cultural life of Europe at this time. The editors and publisher of *War and the Poet* are to be congratulated on having the decency

and good sense to resist such nonsense and include examples of Pound's work" (*Prose* 2:288). See also the later reflection, "The Question of the Pound Award" (*Prose* 3:101–2).

20. For the sake of continuity, Auden also changed the first word in the final stanza (from "Yet" to "So") when he eliminated the previous stanza (*CP* 251).

21. The term "protective lie" is taken directly from Torrey, *The Spirit of Voltaire*, 120.

22. As Auden writes in his review essay on Voltaire, "When he wrote, '*Écrasez l'infâme*,' he had in mind the assumption, under whatever disguise, religious, philosophical, political, that the final absolute truth has been revealed. Allow that assumption, and tyranny and cruelty are not only inevitable but just and necessary. For if I know the Good then it is my moral duty to persecute all who disagree with me" (*Prose* 2:10).

23. See Torrey, *The Spirit of Voltaire*, 257, which refers to Voltaire, *Complete Works of Voltaire*, 20:342. Auden elides the following phrase (in Torrey's translation): ". . . which the vulgar do not know how to admire. I admired still more the intelligence which directs these vast forces. I said to myself . . ."

24. For a reflection on the meaning of Voltaire's dedication to work, see Rachel Galvin, *News of War: Civilian Poetry 1936–1945* (Oxford: Oxford University Press, 2018), 128–29.

25. Both Noyes and Torrey discuss the grounding of Voltaire's belief in a supreme being in terms of the image of the divine Watchmaker: "In a letter to Helvetius, as far back as 1739, he [Voltaire] wrote of the relationships and harmonies of design in the universe. . . . And in the *Philosophical Dictionary* . . . he anticipated the famous argument of [William] Paley, that the watch implies the watchmaker" (Noyes, *Voltaire*, 485); "He [Voltaire] stated clearly enough . . . that it was not Descartes, but Newton, Hartzoecker, and Nieuventyt who persuaded him of the existence of God. Just as a clock implies a clock maker, so this marvelously ordered and regulated world implies a supreme intelligence" (Torrey, *The Spirit of Voltaire*, 231).

26. William Blake, "The Tyger," in *The Complete Poetry and Prose of William Blake*, ed. David Erdman (New York: Doubleday, 1988), 24–25.

27. The fair copy of the poem can be found in Manuscript box: Voltaire at Fernay [*sic*]. Holograph draft of poem with the author's ms. revisions n.d. [Berg]).

Chapter 3: "Civilization Must Be Saved"

1. Harold Laski, *Where Do We Go from Here?* (New York: Viking, 1940), 13.

2. Max Horkheimer, *A Life in Letters: Selected Correspondence*, ed. Evelyn and Manfred Jacobson (Lincoln: University of Nebraska Press, 2008), 173.

3. Horkheimer, *Life in Letters*, 173.

4. Horkheimer, *Life in Letters*, 173.

5. Horkheimer, *Life in Letters*, 174 (written in English).

6. On the funding situation of the Institute, see the illuminating study of Martin Jay, *The Dialectical Imagination: A History of the Frankfurt School and the Institute of Social Research, 1923–1950* (Berkeley: University of California Press, 1996).

7. Some of Auden's conflicted response to Laski is doubtless occasioned, in part, by the programmatic aims of the journal in which his review is to be published: "In a world where all values are transvalued," Klaus Mann writes in the prefatory remarks to the first number of *Decision*, "there is an abundance of new questions to be asked and old ones to answer." See [Klaus Mann], "Issues at Stake: Decision," *Decision: A Journal of Free Culture* 1:1 (1941): 7. Regardless of whether or not Auden had a chance to read Mann's introductory remarks, his review, from its title onward, is a resounding reproof: the "real question" has not changed, nor can it change, and the Nietzschean rhetoric of the "transvaluation of all values" only contributes to the "time of confusion" Mann describes. Because the "real question," for Auden, must be posed "at every moment," there is no interval in which it could alter—and no temporal latitude that would grant an opening for some prescribed procedure to take effect. A similar sentiment is discernible in Auden's other contributions to *Decision*, most notably his review of José Ortega y Gasset's *Toward the Philosophy of History*, where he quotes a few laudable passages but concludes by casting doubt on the premise of its entire outlook: "Whether Dr. Ortega y Gasset's humanism which attempts to replace the worship of God by the study of history is ultimately a satisfactory faith, I doubt, but a review is no place to discuss such a complicated question" (*Prose* 2:129). Whereas Ortega y Gasset displaces attention from the question "where-are-we-now" to "where-have-we-been"—and thus makes the past into an object of reverential worship—Laski goes in the opposite direction. After quickly assessing our current standpoint, he proceeds to describe our future direction. Auden stops his review of Ortega y Gasset at the point where he expresses doubts about the fundamental direction of the Spanish philosopher's theory of history, but in the case of Laski, Auden shows no such restraint.

8. Slavoj Žižek, *In Defense of Lost Causes* (New York: Verso, 2008), 459. For an argument that Auden's "position" is that of a "a sort of liberalism-by-default," see Douglas Mao, "A Shaman in Common: Lewis, Auden, and the Queerness of Liberalism," in *Bad Modernisms*, ed. Douglas Mao and Rebecca Walkowitz (Durham, NC: Duke University Press, 2006), 206–37; here 220.

9. Žižek, *In Defense of Lost Causes*, 2.

10. The term "historical perspective" is drawn from Laski, *Where do We Go from Here?*: "Politics, in short, is unintelligible if we simplify it to the point of

making it into a struggle of right against wrong, of good men against evil. It is unintelligible, also, unless we see it in its historical perspective; otherwise it becomes immune to rational analysis and becomes a tale devoid of meaning" (20).

11. Walter Benjamin, "On the Concept of History" in *Selected Writings*, ed. Michael Jennings and Howard Eiland (Cambridge, MA: Harvard University Press, 1996–2003), 4:391.

12. In response to Klaus Mann's uncertainty about the potential influence of "intellectuals" on "political affairs" and the corresponding role of a "cultural journal" in time of war, Auden tersely rejects its premise, which consists in the proposition that wartime is a special moment in the onward rush of civilization forward or backward. Mann prefaced his "Symposium" with a description of the circumstances that led him to pose the question concerning the role of the intellectual. He had discovered a book containing Voltaire's novels in a house where he had recently stayed, and he recognized a resemblance between Voltaire's time and his own: even as creative work requires a high degree of inspired "merriment," all forms of optimism—the allusion is, of course, to *Candide*'s travesty of Leibnizian doctrine—must be rejected as "foolishness" (Klaus Mann, "Symposium," *Decision: A Journal of Free Culture* 1:1 [1941]: 44). Auden hyperbolizes Mann's contention to the point where it appears less an insight than an error. Not only can certain contemporary conditions be found in Voltaire's time, so can all historical conditions be seen to reflect one another, for the state of civilization simply does not advance or regress. As the subject matter of decision, it is always unqualified, whether one acts in favor of civilization or against it. Questions of historical pessimism and of historical optimism are equally pointless: "The struggle of culture with ignorance and barbarism is continuous and never-ending. War, as such, is only a sharp reminder that civilized life is always in greater danger than we realize, and that we have never done as much to maintain it as we could" (*Prose* 2:104).

13. The monologue was first published in 1934, in the journal *Life and Letters*, under the title "Sermon by an Armament Manufacturer," while its second iteration, also in 1934, occurs in *The Chase*, where it becomes a speech emanating from a Gramophone placed on the stage. Auden placed it in two further settings: in *The Dog Beneath the Skin*, where it is described as a "sermon on Bolshevism and the devil," spoken by a Vicar (*Plays* 574); and then in the 1945 edition of *Collected Poetry* as a prose monologue occupying its own section and titled "Depravity: A Sermon." In a "Note" to the latter, Auden first warns readers that the sermon is not to be understood as a case of "simple anticlericism," which would "flatter" the egos of the laity, and then identifies "two temptations" with which the sermon is concerned: "the constant tendency of spiritual life to degenerate into aesthetic performance; and the fatal ease with which Conscience, i.e., the voice of God,

is replaced by 'my conscience,' i.e., the Super-Ego which, as a writer in *Punch* remarked some years ago 'is very genteel,' and holds one variety or another of the Dualist heresy" (*CP45* 242). For a description of these many alterations and their complex publication and production history, see Mendelson's "Textual Notes," in *Plays*, 549–52. Lucy McDiarmid notes how Auden recasts an earlier epithalamion for Iris Snodgrass and Alan Sinkerson as Iris Crewe and Alan Norman in *The Dog Beneath the Skin*; see Lucy McDiarmid, "Auden's 1931 Epithalamion and Other Generous Hours," *Modern Language Quarterly* 46 (1985): 407–28.

14. See Edward Mendelson, "Revision and Power: The Example of W. H. Auden," *Yale French Studies* 89 (1996): 103–12. In 1928, Eliot wrote "A Song for Simeon," which is often described as his conversion poem. *T. S. Eliot: The Complete Poems and Plays: 1909–1950* (New York: Harcourt Brace, 1980), 69.

15. Although the direction of her argument differs from the one pursued here, see the excellent reading of the figure of Herod in Lucy McDiarmid, *Saving Civilization: Yeats, Eliot, and Auden Between the Wars* (Cambridge: Cambridge University Press, 1984); and *Auden's Apologies for Poetry* (Princeton: Princeton University Press, 1990).

16. In his *Commentary* on Auden's work, Fuller notes the similarity between the figures of Voltaire and Herod, but he understands the difference between them as the expression of an alteration in Auden's attitude toward "humanism": "In his stand against 'superstition', Voltaire becomes a near relation of Herod in *For the Time Being*, except that Auden still at this date [1939] seems to see such humanism as a possible stance"; see John Fuller, *W. H. Auden: A Commentary* (Princeton: Princeton University Press, 1998), 263. The opposition between the figures of Voltaire and Herod should not, however, be attributed to any change in Auden's mode of thinking that might have accompanied his return to Christianity, generally dated between the composition of "Voltaire at Ferney" and *For the Time Being*. Herod is not Voltaire seen afresh through the eyes of faith. This opposition should be understood, instead, as Auden's version of the dialogue between "one-sided reason" and the voice that responds to its accusations.

17. As many readers have pointed out, "The Meditation of Simeon" reflects many of Auden's philosophical-theological views at the time; see, for example, Fuller, *W. H. Auden: A Commentary*, 352. Thus, to cite one example among many, just as Simeon sees Christianity as both the preserver of art in the tumultuous times of late antiquity and the source of modern science, which Gnosticism otherwise would have drained of its energy and inspiration, so does Auden. The same is true in relation to Simeon's pronouncements about the value of Christianity for social life at large: "the course of History is predictable in the degree to which all men love themselves, and spontaneous in the degree to which each man loves God and through him his neighbor" (*FTB* 109). A sim-

ilar view appears in a review Auden wrote in 1944: "In so far as its members love themselves, a society is an earthly city in which order is maintained by force and fear of chaos, bound sooner or later to break down under the tension between freedom and law; in so far as they love God and their neighbor as themselves, the same society becomes a heavenly city in which order appears the natural consequence of freedom, not a physical or logical imposition" (*Prose* 2:230). These resonances between the views expressed in Simeon's monologue and those in Auden's contemporaneous prose writings are by no means isolated occurrences. It is as though "The Meditation of Simeon," which Auden never published outside *For the Time Being*, reappears in fragmentary form, with its claims distributed into various reviews, articles, and prefaces of the period. Far from showing that Auden is using Simeon only as the representative of his own views, the ease with which Simeon's pronouncements are detachable from his concrete situation indicates that in the original context of *For the Time Being* Simeon's intensely "presentist" reflections nevertheless remain detached from the only real question, in Auden's view, "Where are we now?"

18. The draft of Simeon's meditation begins as follows: "Once when I was fifteen years old, and I walked / At three o'clock on a Sunday afternoon / On a narrow causeway in the middle of a saltmarsh / When I suddenly knew what I was going to be. / I was surprised because poetry / Was nothing I had thought about, but not in the least / Excited or alarmed, I simply felt / I had been given the task which I was able to do"; quoted from Edward Mendelson, *Later Auden* (New York: Farrar, Straus and Giroux, 1999), 211. And here is the corresponding passage from "Letter to Lord Byron":

> I shall recall a single incident
> > No more. I spoke of mining engineering
> As the career on which my mind was bent,
> > But for some time my fancies had been veering;
> > Mirages of the future kept appearing;
> Crazes had come and gone in short, sharp gales,
> For motor-bikes, photography, and whales.
>
> But indecision broke off with a clean-cut end
> > One afternoon in March at half-past three
> When walking in a ploughed field with a friend;
> > Kicking a little stone, he turned to me
> > And said, "Tell me, do you write poetry?"
> I never had, and said so, but I knew
> That very moment what I wished to do. (*LI* 208)

Despite the obvious correspondences between the two accounts, both of which describe the moment of a young poet's awakening to his vocation, Auden was already modifying the details in ways that suggest the critical distance between himself and Simeon, even as he was asserting their likenesses. In the figure of Simeon—so obviously associated with his own return to the church and his philosophical-theological reflections on Christianity—Auden was exploring the acceptance of religiosity as either an involuntary event or a negative reflex. In the verse draft of Simeon's meditation, he writes in language that is self-consciously stripped of urgency, and in contrast to Auden in his earlier self-portrait, there is no indication that the hyperconscious Simeon makes a conscious decision at all. The lively specificity of the nouns and verbs Auden chooses for the description of his own decision in "Letter to Lord Byron"—to say nothing of the imbedded line of dialogue—keep the rime royal lines energetically moving forward. By contrast, Simeon's description of the revelation of his calling depends for its animation on uninspired adverbs and adjectives that merely signal excitement, including "excited," but even this unimaginative diction is negated ("nothing," "not in the least") and resolved into the blankness of "simply felt" (*Prose* 2:71). In "Letter to Lord Byron," the concrete description of the "crazes" that had absorbed the adolescent Auden's imagination gives a comic tone to the fateful account of poetic discovery, a characteristic feature of his verse that is entirely lacking from Simeon's tediously dutiful recitation of his "task." The verse draft of Simeon's contribution to *For the Time Being* thus acquires its strange lifelessness, as Auden de-dramatizes the experience of conversion by presenting the corresponding turn to poetry as an empty moment.

19. What appears to be the initial draft of Simeon's soliloquy runs as follows: "I am glad it was fine today." This turns into: "I am glad it was fine today was a winter day / One of those winter days, cold [unreadable word] and very still." After several more similarly framed versions, Simeon explains why the coldness of the day is conducive to his self-reflective condition: "I never felt well during the summer." For both these passages, see W. H. Auden [For the time being] Holograph poem (incomplete), Bound n.d., p. 82 [Berg]).

20. Mendelson reconstructs these passages from one of Auden's holograph notebooks and then astutely notes: "Between writing the draft and finishing the poem, Auden recalled his belief that the poet, by the nature of his craft, is inevitably tempted by his own power. The most suitable allegory for the poet became Herod who massacres the innocent, rather than Simeon the contemplative worshipper" (Mendelson, "Revision and Power," 107).

21. In an earlier draft of this, the last paragraph of "The Massacre of the Innocents," Herod explains why civilization cannot do without the use of violence

and at the same time expresses a much stronger dislike for the military: "This cannot be allowed to happen. Civilization must be saved. And since neither poetry nor philosophy can save it, I suppose we must turn the job over to the military. . . . ~~They are the experts whom we always must send for in the end.~~ How dreary. I detest them, great [two words unreadable] who have no more idea of Justice than this table" (W. H. Auden [For the time being] Holograph poem, p. 147 [Berg]). This could be put in another manner that would be familiar to those who know Auden's work of the period: since neither poetry nor philosophy make things happen, military force is required. His revision indicates that he did not want this association.

22. Laski begins his treatise by describing Hitler as an "outlaw" (*Where Do We Go from Here?* 5). Auden's agreement about the nature of Hitler's regime is predicated on a potential conflict over what the word *law* means. Auden, who had recently published "Law Like Love," in *Another Time*, suspects that Laski has little conception of what it means to act and suffer in the absence of law. For a reading of this poem in the context of reflections on literature and human rights, see Homi K. Bhabha, "On Writing Rights," *Globalizing Rights: The Oxford Amnesty Lectures 1999* (Oxford: Oxford University Press, 2003): 162–83.

23. See the seminal work of Edward Said, *Orientalism* (New York: Pantheon, 1978).

24. See Auden's letter to Theodore Spencer as discussed by Kirsch in his edition of Auden, *The Sea and the Mirror: A Commentary on Shakespeare's "The Tempest"* (Princeton: Princeton University Press, 2003), xxxi. For a lucid reflection on the erotic character of Caliban's address, especially as understood by John Ashbery, see Aidan Wasley, *The Age of Auden: Postwar Poetry and the American Scene* (Princeton: Princeton University Press, 2011), 117–42.

25. See Gayatri Spivak, "Can the Subaltern Speak?," in *Colonial Discourse and Post-Colonial Theory: A Reader*, ed. Patrick Williams and Laura Chrisman (New York: Columbia University Press, 1993), 66–111.

26. For an informative reflection on Auden's relationship to Brecht, see John Willett, *Brecht in Context: Comparative Approaches*, rev. ed. (London: Bloomsbury, 2015).

27. Walter Benjamin, "What Is Epic Theater?," in *Understanding Brecht*, trans. Anna Bostock (New York: Verso, 2003) 1–22.

28. Karl Barth, *Epistle to the Romans*, trans. Edwyn Hoskyns (Oxford: Oxford University Press, 1933), esp. 107, where the term "wholly other" is repeated several times in the context of the credo "justification by faith alone."

29. See Arthur Kirsch's informative introduction to Auden, *The Sea and the Mirror*, esp. xxx–xxxi.

30. Manuscript box: [Sea and the mirror, The. Caliban to the audience] Two typescript drafts of German translation by Elizabeth Mayer with her ms. corrections n.d., p. 44 (Berg).

31. Perhaps the best-known treatment of the concept of molarity can be found throughout Deleuze and Guatarri's *Mille Plateaux*; but as they often indicate that the operative distinction between molar and molecular is anything but a stable opposition or polarity, they never indicate, it seems, that the term *molar*, at least in English, is intimately linked with molecularity through the process of milling down molar units so that they become molecular. For an instance of their disavowal of the strict opposition between molar and molecular, see Gilles Deleuze and Felix Guattari, *Mille Plateaux*, trans. and intro. Brian Massumi (Minneapolis: University of Minnesota Press, 1987), 58–60.

32. See Kirsch's note in Auden, *The Sea and the Mirror*, 95.

Interlude: The Falling Empire

An earlier version of parts of the Interlude appeared in Susannah Young-ah Gottlieb, "The Fallen Empire," in *Auden at Work*, ed. Bonnie Costello and Rachel Galvin, 156–78 (London: Palgrave, 2015).

1. Quoted in John Pudney, "Broadcast About a Ruin" (November 19, 1937), excerpted in *Plays*, 675.

2. For an especially astute reflection on the complexity of Auden's motives for this movement, see Lorrie Goldensohn, *Dismantling Glory: Twentieth-Century Soldier Poetry* (New York: Columbia University Press, 2003), 83–101.

3. One of the more suggestive traces of Auden's experience with Roman history can be found in one version of what was originally the penultimate stanza of "September 1, 1939," which runs as follows: "To testify my faith / That [heavily crossed out word] reason's roman path / And the trek of punishment / Lead both to a single goal: / Individual death, / Each pert philosopher's / Concupiscence or, worse, / Practical wisdom, all / Our public impatience can / Delay but not prevent / The education of man" (Manuscript box: September: 1939. Typescript draft of poem with the author's ms. corrections and deletions n.d. [Berg]). Two sets of lines cross this stanza out—for good reason, one could say, insofar as the stanza, alluding to Schiller's famous *Letters on the Aesthetic Education of Man*, evinces an unwarranted optimism that tends to subvert the direction of the poem. Another alteration, which entered into the final version, points in the same direction: Auden had originally typed "The little points of light" but crossed out the first two words and replaced them with "Ironic," a term that cannot be applied to Schiller's idea of the "education of man." Nevertheless, at least aspects of the deleted stanza run counter to the apparent confession of faith in human perfectibility. The first is the colon at the end of the fourth line, which

indicates that "Individual death"—not general education—is the "single goal." And the other is the troubling concept of "reason's roman path," which suggests that reason, when it undertakes a directed movement (with an origin and a goal) is necessarily imperialistic or imperializing. Reason, in other words, is "roman" when it conceives of itself on a path that is altogether its own.

4. Auden writes at length about the errors and dangers of the planned society—from Plato to Marx to Hitler—which imagines human beings as material to be manipulated in a progressive program whose ends are known, rather than as responsible agents whose decisions are unpredictable. See, among many examples, W. H. Auden, "Who Shall Plan the Planners?" (*Prose* 2:88–89).

5. Many years later, Auden wrote the following about his encounter with Cochrane's treatise: "The discovery of books, previously published, which either through chance or snobberies, social and academic, have been neglected or ignored. Each of the editors, I am sure, could cite a number. For example, I think of two, published around 1940, of first-rate importance and virtually unknown: Charles Cochrane's *Christianity and Classical Culture* and Rosenstock-Huessy's *Out of Revolution*" (*Prose* 4:853).

6. See John Fuller, "Tennyson and Auden," in *Tennyson Among the Poets: Bicentenary Essays*, ed. Robert Douglas-Fairhurst and Seamus Perry (Oxford: Oxford University Press, 2009), 390–408; and Guy Boas, "Notes and Observations: Lord Tennyson and Mr. Auden," *English: The Journal of the English Association* 7:34 (1947): 169–70.

7. Auden is quoting Henry James on Tennyson; see Henry James, *The Middle Years* (New York: Scribner's, 1917), 102.

8. T. S. Eliot, *Selected Essays* (New York: Harcourt Brace, 1932), 343; originally published as the Introduction to Charles Baudelaire, *Intimate Journals*, trans. Christopher Isherwood (London: Blackamore Press, 1930).

9. See Edward Mendelson's note on when Auden's introduction was written (*Prose* 2: 546).

10. Charles Baudelaire, "Correspondances," in *The Flowers of Evil: A New Translation with Parallel French Text*, trans. James McGowan (Oxford: Oxford University Press, 1993), 18–19.

11. T. S. Eliot, *The Waste Land*, in *T. S. Eliot: The Complete Poems and Plays: 1909–1950* (New York: Harcourt, Brace & World, 1971), 39.

12. Eliot, *Selected Essays*, 380.

13. Charles Baudelaire, *Artificial Paradises*, trans. Stacy Diamond (New York: Citadel, 1996), 29.

14. Heraclitus of Ephesus, in *A Presocratics Reader: Selected Fragments and Testimonia* (2nd ed.), ed. Patricia Curd, trans. Richard D. McKirahan and Patricia Curd (Indianapolis: Hackett, 2011), 43 (Diels-Kranz 22b89).

15. This exchange is reprinted, in part, in *Prose* 2:529–31.

16. For further reflections on Auden's relationship to *Horizon*, see Seiler, *Midcentury Suspension*, 114–19.

17. See Cyril Connolly, "Beware the Ides," *Sunday Times*, March 2, 1952, 3.

18. See Connolly, "Some Memories," in *W. H. Auden: A Tribute*, ed. Stephen Spender (New York: Macmillan, 1974), 73.

19. For a description of Connolly as "a child of the British Empire," see Clive Fischer, *Cyril Connolly: A Nostalgic Life* (New York: Macmillan, 1995), 10.

20. Cyril Connolly, "Comment" *Horizon* 20:120–21 (Dec. 1949–Jan. 1950).

21. See Oswald Spengler, *The Decline of the West: Form and Actuality*, trans. Charles Francis Atkinson (New York: Knopf, 1927).

22. Auden read and referenced *The Future of an Illusion* throughout this period; see, for example, W. H. Auden and Louis MacNeice, *Letters from Iceland* (New York: Paragon, 1937), 194; and W. H. Auden, "Psychology and Art To-day" (*Prose* 1:93–105).

23. The only alteration Auden makes in the fair copy of "The Fall of Rome" affects this line: he originally wrote "Watch" and replaced it with "Eye." It is doubtless a very small change; but it nevertheless suggests a displacement of the perspectival "I," which watches from individual viewpoints, and the corresponding emergence of a (singular) "bird's-eye" view, which sees everything at once (see Auden's Holograph notebook. Poems 1947[-1949], p. 5: Fall of Rome, The. Holograph poem n.d. [Berg]).

24. W. B. Yeats, "Sailing to Byzantium," *The Poems of W. B. Yeats*, ed. Richard J. Finneran (New York: Macmillan, 1983), 194.

25. For a discussion of Auden's work in the context of the environmental humanities, see Kelly Sultzbach, *Ecocriticism in the Modernist Imagination: Forster, Woolf, and Auden* (Cambridge: Cambridge University Press, 2016). However, Sultzbach does not discuss "The Fall of Rome."

Chapter 4: Isotopes of Love

Earlier versions of parts of Chapter 4 appeared in Susannah Young-ah Gottlieb, "Auden in History," in *W. H. Auden in Context*, ed. Tony Sharpe, 181–95 (New York: Cambridge University Press, 2013).

1. See especially Auden's adaptation of the basic outline of *Out of Revolution* in his Introduction to *Poets of the English Language* (*Prose* 3:111–13).

2. Denis de Rougemont, *Love in the Western World*, trans. Montgomery Belgion (New York: Harper Colophon, 1974), 211.

3. Auden is quoting from Dante, *Purgatorio*, Canto 19, ll. 104–5: "love is the seed in you of every virtue and of every action that merits punishment." As for why Auden did not translate the line from Dante, an answer can be found in

the following remark from a review of Dante translations he wrote in 1947: "In view of the infinite distance between the common modern meaning of the word *love* and the *amor* of Dante, he [the reader] should read a first-rate study of the subject by M. C. D'Arcy which has recently appeared, *The Mind and Heart of Love*" (*Prose* 2:325).

4. Auden revised the poem and called it "The Council" for his *Collected Poems*. Of the numerous changes, perhaps only one is worth describing: "The Southern harbours are infested with the Jews" becomes "The Southern shipping-lanes are in the hands of Jews" (*CP* 300). Even placed in the mouths of sixteenth-century messengers, the rhetoric of infestation associated with Judaism was obviously too much, for Auden.

5. Auden is revising and rethinking perhaps the most famous line of "In Memory of W. B. Yeats," "Poetry makes nothing happen" (*AT* 98).

6. Auden, however, never addressed Nygren's *Agape and Eros* in print; a relatively full version of the Swedish original first appeared in English in 1938.

7. Auden includes a poem, entitled simply "Nietzsche," among the elaborate notes to "New Year Letter" in *The Double Man* (*DM* 91–92).

8. For a remarkable reflection on Auden's elegies and the conundrums of poetic grief, see Jahan Ramazani, *Poetry of Mourning: The Modern Elegy from Hardy to Heaney* (Chicago: University of Chicago Press, 1994), 176–215; in the context of cross-national mourning, see also Ramazani, *A Transnational Poetics* (Chicago: University of Chicago Press, 2009), esp. 82–85.

9. See Homer, *The Iliad*, trans. Robert Fitzgerald (New York: Anchor Press, 1974), bk. 5, l. 442.

10. Sigmund Freud, "The Theme of the Three Caskets," reprinted in Sigmund Freud, *Writings on Art and Literature*, ed. Neil Hertz (Stanford: Stanford University Press, 1997), 113; the translation here is modified to accord with the German original.

11. Freud, "Theme of the Three Caskets," 115.

12. The four review-essays under consideration are "Sigmund Freud" (*The New Republic*, 1952), "The Greatness of Freud" (*The Listener*, 1953), "The Freud-Fliess Letters" (*The Griffin*, 1954), and "The History of an Historian" (*The Griffin*, 1955).

13. See Hans Eysenck, *The Scientific Study of Personality* (London: Routledge & Kegan Paul, 1952).

14. See Frank Sulloway, *Freud: Biologist of the Mind: Beyond the Psychoanalytic Legend* (New York: Basic Books, 1979); and Adolf Grünbaum, *The Foundations of Psychoanalysis: A Philosophical Critique* (Berkeley: University of California Press, 1984).

15. See Paul Ricoeur, *De l'interprétation: essai sur Sigmund Freud* (Paris: Seuil, 1965).

16. See Mendelson's helpful note to this review, in *Prose* 3:752.

17. Auden first elaborates what he means by the "Helmholtz faith" in his review of the Freud-Fliess letters: "Freud was brought up in and, with a part of his mind, continued until the end of his life stubbornly to believe, what might be called the Helmholtz faith, namely that real knowledge can only be obtained by the methods of the natural sciences, physics, chemistry, biology etc." (*Prose* 3:475). Many years later, Auden summarized the relation in a trenchant manner: "Sometimes, however, [the mating of minds] ends unhappily. One thinks of Fliess and Freud, the one a talented eccentric, the other a genius. It is fortunate for the world that they met, but one is sorry for poor Fliess, his brain picked and then deserted" (*Prose* 4:348).

18. Ernest Jones, *Sigmund Freud: Life and Work, Vol.1. The Young Freud, 1856–1900* (London: Hogarth Press: 1953), 106, 107, 406.

19. Auden supports the last element of historiography by means of long passage from Jones, which begins as follows: "[Freud] felt satisfied that he could trace back the causal links quite comprehensively from the end product to the very beginning, but he was equally clear that were one to proceed in the reverse direction there would be no such certainty" (*Prose* 3:598). Auden proposes a similarly algebraic formulation of the methods of historiography at the end of his review of the Freud-Fliess letters (see *Prose* 3:476).

20. See Sigmund Freud, *Civilization and Its Discontents*, trans. James Strachey (New York: Norton, 1961), 56–76.

21. An account of these developments would far exceed the space available in a note; but here are some of the important elements: Jeffrey Masson, *The Assault on Truth: Freud's Suppression of the Seduction Theory* (New York: Farrar, Straus and Giroux, 1984); Janet Malcolm, *In the Freud Archives* (New York: Knopf, 1984); Shoshana Felman and Dori Laub, *Testimony: Crises of Witnessing in Literature, Psychoanalysis, and History* (New York: Routledge, 1992); Cathy Caruth, *Unclaimed Experience: Trauma, Narrative, and History* (Baltimore: Johns Hopkins University Press, 1996).

22. See George Macauley Trevelyan, "Clio, a Muse," in *Clio, a Muse and other Essays Literary and Pedestrian* (London: Longmans, Green, 1913), 1–55. The point, for Trevelyan, of designating the concept of history in a "poetic" way is to argue for the value of history as literature, not simply as science, and literature, for its part, as a means of liberal education.

23. See Hesiod, *Theogony* (ll. 50–104). in *The Works and Days—Theogony—The Shield of Herakles*, trans. Richmond Lattimore (Ann Arbor: University of Michigan Press, 1959), 125–29.

24. The remark appears in Auden's Foreword to John Ashbery's *Some Trees*. It seems as though Auden was looking for an opportunity to correct the record,

as it were, and indicate that memory for the archaic Greek bards was not the same as memory for modern poets.

25. E. R. Dodds, *The Greeks and the Irrational* (Berkeley: University of California Press, 1951), 81; the ellipses indicate Dodds' citations of classical sources, and the Greek words are here transliterated; the primary textual source for Dodds' footnote is Odysseus' description of Demodocus in Book 8 of the *Odyssey* (ll. 487–91). The "fallibility of tradition" to which Dodds draws attention here is related to changing technology, specifically the technology of writing: "in an age which possessed no written documents, where should first-hand evidence be found? Just as the truth about the future would be attained only if man were in touch with a knowledge wider than his own, so the truth about the past could be preserved only on a like condition. Its human repositories, the poets, had (like the seers) their technical resources, their professional training; but vision of the past, like insight into the future, remained a mysterious faculty, only partially under its owner's control, and dependent in the last resort on divine grace" (81). For a more recent investigation of this issue in relation to the function of the muses in archaic Greek sources, especially Hesiod's *Theogony*, see the influential study of Marcel Detienne, *The Masters of Truth in Archaic Greece*, trans. Janet Lloyd (New York: Zone Books, 1999), esp. 39–52.

26. E. R. Dodds refers to Auden's essay "Criticism in a Mass Society" (*Prose* 2:99) in *The Greeks and the Irrational* in the context of his discussion of the "open society" of Hellenistic-era Greece (237–38); for his reflections on Auden, see his autobiography, E. R. Dodds, *Missing Persons: An Autobiography* (Oxford: Clarendon Press, 1977), 118–23.

27. See Henry George Liddell and Robert Scott, *A Greek-English Lexicon*, rev. ed., revised and augmented by Henry Stuart Jones and Roderick McKenzie (Oxford: Clarendon Press, 1978), 958.

28. Hesiod, *Theogony* (l. 78), in *The Works and Days—Theogony—The Shield of Herakles*, 127. Kleio is the first named, but Hesiod describes Calliope, the last named muse, as the most honored one, for she inspires accurate and swift judgment among those who govern political life. An excellent discussion of *kleos* in the broad context of the Greek epic tradition can be found in the classic study of Gregory Nagy, *The Best of the Achaeans* (Baltimore: Johns Hopkins University Press, 1979), esp. 15–25 and 94–102: "The conceit of Homeric poetry is that even a Trojan warrior will fight and die in pursuit of the *kleos* . . . *Axaiōn* 'the *kleos* of the Achaeans'" (16–17).

29. See Homer, the *Iliad*, 51 (bk. 2, ll. 484–86): "Tell me now, Muses, dwelling on Olympos, / as you are heavenly, and are everywhere, / and everything is known to you—while we / can only hear the tales [*kleos*] and never know."

30. In response to the influential argument Bruno Snell proposes in *The*

Discovery of the Mind, first published in 1959, Auden distinguishes between the bards of archaic Greece (like Homer and Hesiod) and the Greek tragedians, who make the momentous discovery that "artistic reality can be fiction" (*Prose* 4:207). Of the former, he further refines his reflections on the status of the muses, even as he maintains the same thesis, namely that the muses exist to counteract the possibility of change: "To Homer, the Muses are, in the most literal sense, the daughters of memory; to imagine means to recall" (*Prose* 4:206).

31. See, for instance, John R. Clark's detailed description of Clio in Roman houses around the second century CE, where she is seen holding a "diptych in her left hand a stylus in her right": John R. Clark, *The Houses of Roman Italy, 100 B.C.–250 A.D.: Ritual, Space, and Decoration* (Berkeley: University of California Press, 1991), 279.

32. For a contrasting view of Auden's relation to historicism, see Charles Altieri's reading in *The Art of Twentieth-Century American Poetry: Modernism and After* (Malden, MA: Blackwell, 2006); 149–54.

33. A similar mistake would be to abstract Clio from her sisters and make her into a placeholder for something like "sense": "The silence of the Muse is the desire for sense" (Rainer Emig, *W. H. Auden: Towards a Postmodern Poetics* [London: Palgrave Macmillan, 2000], 113).

34. Many of the drafts of "Homage to Clio" are heavily dotted, indicating that Auden was carefully counting the syllables (see, e.g., Auden's Holograph notebook [1955-1965], pp. 14–15, 17–18: [Homage to Clio] Holograph poem n.d. [Berg]).

35. For a marvelous discussion of Moore's performance practice, see Peter Howarth, "Marianne Moore's Performances," *ELH* 87:2 (2020): 553–79.

36. After her brief analysis of the poetic form, Bonnie Costello rightly emphasizes that the poem "is dialogical even without an explicit countervoice" (Bonnie Costello, *The Plural of Us: Poetry and Community in Auden and Others* [Princeton: Princeton University Press, 2017], 208).

37. See Freud's account of the origin of psychoanalysis in Sigmund Freud, *Five Lectures on Psycho-Analysis* (New York: Norton, 1990), 8–9.

38. See Friedrich Nietzsche, *Thoughts out of Season*, trans. A. M. Ludovici and Adrian Collins, vols. 4 and 5 of *The Complete Works of Friedrich Nietzsche*, 18 vols., ed. Oscar Levy (Edinburgh: Foulis, 1909–1914).

39. Friedrich Nietzsche, "On the Utility and Liability of History for Life," in *Unfashionable Observations*, trans. Richard Gray (Stanford: Stanford University Press, 1995), 87; this translation, which derives from the now-standard German edition of Nietzsche's complete writings, does not, of course, correspond to one with which Auden would have been familiar in the 1950s. Because Auden, who was then living in Austria, would have had an easier time finding a

German version than an English one, there is no reason to quote from the older, less reliable translation.

40. Nietzsche, *Unfashionable Observations*, 87.

41. Nietzsche, *Unfashionable Observations*, 87.

42. Edward Mendelson notes that Auden describes the poem in a letter to J.R.R. Tolkien as "a hymn to our Lady." In a footnote, Mendelson highlights the ambivalence of this identification: "In the same letter he praised Tolkien for having solved . . . the problem he had implicitly set for himself in writing this poem: 'how to write a "Christian" piece of literature without making it obvious or "pi" [exaggeratedly pious].' He wrote to Ursula Niebuhr about the 'Anglican problem' of composing a 'hymn to B.V.M. . . . The Prots don't like Her and the Romans want bleeding hearts and sobbing tenors.'" See Edward Mendelson, *Later Auden* (New York: Farrar, Straus and Giroux, 1999), 396.

43. An earlier draft of "Homage to Clio" seems to be more positive about Clio's image: the poet sees her as a "teen-age mother breastfeeding her baby." This and several similar phrases can be found in Auden's Holograph notebook [1955-1965], p. 25: [Homage to Clio] Holograph poem n.d." (Berg).

44. Prompted by Auden's remark, "I think the two most wicked inventions are the internal combustion engine and the camera," an interviewer asked him, "Why do you think the camera is an evil?" Auden's reply: "It turns all fact into fiction to begin with. People see movies of people being burned up in Vietnam. It is just like a movie. They don't react anymore. The camera is all right with comic subjects, but sorrow and suffering and grief it must degrade. In ordinary life, suppose you see someone suffering or grieving. Either you try to help, if you can do something, or you look the other way. Automatically with a photograph you can't do anything because you are not there and it just becomes an object of voyeurism." See *W. H. Auden at Swarthmore*, "An hour of questions and answers with Auden (November 15, 1971)," http://www.swarthmore.edu/library/Auden/QandA_pt6.html. This is also another one of the places where Auden finds company with Rosenstock-Huessy. See especially the epigraph from Rosenstock-Huessy that he places before the late poem, "I Am Not a Camera": "Photographable life is always either trivial or already sterilized" (*CP* 841).

45. Freud, *Civilization and Its Discontents*, esp. 102–3.

46. For a discussion of "Homage to Clio" that compares it with "Spain," see Stan Smith, *W. H. Auden* (Oxford: Blackwell, 1985), 171–73. For a deeply researched and convincing account of Auden's complex relationship to his own poem, see Rachel Galvin, *News of War: Civilian Poetry 1936–1945* (Oxford: Oxford University Press, 2018), 22–23 and 92–94.

47. See Humphrey Carpenter, *W. H. Auden: A Biography* (Boston: Houghton Mifflin, 1981), 215.

48. When Orwell did meet Auden, he liked him, and therefore determined never to meet anyone he'd reviewed again. Auden remained friends with Sonia Orwell.

49. George Orwell, *All Art Is Propaganda: Critical Essays*, ed. George Packer (New York: Houghton Mifflin Harcourt, 2008), 125–26.

50. The line in *Another Time* reads: "The conscious acceptance of guilt in the fact of murder" (*AT* 96).

51. For a complementary reflection on Auden's practice of revision in the context of this poem, see Edward Mendelson, "Revision and Power: The Example of W. H. Auden," *Yale French Studies* 89 (1996): 112.

52. One of the earlier drafts of the final stanza of the poem is rather different from the one he ultimately published. The lines are difficult to decipher, but they unmistakably identify the book with which the poem begins: "The book in my hand / Is called a history but [unreadable] few of its pages / Are your concern {?}" (see Auden's Holograph notebook [1955-1965], p. 24: [Homage to Clio] Holograph poem n.d. [Berg]). The concluding stanza of the poem's published version indicates that Clio is probably unconcerned with the poets—and thus with the book in his hands, if, as I argue, it is his own book of poetry. All this is conjecture, of course, but the stanza on page 24 of the notebook suggests that Auden may have radically reconceived the poem as he developed it: in its original conception, the poet would reveal that the muse of history was unconcerned with books of history (another line of the same discarded stanza reads: "And can be repeated any number of times," thus indicating the reason for Clio's unconcern, insofar as she is always only concerned with the singular relationship); Auden ultimately decided, however, that Clio may be concerned with books of history—but not with books of poetry, including his own, which he holds in his hands.

53. Friedrich Nietzsche, *The Twilight of the Idols*, trans. Richard Polt (Indianapolis: Hackett, 1997), 8, § 24.

Chapter 5: From Poem to Volume

1. Auden often identifies the poet with "the maker" in accordance with the original Greek sense of the word; see, for instance, his casual discussion of the term in a reflection on Jean Cocteau (*Prose* 3:169) and his more elaborate discussion in "The Fallen City" (*Prose* 4:232–33).

2. For an expanded discussion of this issue, see Auden's 1955 BBC broadcast, which became the nucleus for *The Dyer's Hand* (*Prose* 3:541–43).

3. Auden rehearses this same thought in a poem where Dante is explicitly addressed, "The Truest Poetry Is the Most Feigning" (*CP* 619–21).

4. Wittgenstein, *Tractatus Logico-Philosophicus*, § 1. Auden also alludes to

this proposition in "Plains," from *Shield of Achilles*: "Though I can't pretend / To think these flats poetic, it's as well at times / To be reminded that nothing is lovely, / Not even in poetry, which is not the case" (*SA* 27).

5. See Wittgenstein, *Tractatus Logico-Philosophicus*, §§ 6.41–43.

6. This collection of aphorisms is something Auden described as his "autobiography" in the foreword to *A Certain World* (*Prose* 6:3).

7. John Fuller helpfully places this often overlooked poem in the broadest context of Auden's poetic production: "'Reflections in a Forest' follows the familiar Auden procedure of contrasting humanity with nature . . . and underlining the paradoxical advantages of duplicity. Quarelling, lies, bluff, and so on, depend entirely upon a human conception of what is not the case, which trees do not have" (Fuller, *W. H. Auden: A Commentary* [Princeton: Princeton University Press, 1998], 465).

8. Auden once gave Christopher Isherwood a book of poetry by Robert Bridges, in which he inscribed the following lines: "He isn't like us / He isn't a crook / The man is a heter / Who wrote this book" (Christopher Isherwood, "Some Notes on the Early Poetry," *W. H. Auden, A Tribute*, ed. Stephen Spender [New York: Macmillan, 1975] 79).

9. In the original drafts of the poem, Auden was less emphatically negative; instead of saying "no" to Virgil, he asks him a question: "Why, Virgil, did you do it?" (see Auden's Holograph notebook [1945-1961], p. 98: [Secondary epic] Holograph poem (incomplete) n.d. [Berg]). This question turns into one addressed to the reader: "Why did Virgil do it?" (Holograph notebook, p. 99). Even after Auden arrived at the final form of the opening line, he experimented with a different poetic form that, unlike any of Virgil's, would be built around rhyme. Thus, the opening line of the draft runs, "No, Virgil, no, it was a mistake," and in subsequent lines "mistake" is rhymed with "sake" and "make." Hermann Broch, incidentally, published a novel in 1945 with a similar theme, *Der Tod des Vergil*, which first appeared in an English-language version under the title *The Death of Virgil*. Auden was doubtless aware of Broch's novel, but he does not seem to have commented on it.

10. The title poem of *The Shield of Achilles* had revisited, of course, the very same passage in Homer's epic, and so "Secondary Epic" is not only a reflection on Virgil's alteration of the heroic shield but also a self-reflection on Auden's own "secondary" poem. When, in the early 1960s, Auden set about the task of rereading all his work for the purpose of gathering together the poems he wished to preserve for the last version of his *Collected Poems*, he generally placed the poems in chronological order; but in a few instances, he refrains from this organizational principle and interrupts the temporal sequence. This happens perhaps most notably with his decision to place "The Shield of Achilles" im-

mediately before "Secondary Epic." The juxtaposition emphasizes one of the primary points Auden advances in his review of Humphries' translation of the *Aeneid*: "Virgil's conscious imitation of Homer is, of course, not due to a lack of invention; indeed, it is precisely when he copies most closely that the novelty of his vision is clearest" (*Prose* 3:243). The difference between the Homeric and Virgilian shields is perceptible in the difference between the formal features of Auden's two poems: "The Shield of Achilles" elegantly alternates between rime royal and eight-line trimeter stanzas, whereas "Secondary Epic" is composed of stanzas of irregular length, with comic triple-measure tetrameter lines that move loosely between dactyls, amphibrachs, and anapests. Furthermore, the second poem includes a stanza, described as an editorial "interpolation" and marked off by italics; its regular iambic pentameter lines are in marked contrast to the irregularity of the preceding and following stanzas. In "Secondary Epic" the title refers not only to the *Aeneid* but also, as the poem unfolds, to the interpolated lines of a third epic poet, who celebrates the triumph of Alaric, king of the Visigoths, over the heirs of Rome. The formal differences between "The Shield of Achilles" and "Secondary Epic" are further reflected in the poems' respective themes. The first both describes and perpetuates a condition of catastrophic stasis. Just as the images on the shield are necessarily immobilized, so, too, is everything it depicts. Instead of innocently expressing the solidity of the shield, the presentation of immobilized human figures—most chillingly captured in the impassive observation that "Barbed wire enclosed an arbitrary spot" (*SA* 36)—is preparation for their imminent destruction. Without being able to say anything, the shield shows nothing beyond the disquieting moment of "peace" preceding a total war. The end of the poem explains why the shield ultimately belongs to Achilles. Instead of being the "best of the Achaeans"—or perhaps for this very reason—Achilles is the best representative of catastrophic stasis, the one whose metallic head resonates with his short, violent life: "Iron-headed man-slaying Achilles / Who would not live long" (*SA* 37).

11. In a notebook, Auden indicates as much when, after listing the three verse forms mentioned in line 20 of the published poem (rhopalic, anacyclic, epanaleptic), he asks, "Who wrote rhopalic hexameter?" (see Auden's Holograph notebook [1945-1961], p. 38 [Berg]). Auden himself seems to have experimented with several verse forms around epigonic Roman poetry. The first draft interweaves the aforementioned poetic forms with remarks about cooking, which suggests the poem was conceived as a reflection on something like the bifurcation of "taste." A later draft seems to emphasize the historical character of epigonic poetry, since it includes a line stating that only "Teutonic scholars" would be interested in such poetry; but Auden seems to have quickly abandoned

this draft and replaced it with one closer to both the theme and form of the final version, for it begins with the death of the "pleasure-seeking gods" (both drafts can be found in Notebook, p. 39). Auden, it seems, did not want to declare that epigonic poetry was historical; the experience of its historicity had to emerge from the poem itself.

12. See Sigmund Freud, *Beyond the Pleasure Principle*, trans. James Strachey (New York: Norton, 1961), esp. 48–55.

13. For a brief but incisive reflection on Auden's aspiration to be a minor Atlantic poet in the context of the Goethean program of world literature, see the introduction to Homi K. Bhabha, *The Location of Culture* (New York: Routledge, 1994), esp. 11–13.

14. For Auden's amused and amusing attitude about Goethe, see his review of a book containing a selection of Goethe's conversations (*Prose* 5:336–41).

15. Auden, following a long tradition initiated by Goethe himself, often describes the German poet as "simply unchristian" (*Prose* 2: 319). This does not capture Auden's profound relation to Goethe, which is discussed more in the final chapter, where he casts himself as part of the German poet's "stamp" (*HC* 81).

16. See Edward Mendelson, *Later Auden* (New York: Farrar, Straus and Giroux, 1999), 316.

17. Ludwig Wittgenstein, *Philosophical Investigations*, trans. G.E.M. Anscombe (New York: Macmillan, 1955), 3.

18. See Sigmund Freud, *Writings on Art and Literature*, ed. Neil Hertz (Stanford: Stanford University Press, 1997), 182–92.

19. Wittgenstein, *Philosophical Investigations*, 153, §§ 580–81.

20. Wittgenstein, *Philosophical Investigations*, 153, § 583.

21. Wittgenstein, *Philosophical Investigations*, 103, § 309.

Chapter 6: Anthropology, Hell, "Good-bye"

1. Adopting a capacious perspective that is consonant with the one Homi Bhabha develops in *The Location of Culture*, "Limbo Culture" provides a hybridized analysis of the location where an anonymous and pseudo-objective culture establishes its domain; see esp. Bhabha's reflection on the "Third Space," 31–39.

2. Auden repurposes this quatrain as the epigraph for *CSP* (n.p.). In the Prologue to *The Dyer's Hand* Auden affirms that "Poetry is not magic. In so far as poetry, or any other of the arts, can be said to have an ulterior purpose, it is, by telling the truth, to disenchant and dis-intoxicate" (*Prose* 4:473). These remarks are an essential element of the subsequent analyses, commentaries, and remarks as well as his other reflections on the purpose of poetry throughout his career.

For a discussion of this vast topic, see, among others Matthew Mutter, "'The Power to Enchant That Comes from Disillusion': W. H. Auden's Criticism of Magical Poetics." *Journal of Modern Literature* 34 (2010): 58–85.

3. On the term *double bind*, see Gregory Bateson, *Steps to an Ecology of Mind* (Chicago: University of Chicago Press, 2000), esp. 201–27.

4. Auden sketched several different kinds of history, perhaps with the intention of completing a cycle of poems, the titles of which would all begin "History of...." Here is a rendering of the sketch, so far as it is possible to reconstruct it, taken from Auden's Holograph notebook [1955-1965], p. 5 (Berg):

History of Conquerers	(No history. Orders)	
A revolution	(Permanence of one [unreadable word]. N. T.)	
History of art as artifacts.	(one [several unreadable words])	
History of ~~techniques~~ science as techniques	(replace.)	
History of theology	([unreadable word] as heresy) Research	
History of the individual	(autobiography)	
Natural history	(	
Methods	The poetic	
	The moral dualists	
Historic research	[several unreadable words]	
The withdrawers	<u>The</u> hunters	The [unreadable word] beast
	The hermit	The abyssal
	Narcissus	~~charity~~ Love

5. See Friedrich Nietzsche, *The Twilight of the Idols*, trans. Richard Polt (Indianapolis: Hackett, 1997), 23.

6. Martin Heidegger, "The Question Concerning Technology" (originally published 1954), in *The Question Concerning Technology and Other Essays*, trans. William Lovitt (New York: Garland, 1977), 16.

7. Gregory Bateson, *Steps to an Ecology of Mind: Collected Essays in Anthropology, Psychiatry, Evolution, and Epistemology* (San Francisco: Chandler, 1972), 12. He immediately adds a remark that relates metalogue to history: "Notably, the history of evolutionary theory is inevitably a metalogue between man and

nature, in which the creation and interaction of ideas must necessarily exemplify evolutionary process."

8. Bateson, "Culture Contact and Schismogenesis," reprinted in *Steps to an Ecology of Mind*, 71–82; originally published in 1935. Auden, for his part, praises Mead's work in several places (although, Mendelson points out, he generally misspells her name); see, for example, *Prose* 2:65 and 2:391; he also includes quotes from *Growing Up in New Guinea* among the "Notes" to *The Double Man* (*DM* 100–101, 148–49). In 1971 Auden spoke at a seminar chaired by Mead in conjunction with a Nobel Foundation conference that took its title from Wolfgang Köhler's *The Place of Value in a World of Fact* (1938). The minutes of the seminar are available at Columbia University, University Seminar on the Nature of Man, "The Place of Value in a World of Fact," https://magazine.co lumbia.edu/sites/default/files/2021-01/Mead-Auden%20Seminar.pdf (see also *Prose* 6:679–88). Auden and Mead engaged in several arguments, including one about what it means to be a hippie; but the most important heated exchange revolved around the theory of history—specifically, whether the theory of evolution added anything essential to "our concept of man." Mead argued that there was a "distinction between historical and evolutionary change," whereas, after lengthy discussion, Auden's skepticism regarding Mead's distinction could be summarized as follows: human beings have "always known that change occurred."

9. In the early 1950s Bateson published a series of father-daughter conversations, beginning with the oddly titled "Metalogue: Why Do Frenchmen?" which first appeared in a 1951 anthology of contemporary dance criticism and concludes as follows: "D[aughter]: Would it be a good thing if people gave up words and went back to only using gestures? F[ather]: Hmm. I don't know. Of course we would not be able to have any conversations like this. We could only bark, or mew, and wave our arms about, and laugh and grunt and weep. But it might be fun—it would make life a sort of ballet—with dancers making their own music" (Bateson, *Steps to an Ecology of Mind*, 23; originally published in *Impulse 1951* and reprinted in *ETC.: A Re-view of General Semantics* in 1953). Bateson's influential paper, "Toward a Theory of Schizophrenia," where, using Bertrand Russell's theory of logical types, he introduced the term *double bind*, first appeared in 1956. Regardless of whether or not Auden was aware of the "Metalogues" Bateson published in the early 1950s, it is worth noting in this context that they are replete with the expression "sort of"—so much so that it becomes the subject matter of his last instance of the genre, "Metalogue: Why a Swan?" (*Steps to an Ecology of Mind*, 43–47), which includes the following definition of poetry in particular and art in general: "we shall never know why the

dancer is a swan or a puppet or whatever, and shall never be able to say what art or poetry is until someone says what is really meant by 'sort of'" (44).

10. Bateson, *Steps to an Ecology of Mind*, "Only some of the conversations here presented achieve this double format" (333).

11. These questions summarize in their own way a problem that Auden identified in the title of a class he taught at Swarthmore in the academic year 1942–43: "Romanticism from Rousseau to Hitler"; see *Prose* 2:466.

12. Quoted in Edward Mendelson, *Later Auden* (New York: Farrar, Straus and Giroux, 1999), 406.

13. Thekla Clark, *Wystan and Chester* (New York: Columbia University Press, 1997), 25; see also the full discussion in Mendelson, *Later Auden*, 405–7.

14. Mendelson, *Later Auden*, 406.

15. Quoted in Mendelson, *Later Auden*, 406.

16. See Jon Petrie, "The Secular Word *Holocaust*: Scholarly Myths, History, and 20th Century Meanings," *Journal of Genocide Research* 2 (2000): 31–63; esp. 39–40.

17. See Auden's Holograph notebook [1955-65], pp. 48–50 (Berg).

18. For Tolkien's use of the term, see J.R.R. Tolkien, "On Fairy-Stories," in *Essays Presented to Charles Williams* (Oxford: Oxford University Press, 1947), 38–89.

19. Auden is particularly concerned with the incalculable dynamics of marriage in the Laxdaela Saga. Two kinds of marriages thus enter into Auden's last reflection on the relation between poetry and history: the precarious marriage between poet and historian and a similarly precarious marriage that provides the material for the sagas of medieval Iceland. There is no suggestion of an allegorical relation between the two marriages; in other words, Auden does not represent the relationship between the two figures he explicitly describes in terms of allegory—the Poet and the Historian—through the stories of marriage and divorce in the Laxdaela Saga. Yet the two marriages are nevertheless related to each other. Implicitly recalling de Rougemont's argument concerning the invention of romantic love in the twelfth century, Auden distinguishes the representation of love in Icelandic sagas from their continental European counterparts. The reality of the Icelandic saga stands in stark contrast to the myth of Tristan: "By the time the Laxdaela Saga was written, the cult of courtly love had already been invented in Provence and was soon to be spread all through Europe in the verse and prose romances" (*Prose* 5:282). As it turns out, however—Auden spends several pages describing the perplexing events of the narrative—neither of the two marriages under consideration ends happily: the literal marriage never really takes place, while its metaphorical counterpart soon dissolves. And as soon as Auden concludes his retelling of the saga, he abruptly describes the

disparity between the primary world of the Icelandic poets and the secondary worlds of their creation that *seem* to represent social reality with unsurpassable fidelity: "The primary world contemporary with the writers of the saga is not the world they describe. By their time the attempt to create a rural democracy had failed. The family blood-feuds over matters of personal honour had degenerated into ruthless power-politics, a general state of anarchy, which ended in the loss of independence. . . . If as historians, they try to depict the past as objectively as possible, as poets, this past has the attractions of a secondary world, nobler and more intelligible than the present in which they are living" (*Prose* 5:287–88).

20. In only one other passage of his prose writings—taken from a postscript to a section of *The Dyer's Hand* entitled "The Infernal Science"—does Auden mention Auschwitz, where he implicitly describes "The Evil One" as a historian who has altogether abandoned the duty of the historian and thus become a mere statistician: "evil is, by definition, what he believes he already knows. To him, Auschwitz is a banal fact, like the date of the battle of Hastings" (*Prose* 4:643).

21. See, for example, T. S. Eliot, *After Strange Gods: A Primer of Modern Heresy* (New York: Harcourt Brace, 1934), esp. 19–20; for an extensive study of Eliot's anti-Semitism, see Anthony Julius, *T. S. Eliot, Anti-Semitism and Literary Form* (Cambridge: Cambridge University Press, 1995).

22. In the subsequent section of *Secondary Worlds* Auden turns to "The World of Opera," where the poet assumes the function of a librettist, whose work is scarcely recognizable to the audience: "The opera house is not a lieder recital hall and they will be very fortunate if they hear one word in seven" (*Prose* 5:462). The brief return of a statistical formulation is ironic. As poets move from the second to the third section of *Secondary Worlds*, they can survive the divorce with history by becoming fully secondary, no longer marrying but only, in Auden's word, "stimulating" the composer. There is again a marriage, to be sure; but now music and the spoken word are to be united. Even as Auden draws on his own experiences in briefly describing what is required of both "if they are to be successfully married" (*Prose* 5:292), the composer retains the last word.

23. Theodor Adorno, *Prisms*, trans. Samuel and Shierry Weber (Cambridge, MA: MIT Press, 1981), 33: "Cultural critique finds itself up against the last step in the dialectic of culture and barbarism: to write a poem after Auschwitz is barbaric, and this also nibbles at the knowledge why it became impossible to write poetry today."

24. For a discussion of Auden's poem in relation to its location, see Aurélien Saby, "W. H. Auden and the Mezzogiorno," in *Literature and Geography: The Writing of Space Throughout History*, ed. Emmanuelle Peraldo (Newcastle: Cambridge Scholars, 2016), 287–304.

25. For an earlier reflection on culture as at once anthropological and

non-anthropological, see Auden's essay from 1940, "What Is Culture?" (*Prose* 2:72–73).

26. See Auden's Holograph notebook [1945-61], p. 95 (Berg); see also note 28 in this chapter.

27. See especially Dodds' reflections on his use of the distinction between guilt and shame cultures in his introduction, where he points toward the seminal and controversial study of Ruth Benedict, *The Chrysanthemum and the Sword* (E. R. Dodds, *The Greeks and the Irrational* [Berkeley: University of California Press, 1951], 17–18).

28. See Auden's Holograph notebook [1945-61], p. 95 (Berg). Three terms are closely interconnected in this, the apparent nucleus of what would become "Good-bye to the Mezzogiorno": guilt, Gothic, and Goethe.

29. A version of the stanza in which the people whom Auden encounters are described as "without hope" continues with the remark they are likewise "immune to despair" (see Auden's Holograph notebook [1945-61], p. 87 [Berg]). According to the anthropological calculus Auden works out in the process of producing the poem, "Mediterranean despair" is what strikes those who, guided by hope, encounter those without hope.

30. Auden is specifically referring to the following lines in the fifth of Goethe's *Römische Elegien* (*Roman Elegies*): "Oftmals hab' ich auch schon in ihren Armen gedichtet, / Und des Hexameters Maß leise mit fingernder Hand / Ihr auf dem Rücken gezählt. Sie athmet in lieblichem Schlummer, / Und es durchglühet ihr Hauch mir bis in's Tiefste die Brust" (*Goethes Werke*, Weimar edition under the direction of Grand Duchess Sophie von Sachsen [Weimar: Böhhlau, 1887], 1:415). Auden and Elizabeth Mayer were translating Goethe's *Italian Journey* when *Homage to Clio* appeared. They completed the translation in early 1961; see Edward Mendelsohn's informative remarks at *Prose* 4:898. For an analysis of the tradition Auden is consciously following in his understanding of the complexity of the "Italian journey" from and beyond Goethe, see Richard Block, *The Spell of Italy: Vacation, Magic, and the Attraction of Goethe* (Detroit: Wayne State University Press, 2006).

31. The image of the gulf through which Auden thus presents the relation between the two cultures recalls the final images of Caliban's speech at the end of *The Sea and the Mirror*: "It is not in spite of them but with them that we are blessed by that Wholly Other Life from which we are separated by an essential emphatic gulf of which our contrived fissures of mirror and proscenium arch—we understand them at last—are feebly figurative signs, so that all our meaning are reversed and it is precisely in its negative image of Judgement that we can positively envisage Mercy; it is just here, among the ruins and the bones, that we may rejoice in the perfected Word, which is not ours" (*FTB* 58). The

two versions of insurmountable gulfs are themselves separated by a gulf, insofar as Auden's relation to those whom he bids farewell at the end of *Homage to Clio* is the very inverse of Caliban's relation to the audience of *The Tempest*: the first is the self-acknowledged master of his own culture, the second a subaltern servant of his master's. For Caliban, "the essential emphatic gulf" represents an intensification of his own double separation from the audience—separated first by the proscenium arch and then again separated from the dominant culture of those to whom he speaks. In "Good-bye to the Mezzogiorno," the reversal in the position of the speaker means that the image of a gulf reveals itself to be *only* an image, indeed, to use Caliban's words, a "fissured" image, which fails to capture the relation in question—or, more accurately, the radical absence of any relation. The gulf in the experience of time, in other words, is unlike the Gulf of Naples, which the two sides share. In the case of the gulf across which Auden bids farewell, there is no connection, not even the connection of Eros, which is common to all living things. How the gulf looks from the other side—not only does Auden claim no knowledge of this, but he summarily distinguishes himself from those who "go southern" to find out.

32. Carl Jung, "After the Catastrophe," first published in 1945 and reprinted in *Collected Works*, ed. Herbert Read, Michael Fordham, Gerhard Adler, and William McGuire (Princeton: Princeton University Press, 1964), 10:198: "[Collective guilt] cares nothing for the just and the unjust, it is the dark cloud that rises up from the scene of an unexpiated crime. It is a psychic phenomenon, and it is therefore no condemnation of the German people to say that they are collectively guilty, but simply a statement of fact." For a discussion of Auden's use of Jung in the composition of *The Age of Anxiety*, see Gottlieb, *Regions of Sorrow: Anxiety and Messianism in Hannah Arendt and W. H. Auden* (Stanford: Stanford University Press, 2003), 226.

33. See Karl Jaspers, *Die Schuldfrage, ein Beitrag zur deutschen Frage* (1946), translated as *The Question of German Guilt*, trans. Ernst Basch under the pseudonym E. B. Ashton (New York: Dial Press, 1947).

34. Celan, *The Meridian: Final Version—Drafts—Materials*, ed. Bernhard Böschenstein and Heino Schmull, trans. Pierre Joris (Stanford: Stanford University Press, 2011), 12. Within the space of a note it is impossible to trace the strange absence of a relation between Auden and Celan. The latter translated English-language poetry, and the former, as this study shows, was deeply involved in the tradition of German poetry and thought. Each of them being drawn to the term *meridian* around the same time suggests their proximity, despite their distance.

35. Incidental evidence for the profusion of names is the simple fact that Auden seemed to alter the list of "sacred meridian names" in every iteration

of the complete poem. In the typescript as well as in the poem published in *Encounter* the names are "Leopardi / Pirandello, Verga, Bellini" (see *Good-bye to the Mezzogiorno*. Published 1958. Typescript, signed. 3 pages 8vo. With an unpublished three-word note in the author's hand, and with substantive variants in lines 4, 6, 20, 77, 87 and 88. [Berg]). In the poem published as a pamphlet, with Carlo Izzo's translation as well as the one published in *Homage to Clio*, the names are as they appear in the text here. In the version published in *Collected Poems*, they are different, once again. Finally, at the bottom of the typescript, Auden adds a facetiously discreet footnote to the name Monte: "My Last Landlord."

Coda

1. Grace Nichols, *The Fat Black Woman's Poems* (London: Virago/Little, Brown Book Group, 1984), 13.

2. *The Compact Edition of the Oxford English Dictionary*, s.v. "Steatopygia," first used by William John Burchell in *Travels in the Interior of Southern Africa* (London: Longman, Hurst, Rees, Omre, and Brown, 1822), 216. This entry reproduces the one both Auden and Nichols probably consulted.

INDEX

Adorno, Theodor, 14, 23, 68–70, 71, 73–75, 76, 80, 82, 84, 85, 88, 230, 252n1, 252n4, 277n23. *See also Dialectic of Enlightenment*; Horkheimer, Max
Agamben, Giorgio: *The Time That Remains*, 24–25
Albom, Mitch, 42; *Tuesdays with Morrie* (book), 12–13, 35–36, 37–38, 39. *See also* Auden, W. H., works of, "September 1, 1939"; *Tuesdays with Morrie* (film)
Aldridge, Owen, 254n16
Altieri, Charles, 268n32
Arendt, Hannah, 9, 246n7. *See also* Auden, W. H., works of, "Thinking What We Are Doing"
Ashbery, John: *Some Trees*, 173, 261n24, 266n24
Auden, W. H., works of:
  "Academic Graffiti," 20, 190, 204, 211, 215, 217
  "Aeneid for Our Time," 196–97, 198, 200, 271n10. *See also* Humphries, Rolfe

Age of Anxiety, The, 252n6
"Anger," 192
Another Time, 40, 55, 58–59, 124, 160, 184, 250n23, 253n14, 261n22, 270n50
"As Hateful Ares Bids," 254n19
As I Walked Out One Evening, 43, 248n6
"Augustus to Augustine," 7–8, 126, 128–29, 258n17. *See also* Cochrane, Charles Norris
"Bathtub Thoughts (c. 500–c. 1950)," 215, 239–43. *See also* Nichols, Grace
"Caliban to the Audience," 15–16, 30–32, 96, 98, 110–21, 139, 218, 242, 247n26, 261n24, 261n29, 278n31; draft of [Berg Collection], 262n30. *See also* Auden, W. H., works of, *Sea and the Mirror, The*
"Cave of Making, The" 204
Certain World, A, 192, 213, 271n6
Chase, The, 257n13
Collected Poems, 3, 4, 18, 37, 79, 184, 251n28, 265n4, 271n10, 279n35

281

Auden, W. H., works of (*cont.*)
  Collected Poetry (1945), 75, 257n13
  "Consider," 87, 148–49
  "[Contribution to *Modern Canterbury Pilgrims*]," 53, 127–28
  "Council, The," 159–60, 265n4
  "Criticism in Mass Society," 253n12, 267n26
  "Dame Kind," 20, 210, 212, 213, 241–42
  "Depravity": A Sermon," 98, 99, 257n13. *See also* Auden, W. H., works of, "Sermon by an Armament Manufacturer" and "Vicar's Sermon"
  "Dichtung und Wahrheit (An Unwritten Poem)," 19, 20, 41–42, 173, 203–10, 212, 213, 214–15, 220–21, 241. *See also* Auden, W. H., works of, "To Goethe: A Complaint"; Goethe, Johann Wolfgang von, "Dichtung und Wahrheit"
  Dog Beneath the Skin, The, 100, 101, 257n13. *See also* Auden, W. H., works of, "Vicar's Sermon"
  Double Man, The, 159–61
  Dyer's Hand, The, 4, 9, 116–17, 200, 223, 251n32; "Balaam and His Ass," 117; "Postscript: Infernal Science," 192, 225, 229, 277n20; "Prologue: Writing," 9, 49, 273n2; "Two Bestiaries," 147, 179–80, 182 (*see also* Moore, Marianne)
  "Effective Democracy," 76
  Enchafèd Flood, The, 132, 169, 205–6
  "Epigoni, The," 195, 201–3, 212, 216; draft of [Berg Collection], 272n11

"Epithalamion," 13, 54–59, 60, 61–62, 66, 249n20, 250n21, 250n23. *See also* Auden, W. H., works of, "In Sickness and in Health"; Wagner, Richard
"Eros and Agape," 156–59, 165, 170, 175. *See also* Rougemont, Denis de
"Essence of Dante, The," 264n3
Faber Book of Aphorisms, The, 186
"Fallen City, The," 270n1
"Fall of Rome, The," 2, 16–17, 25–26, 129–138, 142–52, 264n25; draft of [Berg Collection], 264n23
"Fog in the Mediterranean," 184, 186. *See also* Camus, Albert
"Foreword to *Some Trees*," 172, 173, 266n24
For the Time Being, 1, 96, 101, 105, 107, 110, 111, 125, 126, 127, 129, 130, 258nn16–17, 259n18. *See also* Auden, W. H., works of, "Massacre of the Innocents," and "Meditation of Simeon, The"
"Freud-Fliess Letters, The," 163, 167, 170, 266n17, 266n19. *See also* Freud, Sigmund
"Friday's Child," 20, 224, 236
"From an Aesthetic Point of View," 215
"Funeral Blues," 13, 29, 43–46, 48–50, 248n8. *See also* Newell, Mike, *Four Weddings and a Funeral*; Obergefell, Jim
"Great Democrat, A," 13, 69, 70–71, 76, 80, 84, 253nn10–11, 255n22. *See also* Voltaire

"Great Divide, The," 7
"Greatest of the Monsters, The," 58, 166–67, 250n24, 251n25, 266n17. *See also* Wagner, Richard
"Greatness of Freud, The," 163, 166–67, 170. *See also* Freud, Sigmund
"Greek Self, The," 267n30
"Good-bye to the Mezzogiorno," 21–22, 230–38, 278n31; draft of [Berg Collection], 278n26, 278nn28–29, 279n35
Hadrian's Wall (radio play), 4–5, 123–27, 200. *See also* Auden, W. H., works of, "Roman Wall Blues"
"Handbook to Antiquity," 177
"Hands," 194–95
"History of an Historian, The," 163, 167–70, 186, 266n19. *See also* Freud, Sigmund
"History of Science, The" 216, 217; draft of [Berg Collection], 274n4
"History of the Boudoir," 215, 217; draft of [Berg Collection], 274n4
"History of Truth, The" 22, 216–17; draft of [Berg Collection], 274n4
"Homage to Clio" (poem), 3, 18, 21, 26, 28, 170–86, 187–90, 193, 194–95, 201, 212, 219, 231–32, 234, 269n46; draft of [Berg Collection], 268n34, 269n43, 270n52
Homage to Clio (volume), 2–3, 6, 16, 18–22, 23, 27, 28, 41, 172, 173, 183, 188–210, 211–25, 230–38, 239, 240, 241, 242, 270n52, 278n30, 278n31, 279n35
"I Am Not a Camera," 269n44
"In Memory of Ernst Toller," 58
"In Memory of Sigmund Freud," 18, 59, 161–63, 164, 173–74. *See also* Freud, Sigmund
"In Memory of W. B. Yeats," 3, 4, 99, 210, 265n5. *See also* Yeats, W. B.
"In Sickness and in Health," 13, 54, 59–67, 249n20, 251n28; draft of [Berg Collection], 250n24. *See also* Auden, W. H., works of, "Epithalamion"; Wagner, Richard
Introduction to *A Selection from the Poems of Alfred, Lord Tennyson*, 131–33. *See also* Tennyson, Lord Alfred
Introduction to *Intimate Journals* by Charles Baudelaire, 135, 136–37. *See also* Baudelaire, Charles
Introduction to *Poets of the English Language*, 264n1
Introduction to *Tales of Grimm and Andersen*, 275n8
Introduction to *The Portable Greek Reader*, 156
"Jacob and the Angel," 2, 105
"James Honeyman," 9, 196
"Jean Cocteau," 270n1
"Letter to Lord Byron," 105, 259n18
"Liberal Fascist, The," 81
"Limbo Culture," 20, 28, 213–14, 221, 222, 223, 224, 236, 273n1
"Makers of History, The," 188–90, 195, 212

Auden, W. H., works of (*cont.*)
  "Marriage of True Minds, A," 266n17
  "Massacre of the Innocents, The," 1, 15–16, 30, 96–98, 102–11, 112–14, 115, 119, 125, 258n15, 258n16, 260n20; draft of [Berg Collection], 260n21. *See also* Auden, W. H., works of, *For the Time Being* and "Meditation of Simeon, The"
  "Masses Defined, The," 256n7
  "Meditation of Simeon, The," 15–16, 97, 98, 105–7, 113, 258n17, 259n18, 260n20; draft of [Berg Collection], 260n19. *See also* Auden, W. H., works of, *For the Time Being* and "Massacre of the Innocents, The"
  "Memorial for the City," 11, 148–49
  "Metalogue to *The Magic Flute*," 28, 217–20
  "Methods of dry farming," 6
  "Mimesis and Allegory," 131, 171, 245n1
  "Miss Gee," 9, 196
  "More Loving One, The," 205, 210
  "Mr. G," 273n14. *See also* Goethe, Johann Wolfgang von
  "Mythical World of Opera, The" (lecture), 277n22
  "Nature, History and Poetry," 171, 175
  "New Year Letter," 87–88, 132, 160
  "Nietzsche," 265n7. *See also* Nietzsche, Friedrich
  "Note on Order, A," 252n2
  "Of Poetry in Troubled Greece," 2
  "Opera Addict," 59
  "Pascal," 253n14. *See also* Pascal

  "Place of Value in a World of Fact, The" (seminar), 275n8
  "Plains," 188, 190, 270n4
  "Poet and Politician," 10
  "Poet of the Encirclement, The," 139–41. *See also* Kipling, Rudyard
  Prolific and the Devourer, The, 81, 253n14
  "Psychology and Art To-day," 252n4, 264n22
  "Public v. the Late Mr. William Butler Yeats, The," 99. *See also* Yeats, W. B.
  "Question of the Pound Award, The," 254n19
  "Reflections in a Forest," 18, 190–94, 196, 201, 213, 215, 271n7
  "Refugee Blues," 58
  "Romanticism from Rousseau to Hitler" (course at Swarthmore College), 276n11. *See also* Auden, W. H., works of, *Secondary Worlds* (lecture series), "World of the Sagas, The"
  "Romantic or Free?" 275n8
  "Roman Wall Blues," 123–24, 126–27. *See also* Auden, W. H., works of, *Hadrian's Wall* (radio play)
  Sea and the Mirror, The, 30, 96, 112, 113, 117, 119, 120, 139, 218, 242, 261n24, 261n29, 262n32, 278n31. *See also* Auden, W. H., works of, "Caliban's Address to the Audience"; Shakespeare, William
  "Secondary Epic," 19, 195, 196–201, 203, 212, 271n10; draft of [Berg Collection], 271n9

Secondary Worlds (lecture series), 225–30; "Words and the Word," 252n6; "World of Opera, The," 277n22; "World of the Sagas, The" 226–30, 276n19, 277n22. *See also* Auden, W. H., works of, "Romanticism from Rousseau to Hitler" (course at Swarthmore College)

"September 1, 1939," 4, 13, 36–37, 38–41, 42, 43, 48–49, 52, 55, 57, 58, 65, 82, 160–61; typescript draft of [Berg Collection], 250n23, 262n3. *See also* Albom, Mitch, *Tuesdays with Morrie* (book); *Tuesdays with Morrie* (film)

"Sermon by an Armament Manufacturer," 15–16, 98, 257n13. *See also* Auden, W. H., works of, "Depravity: A Sermon," and "Vicar's Sermon"

"Shield of Achilles, The" (poem), 271n10

Shield of Achilles, The (volume), 188, 270n4, 271n10

"Sigmund Freud," 163, 164–66, 170, 266n16. *See also* Freud, Sigmund

"Sixty-Six Sestets," 192–93

"Some Notes on D. H. Lawrence," 273n15

"Sonnets from China," 10

"Spain, 1937," 4, 10, 58, 183–85, 269n46

"Spain" (pamphlet), 10, 183–85

"Squares and Oblongs," 9

"Symposium," 257n12

"There Will Be No Peace," 20, 21, 221–25, 236; draft of [Berg Collection], 276n17

"Thinking What We Are Doing," 246n7. *See also* Arendt, Hannah

"To Goethe: A Complaint," 204–5, 234. *See also* Auden, W. H., works of, "Dichtung und Wahrheit (An Unwritten Poem)"; Goethe, Johann Wolfgang von

"Truest Poetry Is the Most Feigning, The," 270n3

"T the Great," 183, 188–90, 195–96, 199, 200, 212

"Vicar's Sermon," 15–16, 96–102, 119, 257n13. *See also* Auden, W. H., works of, "Depravity: A Sermon," and *Dog Beneath the Skin, The*, and "Sermon by an Armament Manufacturer"

"Victor," 9, 196

"Voltaire at Ferney," 14, 70–71, 75–79, 80–89, 190, 253n14, 255n20, 258n16; draft of [Berg Collection], 255n27. *See also Dialectic of Enlightenment*, "For Voltaire"

"Wandering Jew, The," 223–24

"What Is Culture?" 233, 277n25

"What Is Poetry About?" 4–5

"Where Are We Now?" 15, 16, 92–96, 97, 103, 104, 106, 108–9, 113, 256n7. *See also* Horkheimer, Max; Laski, Harold

"Who Shall Plan the Planners?" 263n4

Augustine, Saint, 7–8, 126, 128–129; *Confessions*, 206

Azaria, Hank, 38

Bacon, Francis, 68, 252n2

Barth, Karl: *The Epistle to the Romans*, 115–16, 261n28

Bateson, Gregory: *Steps to an Ecology of Mind*, 215, 218, 274n7, 275nn8–9, 276n10
Baudelaire, Charles, 2, 17, 127, 130–38, 140, 151; "Correspondances," 134–35, 136; *Journaux intimes* [*Intimate Journals*], 131, 133, 146; *Les fleurs du mal* [*The Flowers of Evil*], 133, 134, 135, 136, 137; *Les paradis artificiels* [*Artificial Paradises*], 133, 137–38; "L'Irrémédiable," 132. See also Auden, W. H., works of, "Fall of Rome, The," and "Introduction to *Intimate Journals*"; Eliot, T. S.; Tennyson, Lord Alfred
Beach, Joseph Warren, 254n15
Before Sunrise (film), 248n5
Bell, Kathleen, 252n5
Benedict, Ruth, 278n27
Benét, William Rose, 140–42, 264n15
Benjamin, Walter, 91; "On the Concept of History," 22–23, 95; "What Is Epic Theater?," 115
Berlant, Lauren: *Cruel Optimism*, 26–27
Bessie, Alvah: *Men in Battle*, 10
Bhabha, Homi K., 261n22, 273n1, 273n13
Bible. See individual books, e.g., Corinthians 1, Genesis, Job
Blair, Tony, 94
Blake, William, 57, 87–88
Block, Richard, 278n30
Bloomfield, B. C., 248n4
Boas, Guy, 263n6
Bonhoeffer, Dietrich, 20, 222
Borch-Jacobsen, Mikkel, 247n22
Borgese, Giuseppe Antonio, 54–55, 56, 57
Bower, David, 46

Bozorth, Richard, 249n13
Brecht, Bertolt, 9, 114–15, 196, 261n26; *The Caucasian Chalk Circle*, 114; *The Duchess of Malfi*, 114; *The Rise and Fall of the City of Mahogany*, 114; *The Seven Deadly Sins*, 114
Bridges, Robert, 271n8
Britten, Benjamin, 252n4
Broch, Hermann, 271n9
Bryant, Marsha, 248n7
Buber, Martin, 211
Bucknell, Katherine, 246n10
Burchell, William John, 241, 280n2
Burt, Stephen (Stephanie), 248n3
Bush, George H. W., 37
Butler, Judith: *Frames of War*, 26; *Parting Ways: Jewishness and the Critique of Zionism*, 26; *Precarious Life*, 26

Callow, Simon, 43
Camus, Albert: *The Rebel*, 184, 186. See also Auden, W. H., works of, "Fog in the Mediterranean"
Carpenter, Humphrey, 246n8, 249n18, 252n3, 269n47
Caruth, Cathy, 266n21
Celan, Paul, 236, 279n34
Chancellor, Anna, 45
Chaucer, Geoffrey, 133
Chisick, Harvey, 254n16
Clark, John R., 268n31
Clark, Thekla, 222
Cochrane, Charles Norris: *Christianity and Classical Culture*, 7, 8–9, 126, 128–29, 142, 144, 263n5. See also Auden, W. H., works of, "Augustus to Augustine"
Cocteau, Jean, 270n1
Connolly, Cyril, 144–45, 264nn17–20

INDEX

1 Corinthians, 64, 142. *See also* Paul, Saint
Costello, Bonnie, 249n20, 268n36
Criterion, The (magazine), 133

Dante, 56, 270n3; *Commedia*, 18–19, 161; *Inferno*, 20, 191–92, 193–94, 213; *Puragtorio*, 158, 264n3
D'Arcy, M. C., 264n3
Davenport-Hines, Richard, 249n16
Davies, Chris, 249n9
Decision, a Journal of Free Culture, 92, 93, 256n7, 257n12
Deleuze, Gilles, 262n31
Derrida, Jacques, 251n31
Descartes, René, 75, 206–7, 237, 255n25
Detienne, Marcel, 267n25
Dialectic of Enlightenment: Philosophical Fragments [*Dialektik der Aufklärung: Philosophische Fragmente*], 14, 68–70, 71, 85, 89; "For Voltaire," 68–70, 71, 72–75, 76, 77, 82, 85–86, 88–89, 252nn1–2. *See also* Adorno, Theodor; Auden, W. H., works of, "Voltaire at Ferney"; Horkheimer, Max
Dodds, A. R., 172
Dodds, E. R., 10, 23; *The Greeks and the Irrational*, 172–73, 232, 267nn25–26, 278n27
Du Châtelet (Marquise), 79
Dunoyer, Olympe, 79

Eliot, George: *Middlemarch*, 8
Eliot, T. S., 2, 17, 21, 160, 225, 228, 230, 237, 238, 258n14; *After Strange Gods*, 93, 277n21; introduction to *A Choice of Kipling's Verse*, 139; introduction to *Intimate Journals*, 133–34, 135–36, 146; "The Waste Land," 135–36, 137, 139. *See also* Auden, W. H., works of, "Fall of Rome, The"; Baudelaire, Charles; Tennyson, Lord Alfred
Emig, Rainer, 252n4, 268n33
Encounter (magazine), 279n35
Eysenck, Hans, 265n13

Felicity (television series), 248n5
Felman, Shoshana, 266n21
Ferrante, Elena, 248n5
Fischer, Clive, 264n19
Fleet, James, 44
Forster, E. M., 37, 51
Foucault, Michel, 240; *The Archaeology of Knowledge*, 23; *The History of Sexuality* (four volumes), 23–24, 246n15; *The Order of Things*, 23
Freeman, Derek, 28, 247n23
Freud, Sigmund, 18, 27–28, 94, 161–71, 173–75, 176, 182, 186, 194, 247n22, 265n12, 266n17, 266n19, 266n21, 268n37; *Beyond the Pleasure Principle*, 161, 169, 202; "A Childhood Recollection from *Dichtung und Wahrheit*," 208; *Civilization and Its Discontents*, 169, 182; *The Future of an Illusion*, 145, 264n22; "The Theme of the Three Caskets," 162, 174; *Totem and Taboo*, 169. *See also* Auden, W. H., works of, "Freud-Fliess Letters, The," and "Greatness of Freud, The," and "History of an Historian, The," and "In Memory of Sigmund Freud," and "Sigmund Freud"
Frontain, Raymond-Jean, 249n13
Fuller, John, 258nn16–17, 263n6, 271n7

Galvin, Rachel, 255n24, 269n46
Gay, Peter, 254n16
Genesis, book of, 41, 80, 251n27
Gibbon, Edward: *History of the Decline and Fall of the Roman Empire*, 128, 146
Ginzburg, Carlo, 246n4
Gluck, Christoph Willibald: *Orfeo ed Euridice*, 59
Goebbels, Joseph, 51, 72
Goethe, Johann Wolfgang von, 21, 57, 205, 215, 233–34, 235, 246n5, 273nn13–15, 278n28; *Dichtung und Wahrheit*, 19, 203–4, 208; *Italienische Reise* [*Italian Journey*], 278n30; *Römische Elegien* [*Roman Elegies*], 233, 235, 278n30. See also Auden, W. H., works of, "Dichtung und Wahrheit (An Unwritten Poem)," and "Mr. G," and "To Goethe: A Complaint"
Goldensohn, Lori, 262n2
Gottlieb, Susannah Young-ah, 246n7, 251n27, 252n6, 253n7, 279n32
Grant, Hugh, 44
Graves, Robert, 28, 218
Greene, Graham, 81
Gregory VII (pope), 8, 11, 163
Griffin, The (magazine), 265n12
Grünbaum, Adolf: *Foundations of Psychoanalysis*, 164
Guattari, Felix, 262n31

Hannah, John, 43
Hartzoecker, Niklaas, 255n25
Hegel, Georg Wilhelm Friedrich, 69, 74, 112
Heidegger, Martin: "Die Frage nach der Technik" ["The Question Concerning Technology"], 216; *Sein und Zeit* [*Being and Time*], 206
Helmholtz, Hermann von, 18, 165–66, 170, 266n17
Heraclitus, 138
Hesiod, 267n30; *Theogony*, 171–72, 267n25, 267n28
Hitler, Adolf, 10, 15, 55, 90, 93, 94, 95, 96, 109, 222, 261n22, 263n4
Hölderlin, Friedrich, 4, 51, 57; "Bread and Wine," 9
Homer, 149, 162, 172, 197–98, 200, 203, 267nn29–30, 271n10
Horizon (journal), 144, 145, 264n16
Horkheimer, Max, 14, 15, 23, 68–70, 71, 73–75, 76, 80, 82, 84, 85, 88, 90, 91–92, 96, 252n1, 252n4. See also Adorno, Theodor; Auden, W. H., works of, "Where Are We Now?" and "Voltaire at Ferney"; *Dialectic of Enlightenment*; Laski, Harold
Howarth, Peter, 268n35
Humphries, Rolfe, 196, 200, 271n10. See also Auden, W. H., works of, "Aeneid for Our Time"

Isherwood, Christopher, 10, 12, 51, 52, 249n12, 271n8; translation of *Journaux intimes*, 131, 133–34

Jacobs, Alan, 248n8, 251n26
Jaeger, Werner: *Paideia*, 232
James, Henry, 30, 111, 133, 247n26, 263n27
Jaspers, Karl: *The Question of German Guilt*, 234
Jay, Martin, 256n6
Jenkins, Nicholas, 246n10, 248n3
Job, book of, 61

Jones, Ernest, 27, 266n19; *Sigmund Freud: Life and Work Vol. 1: The Young Freud*, 165–67; *Sigmund Freud, Life and Work Vol. 2: Years of Maturity*, 167–68; *Sigmund Freud: Life and Work Vol. 3: The Last Phase, 1919–1939*, 170
Julius, Anthony, 277n21
Jung, Carl, 234, 279n32

Kafka, Franz, 224. See also Auden, W. H., works of, "Wandering Jew, The"
Kallman, Chester, 13, 52–54, 56, 218, 222
Kierkegaard, Søren, 64, 94, 127–28, 129, 130–31, 132, 251nn29–30
Kipling, Rudyard, 2, 17, 95, 139–42, 143. See also Auden, W. H., works of, "Poet of Encirclement, The"
Kirsch, Arthur, 261n24, 261n29, 262n32
Köhler, Wolfgang, 275n8

Lacan, Jacques, 170
Laforgue, Jules, 134, 146
Landor, Walter Savage, 192–93
Laski, Harold: *Where Do We Go from Here?*, 15, 16, 90–96, 103, 104, 105, 108–09, 256n7, 256n10, 261n22. See also Auden, W. H., works of, "Where Are We Now?"; Horkheimer, Max
Laub, Dori, 246n21
Lawrence, D. H., 180
Leibniz, Gottfried Wilhelm, 26, 71, 190, 257n12
Lemmon, Jack, 38, 41
Lenin, Vladimir, 100
Leonardo da Vinci, 56

Life and Letters (journal), 257n13
Listener, The (magazine), 265n12
Locke, John, 94
Lyotard, Jean-François, 22, 23

MacDowell, Andie, 44
MacNeice, Louis, 10, 264n22
Madonna (singer), 37
Malcolm, Janet, 266n21
Mann, Elisabeth, 54–55, 56, 57, 58
Mann, Erika, 13, 51, 53, 54, 55, 249n12
Mann, Klaus, 92, 256n7, 257n12
Mann, Thomas, 55, 249n12, 250n23
Mao, Douglas, 256n8
Marcuse, Herbert: *Eros and Civilization*, 169
Marquis de Sade, 157
Marx, Karl, 5–6, 9, 24, 55, 74, 215, 250n22, 263n4; *The Eighteenth Brumaire*, 6, 245n3
Masson, Jeffrey, 266n21
Mayer, Elizabeth, 262n30, 278n30; letter to [Berg Collection], 7, 246n5
McDiarmid, Lucy, 250n21, 250n23, 257n13, 258n15
Mead, Margaret, 28, 247n23, 275n8; *Sex and Temperament*, 218
Mendelson, Edward, 222–23, 248n3, 248n6, 250n21, 257n13, 258n14, 259n18, 260n20, 263n9, 266n16, 269n42, 270n51, 275n8, 278n30
Meun, Jean de: *Roman de la Rose*, 157
Milton, John, 100; *Paradise Lost*, 99
Moore, Marianne, 175, 268n35; "The Pangolin," 180, 182. See also Auden, W. H., works of, "Two Bestiaries"
Mozart, Wolfgang Amadeus, 57, 217; *The Magic Flute*, 219–20
Mussolini, Benito, 10, 55, 234
Mutter, Matthew, 273n2

Nagy, Gregory, 267n28
Nation, The (journal), 68, 252n2
NeJaime, Douglas, 249n15
Newell, Mike (director): *Four Weddings and a Funeral*, 13, 40, 43–50, 248n7. *See also* Auden, W. H., works of, "Funeral Blues"; Obergefell, Jim
New Republic, The (journal), 140, 164, 167, 265n12
Newton, Isaac, 87, 255n25
Nichols, Grace: "Thoughts drifting through the fat black woman's head while having a full bubble bath," 240–43, 280n2. *See also* Auden, W. H., works of, "Bathtub Thoughts"
Niebuhr, Ursula, 269n42
Nietzsche, Friedrich, 24, 127, 132, 160, 215, 219–20, 251n25, 256n7, 265n7; *Götzendämmerung* [*Twilight of the Idols*], 186, 216; *Unzeitgemäße Betrachtungen* [*Thoughts Out of Season*, also translated as *Unfashionable Observations*], 177–79, 182, 185–86, 268n39. *See also* Auden, W. H., works of, "Nietzsche"
Nieuventyt, Bernard, 255n25
Noonan, Peggy, 37
Norse, Harold, 52
Noyes, Alfred, 79, 80, 84, 255n25
Nygren, Anders: *Agape and Eros*, 160, 265n6

Obergefell, Jim, 13; "Love, Loss, and Steadfast Commitment Lead a Nation Forward," 49–50; *Obergefell v. Hodges*, 50. *See also* Auden, W. H., works of, "Funeral Blues";

Newell, Mike, *Four Weddings and a Funeral*
Offenbach, Jacques: *La belle Hélène*, 162, 174
Ortega y Gasset, José, 256n7
Orwell, George, 270n48; *Homage to Catalonia*, 183; "Inside the Whale," 183–84
Osborne, Charles, 249n14

Paley, William, 255n25
Pascal, 78–79, 84, 253n14. *See also* Auden, W. H., works of, "Pascal"
Paul, Saint (apostle), 25, 64, 142. *See also* 1 Corinthians
Petrie, Jon, 276n16
Plato, 69, 263n4
Poetry (magazine), 70
Pointon, Ann, 249n9
Pound, Ezra, 198, 254nn17–19; "Impressions of François-Marie Arouet," 79–80, 254n17
Pudney, John, 262n1

Ramazani, Jahan, 247n27, 265n8
Redgrave, Corin, 44
Ricoeur, Paul, 164
Rosenstock-Huessy, Eugen, 12, 269n44; *Out of Revolution*, 7, 8–9, 17, 155–56, 163, 263n5, 264n1
Rougemont, Denis de: *Love in the Western World*, 7, 8–9, 17, 156–59, 165, 170, 251n30. *See also* Auden, W. H., works of, "Eros and Agape"
Rousseau, Jean-Jacques, 71, 251n31; "Discourse on the Origin and Foundations of Inequality among Human Beings," 80
Russell, Bertrand, 275n9

Saby, Aurélien, 277n24
Sahlins, Marshall: *How "Natives" Think*, 28, 30
Said, Edward: *Orientalism*, 30, 110
Sansom, Ian, 248n3
Sartre, Jean-Paul, 5
Schelling, Friedrich Wilhelm Joseph von, 74
Schiller, Friedrich, 262n3
Seiler, Claire, 246n9, 264n16
Shakespeare, William, 250n23; *The Merchant of Venice*, 162; *The Tempest*, 29, 112, 116–17, 118, 242. See also Auden, W. H., works of, *Sea and the Mirror, The*
Sieburth, Richard, 254n18
Singh, Jyotsna: "Post-colonial Reading of *The Tempest*," 29–30
Smith, Stan, 252n4, 269n46
Snell, Bruno, 267n30
Spears, Monroe, 222–23, 224
Spencer, Theodor, 261n24
Spender, Stephen, 11, 125
Spengler, Otto: *The Decline of the West*, 7, 145
Spivak, Gayatri: "Can the Subaltern Speak?," 16, 111
Steedman, Carolyn, 246n6
Stern, James, 10–11, 246n10
Sulloway, Frank: *Freud, Biologist of the Mind*, 164
Sultzbach, Kelly, 247n19, 264n25

Tennyson, Lord Alfred, 132, 135, 198, 263n7; "In Memoriam," 132–33. See also Auden, W. H., works of, "Fall of Rome, The," and "Introduction to *A Selection from the Poems of Alfred, Lord Tennyson*"; Baudelaire, Charles; Eliot, T. S.

Tocqueville, Alexis de, 24
Tolkien, J. R. R., 226, 269n42. See also Auden, W. H., works of, *Secondary Worlds* (lecture series)
Tolstoi, Leo, 57
Torrey, Norman L., 79, 80, 84, 253n10, 255n21, 255n23, 255n25
Toynbee, Arnold: *A Study of History*, 7, 246n6
Trevelyan, George Macauley: "Clio, a Muse," 171, 266n22
Trotsky, Leon, 100
Tuesdays with Morrie (book). See under Albom, Mitch
Tuesdays with Morrie (film), 12–13, 38–39, 40–41, 43, 48–49. See also Albom, Mitch, *Tuesdays with Morrie* (book); Auden, W. H., works of, "September 1, 1939"

Variety (magazine), 49, 50
Verdi, Giuseppe: *Otello*, 59
Virgil, 19, 201, 203, 271n9; *Aeneid*, 196–200, 202, 271n10
Vít, Ladislav, 247n19
Voltaire (François-Marie Arouet), 13–14, 26–27, 68–89, 253n10, 253n14, 254nn16–18, 255nn22–25, 257n12, 258n16; *Candide*, 26, 190, 257n12; *Dictionnaire philosophique*, 80, 84, 255n25. See also Auden, W. H., works of, "Great Democrat, A," and "Voltaire at Ferney"; *Dialectic of Enlightenment*, "For Voltaire"

Wagner, Richard, 57, 58–59, 250n24, 251n25, 252n4; *Tristan und Isolde*, 59–61. See also Auden, W. H., works of, "Epithalamion," and

Wagner, Richard (*cont.*)
"Greatest of the Monsters, The," and "In Sickness and in Health"
Walcott, Derek: "The Muse of History," 31–32, 247n27
Wasley, Aidan, 261n24
Weber, Samuel, 277n23
Weber, Shierry, 277n23
White, Hayden: *Metahistory*, 24, 25
Willett, John, 261n26
Winfrey, Oprah, 38
Winnicott, Donald, 76
Witemeyer, Hugh, 254n17
Wittgenstein, Ludwig, 19, 201, 213; *Philosophische Untersuchungen* [*Philosophical Investigations*], 206, 207–9; *Tractatus Logico-Philosophicus*, 192, 206
Wordsworth, William, 172

Yeats, W. B., 2, 17, 99; "Sailing to Byzantium," 146–48. *See also* Auden, W. H., works of, "In Memory of W. B. Yeats," and "Public v. the Late Mr. William Butler Yeats, The"

Žižek, Slavoj, 15; *In Defense of Lost Causes*, 93–94, 256n8
Zohar, the, 251n27

The authorized representative in the EU for product safety and compliance is:
Mare Nostrum Group
B.V Doelen 72
4831 GR Breda
The Netherlands

www.ingramcontent.com/pod-product-compliance
Lightning Source LLC
Chambersburg PA
CBHW021956220426
43663CB00007B/832